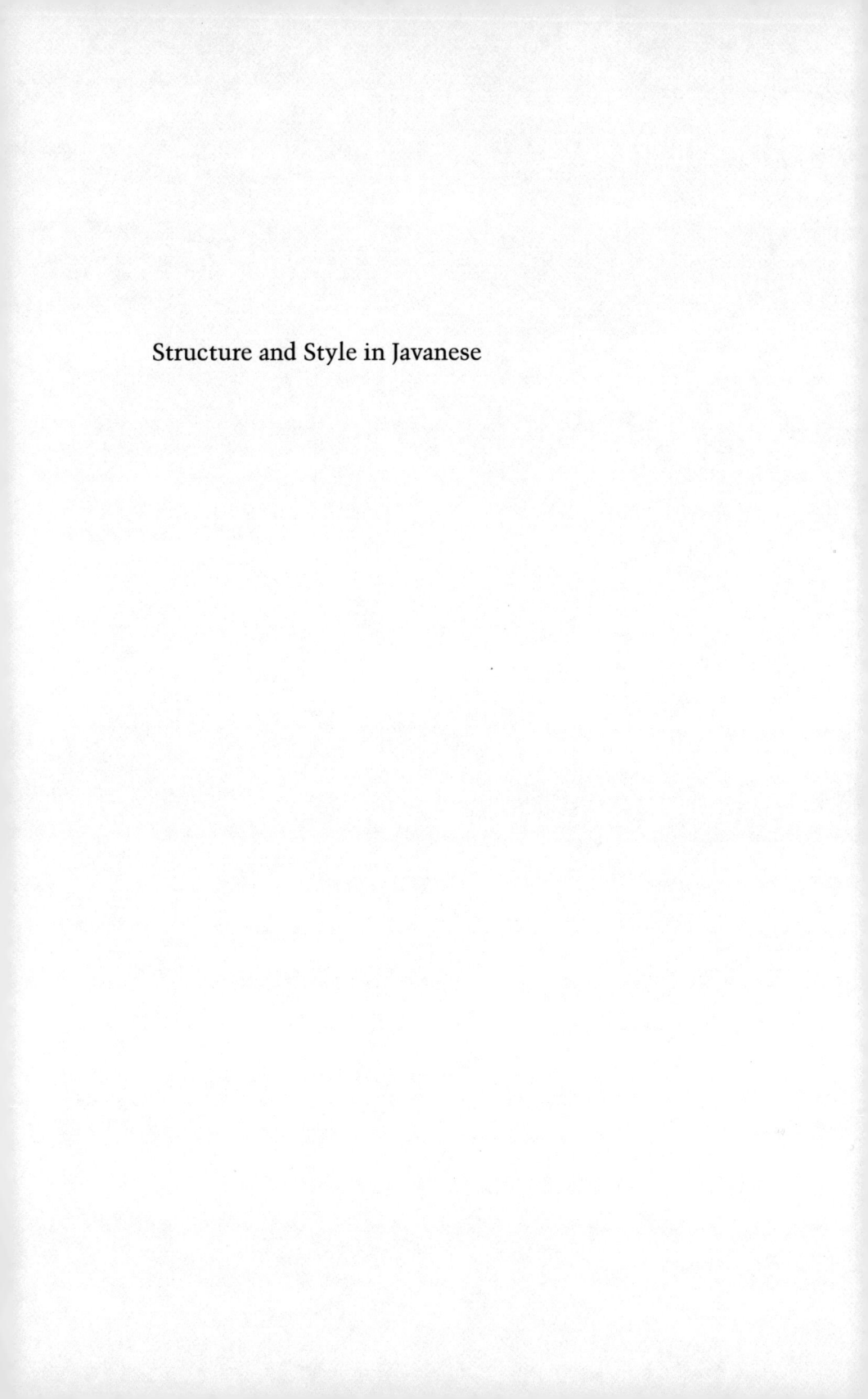

Structure and Style in Javanese

Structure and Style in

Javanese

A Semiotic View of Linguistic Etiquette

J. JOSEPH ERRINGTON

upp

University of Pennsylvania Press / Philadelphia   1988

University of Pennsylvania Press

Conduct and Communication Series

Erving Goffman and Dell Hymes, Founding Editors
Dell Hymes, Gillian Sankoff, and Henry Glassie, General Editors

A complete listing of the books in this series
appears at the back of this volume

Copyright © 1988 by the University of Pennsylvania Press
All rights reserved
Printed in the United States of America

Library of Congress Cataloging-in-Publication Data

Errington, James Joseph, 1951–
  Structure and style in Javanese: a semiotic view of linguistic etiquette / J. Joseph Errington.
    p. cm.—(University of Pennsylvania Press conduct and communication series)
  Bibliography: p.
  Includes index.
  ISBN 0-8122-8103-9
  1. Javanese language—Social aspects. 2. Speech and social status—Indonesia—Java. 3. Java (Indonesia)—Social life and customs. I. Title. II. Series.
PL5161.E78 1988   87-31672
499'.222'0141—dc19   CIP

For the Clelas

Contents

List of tables and figures   ix
Acknowledgments   xi
On notation and transcription   xv

1. Introduction   1
   Speech styles and linguistic etiquette   10
   Referential and social indexicality   14
   Pragmatic salience and sociolinguistic change   17

2. Ethics, etiquette, and the exemplary center   22
   The technical implementation of kingship   25
   Magico-religious legitimation of kingship   28
   Ethics of elite etiquette   34
   Priyayi in Surakarta now   43

3. Status, interaction, and titles   46
   Speech styles: an operational description   49
   Descent and the traditional noble hierarchy   53
   Seniority, status, and etiquette use   69
   Group styles and change in priyayi interaction   73
   Changes in rights to titles   77

4. Basic classifications   85
   Address styles: ngoko, krama, madya   89
   Honorific lexemes   98
   Personal pronouns   104
   Speech style use, change, and pragmatic salience   105

Contents

5. Terms for persons 111
    - Personal pronouns and figurative expressions 115
    - Kin terms, inside and outside the speech styles 134
    - Salience, use, and change 149

6. Deference, reference, and the encoding of status 152
    - Semantics, paradigmatic structure, and pragmatic range 155
    - Speaking for others: *mbasakaké* 160
    - Indeterminacy and semantic domains 162
    - Little-known krama inggil 165
    - Indeterminacy, ambiguity, and vagueness 170
    - Predicates of exchange 174
    - Acts of linguistic exchange 179
    - Deferential directives 185
    - Honorific reference and avoidance 191

7. Address styles and the muting of gesture 194
    - Innovation and standardization of krama and madya 197
    - Ngoko/madya/krama alternations 204
    - Demonstrative pronouns and indexing acts 205
    - Formulaic locutions 212
    - Interjections 219
    - Indexicality and modes of self-presentation 223

8. Signs of politeness 225
    - Style and dialect variation 230
    - Styles and strategies 237
    - Indexicality from the native speaker's point of view 247

Bibliography 257
Index of Javanese words 271
Index of authors 279
Index of subjects 281

Tables and Figures

Tables
1   Terms for descent generation circa 1900   55
2   Titles of descent circa 1900   60
3   Titles of descent after 1939   78
4   Overview of priyayi non-ngoko personal pronoun usage   116
5   Intraset and interset relations by semantic subdomain   163
6   Cross-generation variation in knowledge of krama inggil   169
7   Ngoko alternants of *ngasta*   172
8   Some hyponyms of *digawa*   173
9   Honorific verbs of acquisition   175
10 Honorific predicates of disposal   177
11 Some verbs of speaking   180
12 Inflected verbs of speaking   180
13 Overview of *ngoko/madya/krama* demonstrative pronouns   206

Figures
1   Semiotic/linguistic speech style structure   90
2   Patterns of ngoko and krama address style exchange   93
3   Syntagmatic patterning between three- and two-member sets   97
4   Classification of paradigmatic sets containing honorifics   156
5   Referential and pragmatic ranges of honorifics   159
6   Distribution of knowledge of little-known krama inggil   168

Acknowledgments

When it is difficult to pinpoint the beginnings of a work, it is difficult to open it with a gesture of thanks to those who have helped to make it happen. This book is a considerably revised version of material originally presented in my dissertation, "Changing Speech Levels Among a Traditional Javanese Elite Group," submitted to the Departments of Linguistics and Anthropology at the University of Chicago in 1981. It is based on research in 1979 and 1980 but also on my experiences while a student in Java in 1977 and 1978. Because my work in Java was shaped in part by instruction in Indonesian and Javanese which I received in 1976 and 1977, and in anthropology and linguistics between 1973 and 1976, my experiences over eleven years or so have found their way into this work, and I am indebted to more persons than I can even mention.

My first encounter with spoken Javanese was under the tutelage of Dr. Soeseno Kartomihardjo in the summer of 1976, and I am grateful for his considerate instruction. I learned Indonesian under the supervision of John Wolff before and during my first trip to Java, and am grateful to him and my instructors for their patient help. Before doing research in Surakarta I studied Old Javanese and Modern Javanese at Universitas Gajah Mada in Yogyakarta in 1978. To members of the Jurusan Bahasa Nusantara of the Fakultas Sastra I owe sincere thanks for their patience and willing help with academic and nonacademic matters alike. My tutor in spoken Javanese during this time, Shita Laksmi Prawirohardjo Van Ness taught me how to get closer to the ways people speak and so to the people themselves; I owe her a great debt for her insightfulness, helpfulness, and skill.

Acknowledgments

The research was carried out between February 1979 and August 1980 with indispensable help from several agencies and persons. Financial support came from the National Science Foundation with Michael Silverstein as primary investigator, and from the Social Science Research Council. Institutional support from the Republic of Indonesia was provided by the Indonesian Academy of Sciences (Lembaga Ilmu Pengetahuan Indonesia). I am grateful to all of these organizations; all opinions expressed in this work are, however, my own, and are not to be attributed to any of these agencies. During my stay in Yogyakarta and Surakarta I was fortunate to have Soepomo and Gloria Poedjosoedarmo as advisors and friends; my thanks go to both. To Professor Soepomo and IKIP Sanata Dharma too go my thanks for official regional sponsorship.

In 1985 I had the opportunity to use the archives of the Royal Institute of Linguistics and Anthropology and the library of Leiden University in the Netherlands. I am indebted to Yale University for a Junior Faculty Research Fellowship that supported this research. Among the many gracious and helpful people, including those on the library staff, who made my stay there pleasant and productive I must in particular thank Stuart Robson for his knowledgeability, availability, and hospitality. Drs. Singgih Wibisono, then resident in Leiden, was also especially generous with his time and views on certain points of usage I was then investigating.

After this work was largely completed I returned to Java in December 1986 for nine months of research, different from that reported in this work, but which allowed me to check specific points, remedy inevitable oversights which had become apparent in my notes, and ask again about unclear issues. So the National Science Foundation, the Wenner-Gren foundation, the Social Science Research Council, and Yale University also deserve my thanks for this side dividend to research they generously supported. To Rama Danukusuma, rector of IKIP Sanata Dharma, I am also grateful for personal as well as institutional support during this brief stay.

Personal and intellectual debts are not always apparent until well after they have been taken on and gathered interest, and I doubtless owe some debts I do not know I have accumulated to persons I cannot yet name. Clearly, though, I owe thanks to Michael Silverstein, who supervised the dissertation on which this work is largely based, and to many of my teachers and advisors: Milton Singer, Paul Friedrich, Jerry Sadock, John Wolff, and Alton Becker cannot go unmentioned. Harold Conklin and Keith Basso have both shaped my thinking in ways that may not be apparent in these pages, but their contribution is nonetheless real. My gratitude goes also to Dell Hymes for his encouragement and useful criticisms of a previous version of this work.

The irony of acknowledgments like this is that the persons who had the most to do with this work, whom I call "speakers" and "informants" but think of more as friends and teachers, must go unnamed. The English words ring as hollow as would any lengthy testimony to their graciousness in the face of ineptness, obtuseness, and peculiar, repetitous questions. For their willingness and ability to make me feel less like a stranger and more like a friend I give them all my heartfelt thanks. I hope that those inclined to peruse this work are not too disappointed, and I ask for their forgiveness in advance for the mistakes it contains.

15 June 1987
New Haven, Connecticut

On Notation and Transcription

I have tried to achieve a reasonable compromise among convenience, consistency, and accuracy in transcribing Javanese words and names in this work. Because Javanese metalinguistic terminology is used throughout, I have elected to forgo italicizing the most crucial elements of the technical vocabulary. The word *priyayi* is also not italicized after its first use in the body of the text.

Single quotation marks ('like these') are used only for glosses and for marking reported speech within quotations from speakers in the body of the text. Double quotation marks ("like these") serve as "scare" quotes and to mark quotations from informants.

I have adapted the broadly phonemic orthography developed at a workshop on spelling systems for ethnic languages that was sponsored by the Department of Education and Culture of Indonesia in 1973. For a concise history of standard Javanese orthography see Subalidinoto and Marsono 1975. The system used here differs only insofar as diacritics are used to distinguish mid-high front /é/ from mid front /è/ and shwa /e/. Such conventions were in common use before 1973 and are still recommended for printed instructional literature.

Javanese has voiced and voiceless postalveolar stops transcribed /dh/ and /th/, respectively; these contrast phonemically with interdental /d/ and /t/. The velar nasal (engma) is transcribed as /ng/. Palatal voiced and voiceless affricates are transcribed as /j/ and /c/, respectively, and contrast with sequences of dental stop and glide /dy/ and /ty/. The low back unrounded vowel transcribed here as /a/ contrasts phonemically with mid back /o/ and has a central low unrounded allophone also represented as /a/. Patterns of vowel harmony and allophonic variation in Javanese are not considered here.

Spellings of proper names and titles are often inconsistent because many have been romanized in different ways at different times by different people; in the literature one commonly finds *oe* alternating with *u*, *o* rather than *a*, *j* rather than *y*, and so on. I have taken the liberty of transliterating titles of works cited and examples from the literature in Javanese characters with the modified orthography described above. Proper names are transcribed in accordance with precedents in the literature, my knowledge of the preference of the author in question, and other factors.

Structure and Style in Javanese

1

Introduction

Even if the Javanese did not number more than sixty million[1] and were not the dominant ethnic group in Indonesia, the syncretic complex of Javanese cultural tradition would be of considerable interest. Areal and social diversity notwithstanding, *cara Jawa*, or 'Javanese way', distinguishes Javanese from other ethnic groups in Indonesia and Southeast Asia at large. The phrase *cara Jawa* can be used to refer to Javanese language in particular as well as Javanese practices in general, and the famous system of Javanese "speech levels" is in many ways emblematic of the complexities of Javanese social life. These elaborately distinguished ways of speaking are striking and obviously expressive means for mediating social interaction.

I first encountered the speech levels, as have many others, in the widely reprinted description from Geertz's ethnography of Javanese religion (1960:248):

> [A] number of words (and some affixes) . . . are made to carry in addition to their normal linguistic meanings what might be called a "status meaning," i. e., when used in actual conversation they convey not only their fixed detonative [sic] meaning ("house", "body", "eat", "walk", "you", "passive voice") but also a connotative meaning concerning the status of (and or degree of familiarity between) the speaker and hearer.

1. According to population figures for 1985 projected in the 1980 census (*Statistik Indonesia*, Table III.1.2, quoted in *Indonesia Reports* no. 7, Culture and society supplement) the populations of the provinces of Central and East Java, and the special district of Yogyakarta, where ethnic Javanese are concentrated, total more than 61.5 million. Some of these are members other ethnic groups, mostly Madurese and Chinese, but there are many other ethnic Javanese living on other islands (mostly transmigrants) and in other areas of Java (mostly Jakarta).

2   Introduction

There is a longstanding scholarly precedent for Geertz's decision to sketch this peculiarly Javanese institution as part of his account of the cultural tradition of the Javanese elite, the *priyayi* (1960: 227–352), because foreigners and Javanese alike have long attributed the best, most highly refined forms of Javanese language and art to this traditional noble and courtly class.

Priyayi were traditionally servants and descendants of kings, inheritors and transmitters of an elaborate cultural tradition that has long fascinated academics, mystics, musicians, dancers, artists, and tourists. Although the priyayi elite community has always been tiny, and traditional priyayi status is anachronistic in "modern" Indonesia, priyayi continue to be regarded by Javanese as speakers of the "best," most highly elaborated dialect of the language. This reputation has only been augmented by a century and a half of scholarly study, which has focused especially on the priyayi dialect of Surakarta.

I first went to Java in 1977 to study Javanese and Indonesian in the East Javanese city of Malang. There I got some sense of the enduring fame of the image of ideal, refined priyayi conduct every time someone to whom I addressed my faltering Javanese told me that I should study in Surakarta or Yogyakarta, that in those traditional royal polities on the rice plains of the south-central part of the island Javanese is at its most refined (*alus*). In 1978 I had the opportunity to follow this advice when I moved to Yogyakarta, self-styled gateway to Javanese culture, to study Javanese literature at Gajah Mada University and spoken Javanese with a tutor and acquaintances. There I also read some older scholarly and pedagogical literature, and so became aware of real differences between the substance of those descriptions and the ways my acquaintances, priyayi and otherwise, were speaking and telling me about Javanese. I did not then so much identify topics for later research as develop some first inchoate impressions that appear in retrospect to have shaped my thinking about the speech levels in three ways.

Priyayi speech level usage is famous for its remarkable structural complexity—half a dozen or so second person pronouns, five words meaning 'give', ten distinct "levels," and so on—generally presented in the literature in overtly or covertly prescriptive, ideal-typical ways. The impression thus conveyed of exotic nuance and complexity is not inaccurate, insofar as Javanese contains hundreds of "polite" vocabulary items that combine in structurally complex ways. But these prescriptive treatments fail to capture the dynamic expressiveness and interactive unity of speech levels in social interaction. By the same token, most treatments speak hardly at all to longstanding dynamics of change and variation in speech level use. Even before the huge social disruptions of traditional society following the Japanese occupation in 1942, and the establishment of the Republic of Indonesia in 1945, there were ongoing changes in speech level use among all Surakartans, and among priyayi in particular. The fact if not the nature of such change was obvious from discrepancies between the descriptions I read in older texts and the usage I heard and learned among friends and teachers.

Change and variation in Javanese speech level usage later became the primary focus for my research, and for this book. Although I have tried to develop a fairly broad social perspective on such change—broader, at least, than is common in the linguistic literature—I do so by maintaining a fairly narrow social focus on priyayi speech level usage. My motivation is not prescriptive but practical: to describe everything comprehended by the deceptively simple designation "speech levels" would be to deal with a large number of structurally and functionally variant systems used by Javanese of different social classes, generations, and dialect areas. One need not reflect too long to be impressed by the sheer amount of information required to move beyond one dialect. The privileged position of the priyayi dialect tends to be perpetuated, moreover, by the availability of a fairly rich scholarly literature going back to the middle of the nineteenth century.

A second tendency of these older writings is to abstract the speech levels from the larger social and cultural complex to which they are integrally related. Priyayi repeatedly told me that all aspects of conduct, not just speech, are subject to interactional norms and aesthetic evaluations as relatively refined (*alus*) or coarse (*kasar*) conduct. Learning the speech levels was not the same as learning proper Javanese conduct (*cara Jawa*), they said, since all aspects of conduct and self-presentation need to be enacted and evaluated interactionally. Several older priyayi were fond of saying that using Javanese is a kind of art (they used the Indonesian word *kesenian*) for dealing properly with others. Such hyperbolic statements contain a kernel of truth, insofar as the ethics and aesthetics of priyayi conduct interpenetrate.

Priyayi sociohistorical circumstances and views of etiquette are sketched in the next chapter to provide background information important for understanding strategies and norms for priyayi speech level usage. To adopt a conventionally humble demeanor (linguistic and otherwise) has long been for priyayi not just ethically proper but an especially congenial interactive means to individual social ends. The "code" of verbal politeness can be located in a priyayi ethics of interaction by adducing links between traditional priyayi conceptions of etiquette and the patterns of change in speech level vocabularies dealt with in later chapters.

The third striking lesson I learned while in Yogyakarta was that Javanese do not conceptualize talk about the speech levels in the terms I was learning in the classroom and from books. Even casual conversations about why I was in Yogyakarta led Javanese of all backgrounds to remark on the difficulty of the speech levels in ways which differed from what I was reading in the literature. Most of the literature is framed with Javanese metalinguistic terms that are structurally and analytically precise but have little in common with "ordinary" Javanese ways of talking about talk. This matter was to become practically important during my research on speech level use when I elicited priyayi reports on their own and others' usage. They described the particular examples I proffered with evaluational criteria I have described in detail elsewhere (1985b:76–97), but they responded to my broader questions about how persons speak (or once spoke) to one another in ways that were difficult to reconcile with statements in the older literature. Views on interaction I encountered while a student thus became a practical issue for research, and an issue for this sociolinguistic description.

At the end of my studies in 1978 I decided to move to Surakarta, some sixty-five kilometers to the north and east of Yogyakarta, to do research shaped by these half-recognized problems. The political rivalry between the Sultan of Yogyakarta and Susuhunan of Surakarta has long since given way to a more genteel artistic competition, and some reasons Yogyakartans claim ascendancy for their city over Surakarta—as first home to the government of Indonesia, the city of students, and domain of a still-ruling Sultan who is a national figure—were also the reasons I decided to leave. A few short visits gave me the feeling that Surakarta was a little more behind the times and possessed something of the easy-going pace already largely absent (and much lamented) in Yogyakarta. The relative paucity of foreigners (*landa*) in Surakarta, which has a much less developed tourist industry than Yogyakarta, made for fewer and different preconceptions about me among casual acquaintances, as well as for easier entrée, with the help of introductions from priyayi friends in Yogyakarta, into the city's priyayi social circles.

Under the Dutch aegis Surakarta's two-century-old courtly priyayi community developed what Peacock (1971:72) has aptly called a "hothouse" culture. Long before it became a subprovincial capital in postcolonial Indonesia its kings were figureheads, the last of whom headed a court that was being deserted by priyayi who moved in the late 1930's to new coastal centers of economic and political power.[2] After the Japanese invasion and the revolution for Independence, Surakarta was finally and abruptly brought into a national context and a new political reality. It is difficult to look at Surakarta now, a rapidly growing, sprawling city of half a million people, and imagine what it was like when my older acquaintances were born there seventy years ago. Once a royal exemplary center, it is now an Indonesian subdistrict capital and commercial center; priyayi houses once surrounded by rice fields now look out on six-lane highways complete with street and traffic lights. Traditional pavilionesque priyayi residences still stand behind some of the dirty whitewashed walls in crowded residential areas (*kampung*) named for the nobles who once lived there, but many have fallen into disrepair or been sold by priyayi who cannot afford the rising costs of proper maintainance. An open pavilion requires surrounding space for some slight measure of privacy, which is increasingly impractical in a city located in one of the most densely populated nonurban areas of the world.[3]

After six months living in a small house in a nondescrept *kampung* I and my wife moved to a set of rooms close to but detached from a traditional house in a walled-in compound still belonging to a high-ranking priyayi family. From this convenient base I continued

2. For figures that reflect the general pattern of this migration, and further discussion of the social changes that led to it, see Errington 1985b:54–58.
3. For insightful descriptions of the contemporary Surakartan scene, see Siegel 1986.

to develop a network of priyayi acquaintances; my purposes and presence in tightly knit priyayi circles were legitimized in part by this connection. Over eighteen months I became acquainted with members of a dozen priyayi households, developing acquaintanceships whenever possible with members of two or three generations in each. Visits which were at first rather formal gradually developed into a more easy-going, semiroutine series of morning and afternoon visits punctuated by attendance at ceremonies and outings. I interviewed, questioned, and chatted with them in more and less structured ways; gave some of my younger acquaintances English lessons; talked about, observed, used, and was corrected in my use of "proper" etiquette, linguistic and otherwise.

These are not unsophisticated people. Priyayi were for sixty or seventy years members of a Dutch-educated and Dutch speaking intelligentsia, and are now an important segment of a broadly Western-educated Indonesian elite. Virtually all my older priyayi acquaintances went to Dutch-language schools (some in the Netherlands, where they took doctorates in law), speak Dutch (some also German, French, and English), and know much of the world beyond the confines of their city. This group includes retired and semiretired college and high school teachers, writers, politicians, and artists. Their views of their traditional priyayi heritage differ. Some regard themselves (or presented themselves to me) as members of the shrinking class of guardians of traditional Javanese values that are being lost in an age of modernization. Others conveyed the image of men and women of two worlds, with a remembrance of the good aspects of their parents' and grandparents' Surakarta, but also an awareness of needs and opportunities of the new nation. All felt quite qualified and willing at the outset to take the education of a well-intentioned foreigner in hand.

Virtually all have influential relatives in the new urban center, Jakarta, where many lived for long periods of time. Their children are urbane in a different way. They have grown up in a different social milieu, been educated in different ways, and aspire to a different type of elitehood. Because priyayi have long been among the wealthier and most education-conscious members of an increasingly education-conscious society, their children routinely graduate from high school and more often than not from college. Many households within the extended families I came to know had left Surakarta, and many had a member or two living abroad, permanently or temporarily, as a student, government official, or expatriate. The female head of one household liked to say half-seriously that I had come to Surakarta in exchange for her son, a year younger than I, who was then in Minnesota working on a doctorate in economics. Not all priyayi travel quite as far in search of an education, but they do commonly leave Surakarta to find work, schooling, or both. They leave usually as much out of desire as necessity, because they are often anxious to move out of the city which their parents find peaceful but is for them something of a backwater. Some were more interested in what I could tell them about disco than English, and were often amused by picayune questions about old-fashioned forms of linguistic politesse their parents took seriously but they barely know and rarely use.

Linguistic and social change in Surakarta over the last fifty years has been obvious and subtle. By the 1920s Dutch was widely known to priyayi as an elite ingroup code largely free of the socially significant distinctions encoded in the speech levels. Malay too was a language used in the colonial context, although it had little of the prestige of Dutch. Both languages made possible a very new kind of interactive free play, not just as new languages for communicating new ideas but as vehicles of verbal interaction largely free of the precise, obligatory, and ubiquitous marks of status differences in Javanese. The fate of the two languages was very different. Dutch, banned by the Japanese, still carries the stigma of the colonialist elite even if it also serves as an ingroup code among older members of the Dutch-educated postcolonial elite.[4]

Malay has evolved into *bahasa Indonesia*, the national language that has superseded Dutch in all respects. It is the language of offices (or at least of officials acting in official capacities), of schools, intellectual discourse, and the mushrooming "modern" national culture: movies, novels, pop songs, television, radio news and soap operas are all the province of the national language. The growth and acceptance of Indonesian by people of all strata of Indonesian society, and its

---

4. See on this point Tanner 1967 and Anderson 1966. It is still quite common for some of my older informants when talking with older friends to intersperse freely their Javanese with Dutch.

rapid spread even to the rural peasantry, are remarkable aspects of Indonesian nation-building.[5] For Javanese speakers Indonesian is a relatively flexible means of communication that does not carry, as did prewar Malay, a feeling of stiffness, formality, and lack of ethnic identification. Before the war, as one priyayi said to me, Malay was not *luwes* ('supple'), but hardly more than a decade after the declaration of independence it had become less a non-Javanese and more of a national language for urban speakers.[6] Indonesian has progressively displaced Javanese in a wide range of prestigious contexts, and has entered the repertoires of more and more Javanese.

It would have been surprising to find little substantial change and variation in the structure and use of the speech levels, given their structural intricacies and integral relation with a highly stratified priyayi community that has changed dramatically in the last fifty years. Knowledge of the speech levels is changing and, many Surakartans claim, dying out; Indonesian's impact on use and knowledge of Javanese is a widely discussed issue in both scholarly and popular literature. Most of my acquaintances, young and old, noted more or less regretfully that these days young people do not use "good Javanese:" they run to Indonesian.

An ethnographically grounded account of linguistic interaction in Surakarta would deal, then, not just with structure and use of Javanese speech levels, but with a wide range of code switching and code choice involving Indonesian as well as Javanese. Some occasions and texts of interaction that would provide the basis for such an ethnography of speech have been collected by Wolff and Poedjoseodarmo (1982) and myself, and discussed pedagogically by Keeler (1984), but the inseparable issue of bilingualism is held in abeyance here to focus more narrowly on one kind of linguistic descriptive background that

---

5. Some sources relevant to this process are cited and discussed in Errington 1986.

6. As one Javanese observer remarked: "When I was young . . . if I heard people speaking Malay I felt it was as if they were treating each other as different kinds of people, it lacked intimacy, they weren't 'treating the other as a sibling' [*sumanak*]. Unless one was talking with a friend of the same level, using krama was too formal, ngoko was too coarse, and in that situation one would use Malay. Is it still that way? Not at all." (Prawirohardja 1958:32)

would in any event be presupposed for a wider-ranging ethnographic account.

Two major kinds of change in Javanese usage can be adduced here as symptoms of the changing composition of Surakartan society. First, it no longer follows from the fact that priyayi are the "best" speakers of "good" Javanese that they are necessarily models other speakers are particularly concerned to emulate. Second, the rise of a relatively heterogeneous educated class has made for changing conceptions of social status, patterns of proper interaction, and norms for linguistic etiquette in the community at large. The social circumstances in which priyayi born after 1950 or so have grown up differ radically from those of their predecessors, and younger priyayi are less conscious of any ascribed status as holders of social privilege or standardizers of a language. Their use of linguistic etiquette differs in obvious and unobvious ways from that of their grandparents and parents, who label many widespread features of contemporary usage, including their own children's, as 'wrong' (*salah*) and 'errors which are widely accepted' (*salah kaprah*). Even linguistically conservative priyayi must accept such usage, even if they do not adopt it, because traditional patterns of and norms for etiquette use are increasingly anachronistic in contemporary Surakarta. But to say that Javanese speech levels are dead, or even, as a whole, are moribund, is oversimplistic. Rather, they are changing along with the community of Javanese speakers and social contexts in which they mediate interaction.

This book is an account of some aspects of such sociolinguistic variation, dealing with changing vocabularies of priyayi linguistic etiquette insofar as they can be studied through a literature dating back to the mid-nineteenth century, reports of use, and observed use among priyayi who were born as early as 1920 and as late as 1965. It elaborates and documents a short sketch of speech level change (Errington 1985a) and counts as something of a companion work to an earlier monograph (Errington 1985b) that deals with syntagmatic, combinatory patterns of speech level vocabularies in structurally unitary styles of address. The earlier work, based on related findings gathered during research on which this work is largely based, was oriented to changes in priyayi repertoires of address styles—patterned combinations of the speech level vocabularies—and the ways those changes can be interpreted as linguistic reflexes of social change in the priyayi community. It is artificial but convenient to distinguish analytically these two descriptive foci, and to rehearse major conclusions of the earlier work where they bear on specific points considered here.

Although this work speaks in part to the social background of structural linguistic change, it is focused primarily on changing memberships of the speech level vocabularies, and the structures of paradigmatic sets of stylistically opposed speech level terms. Of central interest here are linguistic and semiotic principles that help organize a description of the structures of the speech level vocabularies, and patterns of use that have changed those structures. Changes in the speech levels are presented with an eye to the sociohistorical circumstances and changing cultural perspectives of speech level users, and though cast in the idiom of code description this approach allows a place for speakers' points of view, since speakers' strategic speech level use has had longstanding effects on the structures of the speech levels and norms for their use.

The strategy is to introduce structural, ethnographic, and historical considerations that bear on an account of speech level structure, and to organize descriptions of linguistic particulars by systematically applying a few basic linguistic and sign theoretic distinctions. These are at least expositorily useful notions for the Javanese case, but are also abstract enough to allow for comparison with other cases of linguistic etiquette. For the sake of expository clarity, I do not explore parallels with other cases here. The broad terms with which this account is framed can be introduced along with some of the reasons why the "speech levels" are better thought of as "speech styles" and as integral parts of "linguistic etiquette."

Speech Styles and Linguistic Etiquette

Well before starting research I had recognized that phrases like "speech levels," "vocabulary of courtesy" (Gonda 1948), "verbal politesse," "linguistic decorum," "linguistic etiquette," and the Dutch *taalsoorten* convey little of a Javanese phrase to which they stand as very rough equivalents: *unggah-ungguh ing basa*, which is better translated as 'the relative values of language'. Priyayi understand conduct to be a matter of gauging one's own status and social relations vis-a-vis others, what can be called the *unggah-ungguh* of a social relation, and adopting the appropriate demeanor or behavioral style in interaction with them. As one elderly gentleman instructed me: "Whenever two people meet they should ask themselves: 'Who is this person? Who am I? What is this person to me?' (Here he held out his hands, palms up, as if they were pans of a scale.) That's *unggah-ungguh*." Proper linguistic and nonlinguistic behavior, endowed with diffuse but very real moral import, manifests one's evaluation of the *unggah-ungguh* of a social relation based on social parameters schematically described in Chapter 3.

The phrase "*unggah-ungguh* of language" suggests an integral relation between stylistically differentiated speech varieties, the larger complexes or gestalts of stylized behavior of which speech is part, and interactional contexts to which ordered behavior is oriented. Etiquette or *tata-krama*, 'the order(ing) of conduct', counts as a conceptual rubric for all modes of self-presentation and guided doings (Goffman 1974:35), including speech, which key to the *unggah-ungguh* of a social relation. Speaking is integrated with other more or less refined (*alus*) facets of behavior—sitting, standing, pointing, composing one's countenance, and so on—and is realized with them in social context.

The complexities of speech level structure make it is easy to overlook the dynamic fluidity and potential for latent expressiveness of speech level use, and to overlook also the kinds of expressive switch between levels that may occur in a single interactive encounter and even a single utterance. This is one reason why I prefer, like Uhlenbeck (1978:307), the term "speech styles" to "speech levels," which may connote a sense of categorical rigidity. It is easy also to overlook many aspects of speech behavior that are analytically independent of the speech style system but are also subject to normative modulation in relatively polite, refined conduct. Examples to be taken up here are acts of reference and address to persons (discussed in Chapters 3 and 5), that may involve terms which are not at all elaborated in the speech style system—proper names, titles, some kin terms—but are nonetheless tremendously expressive of respect or intimacy; different ways of issuing directives in a single speech style (discussed in Chapter 6) that may be more or less explicit, unrefined (*kasar*), and impolite; and the use or abstinence from use of certain interjections (discussed in Chapter 7), the modulation of intonational patterns, and other features that contribute to the relative refinedness and what Geertz (1960:240) usefully calls the "flatness of affect" of speech.

All these aspects of "ordered conduct" have integral places in priyayi linguistic etiquette. For the purposes of this description, which touches on variation in principle distinct from lexical speech style variation, it is useful to keep in mind the difference between the "social meanings" (as Geertz puts it) of the system of speech styles, of the broader sphere of linguistic etiquette that subsumes them, and the still more general interactional domain which is the 'ordering of conduct', or etiquette in general. All stylistically elaborated other-oriented action may be more or less refined, and more or less appropriate in a given context.

As language, speech styles are structured, conventionally significant vehicles of communicative intention used and construed in occasions of speech through knowledge of a language system or code. The specifically linguistic face of Javanese linguistic etiquette resides in the propositionality and semantico-referential significances of speech and its elements (Silverstein 1976), what Geertz calls the "normal linguistic" or "denotative" meanings in the passage quoted previously. As a means for referring and predicating, representing states of affairs, and communicating intentions, Javanese is an instrument for speaking *of* things, and the speech styles are styles of doing the "same" semantico-referential work encoded systematically in "words" that share a given "meaning."

It is obvious but nontrivial that Javanese speech styles count as stylistic subsystems that are superimposed on the semantico-referential apparatus of the language and partake of its systematic properties. In more technical structuralist terms, the code of Javanese associates multiple stylistically opposed signifiers (sound shapes) with a given signified (semantic concept). (Some notable exceptions to the rule of transparent semantic correspondences are discussed in Chapter 6.) Such many-to-one sound to sense relations are intuitively presupposed in authors' and native speakers' statements about the semantic comparability of stylistically opposed sound shapes, which commonly define a "word" of one speech style with a "word" from another: "Word *A* of style *Y* means the same as word *B* of style *Z*" or

Introduction 13

"Word *A* has *B* for its equivalent in style *Z*." The speech styles articulate as an oppositively and combinatorily structured Saussurean system, entities which alternate and co-occur in patterned, well-formed ways that are necessary for contextualized pragmatic interpretability of use. System structure—internal patterns of alternation and combination, and internal sense relations within and across stylistically distinct vocabularies—are the foci of most descriptions of the speech styles, which provide little detail about the system's implementation in use.

As etiquette the speech styles have context-bound symbolic import, what Geertz calls "status" meaning or "connotative" meaning in use to speak *to* or *address* someone. Styles are chosen from style repertoires, used and interpreted as part of a larger interactive whole: the here and now, *hic et nunc*, of ongoing social interaction. The fit between an occasion and context of use of a given speech style can be thought of as pragmatically meaningful, insofar as its "meaning" can only be characterized vis-a-vis socially established features of contexts of use. These relations between use and context are dealt with normatively by scholars and native speakers alike, insofar as they link stylistic types with feature types of appropriate contexts, or describe particular instances of speech style use in actual cases of interaction.

Such *metapragmatic* statements (Silverstein 1976:48) through which speech events and norms of use are conceptualized and objectified as objects of description can thus be relatively abstract or concrete. To say that the speech style called *krama* is refined is to say in abbreviated manner that tokens of that style type normatively presuppose contexts in which it is appropriate to behave in a refined manner. On the other hand, to tell someone (for instance, an ignorant foreigner) to use a particular second person pronoun to some other person is to advise or instruct that person on the nature of his or her social relation with another, vis-a-vis features of usage and associated norms for appropriate conduct.

The "social meanings" of speech styles are realized, then, at the juncture of encoded stylistic opposition and normative typifications of context on one hand, and the experience of face-to-face interaction on the other. To use Javanese linguistic etiquette or understand priyayi metapragmatic statements requires tacit knowledge of particular features of context types assumed to bear normatively on use—social status distinctions, kin relations and role relations, and so on—that priyayi conceptualize and describe in ways taken up in chapter three.

Dynamic relations between shared norms and particular contexts are usually downplayed in structural linguistic descriptions, but obtrude quite clearly in Javanese linguistic etiquette use, because an indefinite number of social factors that elude normative typification may bear on particular occasions of interaction. Normative descriptions made by both authors and native speakers tend to draw attention away from such context-specific, code-contingent factors, and to downplay the reciprocal relation between conventions for and occasions of use. Speech styles are assimilated to communicative and social projects that are informed but not wholly determined by norms of use, and strategic style use may impute features to and perhaps transform intersubjectively constituted speech partner relations. There is a disjunction and potential tension between general norms and particular occasions of interaction which is important here to make sense of change in the structure of the speech style system.

This description of structural change is written with an eye to the double, interpenetrating significances of Javanese speech styles as vehicles of semantico-referential meaning (a means for speaking *of*), and behavioral styles for engaging in and mediating face-to-face interaction (a means for speaking *to*). This double significative character of linguistic etiquette—these two respects, as Peirce would put it, in which uses of speech styles stand for something to somebody—is a central focus of this work.

Referential and Social Indexicality

There are specific points of congruence or coincidence between these two kinds of speech style "meaning," referential and social. Like all languages, Javanese encodes deictic elements that serve referentially by virtue of existential connections between occasions of use and features of spatiotemporal contexts of use (Lyons 1977b:636ff.). Descriptions of the encoded meanings of deictic forms must recurringly incorporate descriptions of feature types that are instantiated in different contexts. As Jakobson (1971:130–147) insightfully pointed out, referential deictic categories anchor code to context by encoding

Introduction 15

context features presupposed for use of deictic elements, whose referential or denotative values therefore shift, to use Jespersen's word (1964:123), from one occasion and context of use to another. There is a correspondence between the referential significance of encoded context-dependent deictic elements, and the social significances of speech styles like those in Javanese that is intuitively clear and neatly captured by Fillmore's term "social deixis" (1975a:76–86).[7] Both types of "meaning" are conventional, yet always realized in ways crucially dependent on aspects of context of use.

This basic significative fit is explored here, though, in different terms that allow for a different expository emphasis and foreground different descriptive goals. The term "social deixis" makes it easy to privilege implicitly semantico-referential deictic significances of speech, and to make referential deixis a model or prototype for understanding context dependent social significances of speech styles like those in Javanese. I adopt a broader, Peircian sign-theoretic notion of *indexicality* to subsume "referential deixis" and "social deixis" as related linguistic significative subtypes under a broader symbolic or semiotic rubric. In this I follow the line of thought developed from Saussurean semiology and Peirce's semiotic by Benveniste (1971), Jakobson (1971, 1980), and Silverstein (1976, 1977a, 1977b) to examine various indexical semiotic processes that interpenetrate in linguistic communication.

The term "semiotic" is used in enough more or less specific, more or less fashionable ways that it may seem gratuitous if not misleading to introduce it here. But I intend it in a technical sense to refer to Peirce's writings on the theory of signs, from which I borrow this descriptive notion. For present purposes it suffices to describe as indexical the significative nature of all representative entities (or signs) whose representative character depends crucially on an existential, dynamic link between that sign and whatever that sign represents. Deictic elements like personal pronouns, for example, are referential indexical signs that are deprived of their representative nature (as terms of reference for speech partners) if features of a contextual whole of which their tokens are part (secured uptake with copresent

7. This has since been developed as a rubric in linguistic pragmatics by Brown and Levinson 1978:317–19 and 1979, Levinson 1983:89–94 and Levinson 1979, briefly discussed in the conclusion.

person/addressee) are absent. Deictic referential elements have distinctively indexical *modes* of reference.

But indexical significances accrue to many other aspects of communicative behavior that stand in dynamic, existential relations to what they represent. A physical gesture of pointing is prototypically indexical; an interjection is indexically significant of a copresent momentary attitude of its user; the social "meaning" of a choice of speech style can be construed only as part of a social context in which it mediates social interaction, indexing an essentially subjective and occasional[8] evaluation of immediately experienced social context.

The semiotic rubric of indexicality serves here to describe structural complexities of the speech style system while capturing the common semiotic basis of the referential code of Javanese and linguistic etiquette. By taking seriously the notion that diverse modes of symbolic behavior share underlying semiotic traits, we can deal explicitly with interpenetrating symbolic aspects of linguistic and nonlinguistic conduct, describing 'the relative values of language' (*unggah-ungguh ing basa*) and linguistic etiquette as integral parts of 'the ordering of conduct' (*tata-krama*), which is etiquette as a whole. The interplay between referential and stylistic indexical significances of speech style use is a crucial and recurring leitmotif in this work. It figures in the classification of speech style elements introduced in Chapter 4, where broad distinctions between linguistic signs that are referential or not, referential of persons or not, and indexically referential or not, yield a semantic classification with clear correlates in the system's structure. This same interplay underlies and helps to describe changes in the highly mutable inventories of personal pronouns and kin terms discussed in Chapter 5, and the se-

8. It would be misleading not to acknowledge that I first encountered the phrase "essentially subjective and occasional," which has found its way into other parts of this work, in Husserl's investigation of expression and meaning (1971:315). I agree with Brown and Levinson (1979) that sociolinguistics must come to grips with communicative intentionality, and believe that Husserl's neglected remarks (especially in his Logical Investigations I and II) on the relation of convention to communication are important for dealing with this problem. Rather than explore the relation of pragmatic salience to communicative intention and larger philosophical issues, I restrict myself here to developing the notion in service of specific descriptive goals.

mantic and syntactic peculiarities of honorific performative directives presented in Chapter 6. It informs likewise a description of structural peculiarities of refined linguistic deictic usage in Chapter 7, and suggests some general conclusions about other aspects of speech that count for priyayi as relatively polite and refined. These are styles of conduct in which the immediate affect of indexically significant behavior—linguistic and nonlinguistic, referential and nonreferential—is normatively muted.

Pragmatic Salience and Sociolinguistic Change

All of this is quite distant from what one reads in most descriptions of the speech styles and hears from native speakers, but this approach was stimulated by real differences between the two descriptive viewpoints presupposed by these sources of information. The conceptual gap between them induced me to try to develop an analytic approach that could reconcile traditional accounts with the priyayi metapragmatic idiom, scholars' and speakers' ways of talking about talk. Enough information about the structure of the speech style system can be drawn from a half-dozen or so descriptions of priyayi usage to develop this classificatory approach, even if the metalinguistic vocabularies used to frame those treatments draw attention away from some system-internal structural contrasts. I might not have recognized these incompletenesses had native speakers' unstudied observations not drawn my attention to them. Priyayi have surprisingly little use for the metalinguistic vocabulary in the literature, and I spent much research time asking people very broad questions about how they and others use (or used) linguistic etiquette.

For older speakers, providing responses to these questions turned out to be inseparable from the task of providing the foreign student with prescriptions for proper use. Some operationally important points emerged from these conversations. Priyayi devoted much more attention to particular aspects of linguistic usage than to the broader contrasts in style usage described at length in the literature. In fact they made use of particular classes of speech style variants as a kind of metapragmatic vocabulary. The ways they directly or indirectly corrected my usage, instructed others in how to address me, and changed their linguistic usage to fit their changing relations with me and others led me to see that more rides socially on use of some speech elements than others. These relatively interactively important elements I have come to think of as relatively *pragmatically salient*.

Some of the pragmatically salient speech elements used in metapragmatic ways by priyayi are only marginally elaborated in the style system, which is one reason why it is important to integrate a description of the speech styles with a general treatment of linguistic etiquette. On the other hand, the single most important metalinguistic vocabulary in their descriptions of use includes personal pronouns, which are so elaborated in the speech style system as to elude complete classification with the metalinguistic terminology received from the literature. This point was at first only operationally important in my efforts to gauge the accuracy of different native speakers' reports on usage. As I compared what I observed myself with reports offered by different speakers or single speakers on different occasions, and with what I knew of the literature, I found that speakers were generally better able to describe some kinds of use than others. Their statements about salient elements were most accurate, most often spontaneously mentioned, and most easily elicited. Speakers conceptualized usage by foregrounding terms referential of persons as relatively crucial mediators of face-to-face social interaction.

As a term for alluding to something like speakers' "awarenesses" of the specifics of use, pragmatic salience is innocuous enough. But comparison of the literature and cross-generation variation in contemporary usage shows that sets of stylistic variants that have changed relatively rapidly are also relatively pragmatically salient, and so the notion bears on an account of historical change in patterns of use, which is the primary goal of the research. Some linguistic elements—notably titles (Chapter 3), personal pronouns (Chapter 5), and kin terms (Chapter 5)—have been relatively mutable in their social import as the result of patterns of strategic use largely unrecognized and undiscussed in the code-oriented literature. Other less pragmatically salient vocabularies have been relatively stable, and have changed through analogical sound pattern extension stimulated in part by the covert dialectal functions of these elements. Changes in these less pragmatically salient vocabularies have been largely unnoticed or sociocentrically misunderstood by speakers.

Speakers' awarenesses of use are linked to knowledge of strategies of use, and so indirectly to the dynamics of variation and change in the code. Linguistic signs' modes and objects of reference correlate not just with the structural complexity or elaboration of their paradigmatic sets, but also with speakers' awarenesses of their roles as mediators of verbal interaction, susceptible to strategic use. Through such strategic use within different social strata, structural change has gradually and recurringly come about.

To look for links between structural change and communicative function is nothing new in sociolinguistic analysis, but to invoke a notion of "native speaker awareness" as an explanatory link between the two as I do here may be more questionable or controversial. Although I might have drawn these correlations between referential function and stylistic elaboration from the literature without relying heavily on speakers' conceptions of use, or even without going to Surakarta, I would have gained little sense of the interactive forces that have been exerted on the code. The notion of pragmatic salience has finally proved most useful for my effort to explain these broad contrasts, and to reconcile the two broadly different models of variation and change that prove descriptively useful.

Put crudely, and in ways to be emended and qualified, two different sorts of social pressure have affected different speech style vocabularies, which have changed in ways that reflect their contrasting social significances in Javanese usage at large. A progressive leveling of pragmatically salient markers of status and status differences has been complemented by decreasingly appropriate asymmetric exchange patterns broadly parallel to patterns of pronominal use described by Brown and Gilman (1960). Less salient variants are not just relatively polite (or appropriate) vis-a-vis contexts of use, but are also standard or substandard as parts of dialects of socially stratified priyayi and non-priyayi subcommunities. Changes in these vocabularies have articulated in ways usefully summarized with Labov's mechanism of linguistic change (1972). The mechanistic metaphor is less suited to shifts in Javanese lexicons of polite speech than to systematic changes in phonological systems of dialects, but it provides a partial, useful picture of change and variation in the standard priyayi dialect occurring on the periphery of native speakers' interactive awarenesses.

To develop an account of general contrasts in the structures, referential significances, and social significances of speech style components, I have had use for these two different ways of understanding linguistic variation in context and encountered two broader descriptive issues. One has to do with the semiotic basis of this description of Javanese linguistic etiquette, which is invoked by the notion of pragmatic salience. The other has to do with dynamics of sociolinguistic change which arise from the interplay between norms for code use and speakers' instrumentally oriented awarenesses of speech components as mediators of social relationships.

The route to these general issues is circuitous, passing through sketches of priyayi culture and social structure in Chapters 2 and 3 to a semiotic/linguistic description of speech style structure in Chapters 4 through 7. Although the account is framed with concepts generalizable far beyond the descriptive particulars presented, and adopts a perspective far more abstract than those of speakers of the Javanese I know, it has grown out of my effort to make sense of diverse specifics that are integral parts of a single linguistic system. For all of its complexity, Javanese linguistic etiquette shares formal and functional traits with other linguistic codes and with simpler, less exotic cases of verbal politesse.

That the second person pronoun paradigm is the most complex and changable in the speech style system, for instance, should not be terribly surprising; this is, as one foreign student of the speech levels wrote almost a century ago, "in the nature of the situation" (Walbeehm 1896:17). More surprising would be comparable structural elaboration or mutability in stylistic alternants of the causative verbal suffix, or coordinate conjunctions, or any number of other structurally distinct elements of the linguistic code. It is to the "nature of the situation," intrinsic properties of the structures and significances of speech embodied and highly elaborated in Javanese linguistic etiquette, that this account is devoted. By describing the system as a part of priyayi linguistic etiquette in broad terms, I do not try to minimize the system's elaborateness so much as reduce its exotic appearance. A fairly abstract, sign-theoretic point of view also helps to account for complexities of priyayi usage in ways that suggest some basic principles of stylistic elaboration adducible from less overtly complex cases of linguistic etiquette.

The prospect of theoretically interesting conclusions may help maintain interest in the complex particulars of an unusual situation, and an appropriate way to broach those particulars is to consider very broadly the cultural heritage and sociohistorical circumstances of priyayi, and the ways present circumstances have been shaped by the same forces shaping the forms of priyayi linguistic etiquette.

2

Ethics, Etiquette, and the Exemplary Center

> The appearance of the Honored Lord
> did not differ from that which was usual
> when the times were still prosperous,
> but in his heart were darkening clouds
> as he continuously brooded over
> the destruction of the capital;
> the *kraton*
> and all of its treasure
> were as good as destroyed,
> burned to nothing by the Chinese enemy.
> (Ricklefs and Poedjosoedarmo 1967:94)

During the political turmoil of the mid eighteenth century Pakubuwana II, king of Java, founded Surakarta on the west bank of the Solo River. Located approximately halfway between the peaks of the volcanoes Lawu and Merbabu as the crow flies, it was built to replace the former capital named Kartasura, some fourteen kilometers to the west, where the king is described in the passage quoted above as he brooded over the desecration of his palace.

The Kartasura *kraton* (from the word *ratu* 'king', thus, 'place of the king') had been founded in 1680 by Mangkurat II as a new seat for his kingdom after he won a power struggle with his siblings. By conquest and alliance, his grandfather, Sultan Agung, had come to dominate all of Java and so founded what is now called the latter Mataram Empire. But Sultan Agung's son Mangkurat I, who took the throne at his death, quickly earned a reputation as a cruel, unpredictable leader

Ethics, etiquette, and the exemplary center 23

who stopped at nothing as he sought to consolidate his hold on the northern coast, traditionally a major locus of political unrest and rebellion against the inland monarchs. In a palace coup Mangkurat I was deposed, and the victorious faction placed one of his sons, Mangkurat II, on the throne. The East Indies Company played a central role in this first of many acts of direct political interference by the Dutch among the royal houses of Mataram.

By the turn of the century the struggle for supremacy among the elite broke into armed conflict, and in the first of the Three Wars of Succession the throne fell to Mangkurat III. He was soon dethroned (again with the help of the Dutch) but his uncle, who took the throne with the title Pakubuwana I, soon died, in 1719. Another in the line of Mangkurat took the throne but lived only four years, and in 1723 Pakubuwana's son became king with the title Pakubuwana II.

Central Java was not the only area of the island where there was trouble during the late seventeenth and early eighteenth centuries. Ethnic tensions had been building in Batavia (site of the present Jakarta, on the northeast coast); in the face of hostility on the part of natives, Dutch and newly arrived Chinese immigrants became increasingly distrustful of each other as well. In 1740 the tension exploded in a massacre of Chinese; the survivors evacuated Batavia and moved east in roving bands, raiding as they went. When the Chinese reached the area of Semarang (on the north central coast), they were joined by some discontented nobility seeking to improve their lot, and en masse they moved south to Kartasura where they looted and razed the palace of Pakubuwana II. The king was able to escape, and after the rebellion was put down (again the Dutch played an important role) he returned to the site of his destroyed palace (see Rickleffs 1974, 1983). Although he was able to reestablish residence, and was still recognized as the lord of the land, he decided to move the site of his *kraton*.

This sketch of a chapter in Javanese history contains elements of old Java and the Java that was to be. In the turmoil surrounding succession to the throne and the struggle for supremacy, the cycle of Javanese politics—formation, fragmentation, and dissolution of power centers—was continuing. The Dutch had come onto the stage of Javanese politics at a time of dissolution when the land, like the royal house, was in chaos, and this unprecedented foreign presence her-

24   Ethics, etiquette, and the exemplary center

alded the beginning of a new stability. First as kingmakers, later as outright colonialists, the Dutch divided and fixed the powers of the nobility, and then gradually eroded the power of their kings. It might have been a foreshadowing, what the Javanese call a *pralambang*, that two people were sent out by Pakubuwana II to seek a site for the new palace: a trusted official, a *tumenggung*, and the Dutch military commander Hohendorff.

The royal palace in a traditional Javanese kingdom was always much more than the place where the king lived; it was a locus of administrative and magico-religious power, an exemplary center of royal glory. There crucial political decisions were made for the kingdom, but there also was celebrated the king's status as receptacle of God-granted right to rule, manifested and inculcated in the "cult of glory." It is not hard to understand Pakubuwana II's distress that his palace, an extra-ordinary locus of power, had in a real sense been desecrated. Because its physical destruction threatened likewise to destroy his legitimacy, his decision to move may be interpreted as an attempt to renew that legitimacy, as well as the peace and prosperity of the realm. If the old capital proved to be ill-fated, he could maintain and at the same time alter his connection with the past by reversing the two elements of its name. His hopes, as it turned out, were justified in a way he surely had not foreseen. Although the symbolic status of his noble house was to be preserved for an unprecedented two centuries, that stability cost his descendants their temporal power, which the Dutch usurped as they progressively divorced the court from their subjects.

This episode in Javanese history may convey some sense of the importance in traditional Java of the conception of exemplary center and ideology of kingship which informed not only Pakubuwana II's decision to found a new city but also the ideally refined, ritualized forms of conduct that were renewed there by his courtiers. As part of the cult of royal glory celebrated in the courtly milieu, stylized markers of social status set off the palace and courtiers from more mundane places and people. Priyayi, persons "close to the king," made use of a system of etiquette that governed both means and ends of interaction. In the traditional priyayi scheme of things, etiquette cannot be conceptually separated either from priyayi understandings of the palace as the place of the king, or the nature of social relations between ruler and ruled, between royal courtiers, or between master and servant.

The Technical Implementation of Kingship

Because the island's geomorphology long promoted regional disunity and factionalism, precolonial Java saw repeated conflict between agrarian inland kingdoms of the south and the north coast mercantile centers (Schrieke 1957:102ff.). Inland agrarian kingdoms in general, and Surakarta in particular, depended for their power and concomitant orderly functioning "first and foremost on the peasantry, whose labor provided the means necessary not only to till the soil but also to do the work of maintaining and sustaining the state . . . " (Moertono 1963:137).

Traditional kingdoms were identified not so much by their borders as by their royal capitals, less by their peripheries than their centers. Javanese, like other Indonesian languages, has a single word which can be glossed as 'royal city' and 'country', both traditionally spoken of as *negara* (in refined language *negari*).[1] In the royal city was the residence of the king, the *kraton*, and the administrative center of the royal polity. Territorial authority and revenues were distinguished in accordance with a given area's proximity to the city and *kraton*. In a concentric circle around the *negara* lay the *negara agung*, literally the 'great country', in which the king's closest officials and family were awarded appanages (sometimes called *palungguhan* 'place to sit'). As source of both royal income and support for royal dependents it was the "heart of the country" (Rouffaer 1921:596) crucial to the welfare of the noble elite as a whole.[2] Within the *negara agung* and the *negara* itself authority was traditionally delegated to counselors called *wedana*, who were overseen by the prime minister, or *adipati*.

Encircling the *negara agung* was the *mancanegara*, 'outside the

1. For discussion of the related Balinese situation, see Geertz 1980. As recently as 1986 I heard one older peasant tell another of her trip to Surakarta as a trip to the *nagari*.
2. The most common measurement of the size of appanages and the kingdom itself was not a unit of land area but a count of tenants by the *cacah* 'household'. See discussion in Moertono 1963:117, and van den Haspel 1985.

negara', territory ruled by monarchs who were less tightly tied to the *kraton* and acknowledged their fealty by paying tribute at the *kraton* in ceremonies of great pomp once or twice a year. These 'lords of the land' (*bupati*) had less restricted administrative prerogatives, and together with the *adipati* and *wedana* formed the highest stratum within the royal government, part of the group often referred to as *priyayi luhur* 'exalted priyayi' or *priyagung* ('great priyayi'). Outside of the *mancanegara* lay the *pasisiran*, 'the coast', over which inland royal houses rarely exercised any real control. Everything else was *tanah sabrang* 'land across the water'.

Most peasants did not owe fealty directly to the king but to such a local lord whose descent, though at least putatively noble, was often traced to a royal line other than that of the reigning king. In delegating power to such persons kings followed "one of the basic principles of administration in Java: choose officials with regional responsibility primarily on the basis of [their] influence in the community" (Moertono 1963:85). The king's delegates in outlying areas with which communication was difficult were a relatively heterogeneous group who could threaten the regime as well as support it, and indirect channels of communication allowed for forestalling of damaging losses of face in case of latent hostility or disagreement.

The king's control in these outer areas was de facto consensual because he perforce relied on subordinate lords for the economic and military support needed to launch expeditions of conquest or reprisal, which were undertaken only after careful weighing of alternatives. As Ricklefs (1974:22) puts it:

> Rebellions could only be put down successfully if a large enough number of local aristocrats, princes, and other notables were sufficiently opposed to the rebellion to send their men to march in royal armies ... even a relatively small amount of opposition, if not immediately dealt with, might ultimately lead to the total collapse of royal power.

Potential rebellion could often be prevented only by relying on checks and balances, avoiding as much as possible "disturbing open clashes that were not absolutely necessary" (Moertono 1963:41).

The 'place of the king' was in this respect a kind of fulcrum to exert military, familial, and political leverage on members of a sometimes fractious local nobility in relatively distant locations. Because difficulties in overseeing delegates were directly proportional to an appointee's distance from the palace, so too the potential seriousness of a threat that person might pose was directly proportional to his proximity with the *kraton*. At the palace the king was on his firmest political ground; it was the place to which potential troublemakers could be summoned, separated from a local base for any suspected power-building, and put within easy reach if sterner measures were necessary.

An extended network of familial ties radiated out from the *kraton* as personalistic avenues for establishing and maintaining political power. Alliances could be established by marrying into the family of some local nomarch whose fealty could thereby be commanded; such affinal relations helped to forestall revolt and also opened the possibility for direct, intimate communication with the king via his wives, at once personal extensions of his power and symbols of his fecundity.

Within the administrative hierarchy power was delegated across strata of priyayi society in ways that can be described conveniently if not perfectly with the Weberian model of the patrimonial state (Schrieke 1957, van den Haspel 1985:81, Anderson 1972:33). Royal power devolved and concretized away from the *kraton* in self-regulating spheres of dominion, formed and centered around the king, as relations between ruler and peripheral subject became looser further from the royal center. Disputes within a given administrative sphere were normally resolved without being referred to higher governmental strata, and so economic, military, and juridical dominion all came to reside in the persons of individual nobles and officials. As overseer of this streamlined but abuse prone system, the king intervened only to deal with troubles which spread beyond an official jurisdiction or were perceived to threaten his rule.[3]

Concomitant with such personalized political power were patron-client relations that linked commoners, officials, and nobles across hierarchical levels throughout the polity. Strong vertical connections across strata came into being at the expense of horizontal ties be-

3. The traditional Javanese polity, then, could be taken as an instance of that more general areal phenomenon called by Tambiah the "galactic polity," and if Surakarta came to resemble what he calls the "strong" version of the galactic polity it was, as Tambiah suggests (Tambiah 1976:124), unusual and, in fact, artificial.

tween members of a single hierarchical strata, as clients of a given patron identified more strongly with their immediate superior than with each other (Scott 1972). These "diffuse, long-standing [relations of] affect-laden mutual obligation," in which "personalistic power accumulated through the role of influencer as provider, protector, educator, source of values" (Jackson 1972:345), are still often described in explicitly familial terms as relations between father (*bapak*) and child (*anak*)—holistic and personalistic rather than explicit and contractual. Relations between intimately and asymmetrically related superior and inferior were ideally represented by the relation of the king and prime minister, which was taken to be paradigmatic of all relations between superior or 'lord' (*gusti*) and inferior or 'servant' (*kawula*). The prime minister was thought to be so finely attuned to and aware of his lord's desire that the most indirect indications of the royal will sufficed to communicate necessary steps to be taken. Such idealized forms of communication likewise permitted the king to involve himself only indirectly and perhaps face-savingly with mundane governmental particulars.[4]

Spheres of such power ideally articulated in a geopolitical pattern likened by Tambiah (1976:102) to the *mandala*, radiating out and pulling away from the apex and center of the kingdom that exerted countering centripetal force from the person of the king and the place of his residence, a political but also an exemplary center (Geertz 1973:331). The king's legitimacy was supported not just by the adroit, discreet balancing of external and potentially disrupting forces, but also by the inculcation of the charisma of God-given right to rule. Stylized and highly ordered interaction helped to set the king, his palace, and his servants off from the rest of the realm as a symbolic manifestation of his and his delegates' magico-religious legitimacy.

Magico-religious Legitimation of Kingship

The exercise of political power from a Weberian perspective can be thought of as one side of a coin, on the other side of which is the kind

4. On the significance of the *kawula/gusti* relation as an image in priyayi mysticism, and conceptions of self and self-conduct, see Geertz 1960 and Errington 1984.

Ethics, etiquette, and the exemplary center   29

of "indigenous political theory" and ideology of power and kingship articulated by Anderson (1972). The traditional Javanese conception of the palace and king is of a piece with an understanding of the royal state as world writ small, a microcosmic "image of the Great Cosmic Order, in which gods maintain absolute dominion" (Moertono 1963:4), to which the realm is indissolubly linked. The stability of each is dependent on the other: if God (in the later monotheistic tradition of Islam espoused by rulers of the latter Mataram empire)[5] rules the universe, then the state as its replica must have within it an image of the One who creates, preserves, and destroys, "a power which, as a part of the Great Cosmic Order, no subject people dare restrict or disturb.... At the center and pinnacle ... is the monarch" (Moertono 1963:57). The palace was a point of direct correspondence between the iconically related, overlapping realms of God and man, and the king as such was God's representative or 'shadow' (*warana*) on earth.

Consonant with this conception of kingship is a conception of power, insightfully described by Anderson, as a tangible property or attribute of persons and things, rather than a property of relations between people. Power is a gift God may bestow or take away, a "mark of divine consent" (Moertono 1963:56) called *wahyu*. The *wahyu* of kingship was traditionally marked by a sign of fitness to rule, a 'light' (*cahya*) sometimes manifest in the countenance of the legitimate king.[6]

> His highness the king ... confirms his office of *kalipah*, meaning the viceroy of the Greatest of Princes [i.e. God]; so it is that he holds the light

---

5. Islam had been syncretized to Javanese religious conceptions by the time Sultan Agung officially adopted it, and so the Arabic terms mentioned later should not be misunderstood or interpreted independently of the Javanese context.

6. *Wahyu* should not be confused with *sakti*. In Javanese *wahyu* refers to God-granted ability and right to serve some function. *Sakti* is supernatural power, derived from instinctual deprivation (*nglakoni*), study, and other practices. As one of my older informants said: "*Wahyu* comes from God, and there are many different kinds. There's the *wahyu* of being president, of being governor, of being a *pesindhèn* (singer with a *gamelan* orchestra). If a *pesindhèn* has *wahyu* she doesn't have to practice a lot; she's got a beautiful voice and everyone wants to hire her. Anybody can get *sakti* if they have the desire, study, and have a good teacher."

[*cahya*] of *wahyu* in three ways. He holds [lit. 'holds in his lap'] the *wahyu* of *Nurbawah*, which means he stands as the king *Binatara*, ruling the world. He holds the *wahyu* of *Kukumah*, meaning that he holds dominion and judges everything in the world. He holds the *wahyu* of *Milayah*, meaning that he [is the one who] has the power to be the compass point and protector [lit. shade] of all his subjects. (Surakarta n.d.: 7)[7]

The *wahyu* of kingship passes at death to another ordinarily descended from the king.[8] Royal power is in this conception absolute, like its source: the preservation of order and peace was the goal and ultimate justification of royal rule symbolized by the two *wringin* ('banyan') trees that traditionally stood only at the gates of the palace as a place of shaded protection.

Alignment with magical and spiritual powers served to augment royal power and legitimacy. Kings descended from Sultan Agung were believed to have inherited his marriage alliance with the Goddess of the South Seas, *Roro Kidul*, whom Sultan Agung had attracted through the power of his meditation.[9] Kings' power extended to the realm of spirits, who were obliged to obey his summons and do his will. For this reason courtiers physically close to the king in the palace were in a supernaturally dangerous place, liminal between the profane realm of ordinary society and the heavens, and were obliged to bear various symbolic marks of status (*kalung samir*) as royal ser-

7. This work, the *Serat Wewaton Tata-Krami Kedhaton*, is a late nineteenth century compendium of court etiquette. *Krami* and *kedhaton* are stylistic variants on *krama* and *kraton*, respectively. In this treatise there is an explicit attempt to reconcile the physical and supernatural statuses of kings in a passage that says explicitly that, as king, the ruler has no kin. "But because he still has the aspect of humanity [a 'servant', *kawula*] there is one acknowledged as his son and successor ... " (Surakarta n.d.:14).

8. On strategies adopted by usurpers of thrones to claim descent from mythohistoric kings, see Schrieke 1957.

9. Sultans of Jogjakarta and Susuhunans of Surakarta alike claim to maintain this supernatural relation. According to one story I heard, the nature of the alliance changed with the accession of Pakubuwana X in the late nineteenth century. One day while his father, Pakubuwana IX, was with his consort in their room in the top floor of the seven story Sangga Buwana (constructed just for this purpose), his young son and future successor, who was playing there, fell. Roro Kidul exclaimed in pity and concern, "Oh, [my] grandchild" (*O nggèr*). In so doing she transformed the alliance from one between husband and wife to (grand)mother and (grand)child.

vants under the king's protection. Supernatural power inheres too in relics of inheritance, *pusaka*, the most powerful and holy (*kramat*) housed in chambers near the king's own rooms (*dalem*) in the palace, which were forbidden to all save appointed female servants and nobles who cleaned them on calendrically auspicious days. These objects, like the person of the king, were potentially dangerous to those not sufficiently powerful to be in proximity with them.[10]

It follows from this conception of kingship that there can be only one king, for God can have only one supreme representative on earth. It follows too that his power, being concrete, is subject to physical limits as it radiates out and away from his person, like a source of light that loses intensity as it diffuses. Mere presence in the palace may allow one to partake or be imbued with some of that power, but is also potentially dangerous, because manifestations of that power would be first and most strongly felt there. Power, as Anderson notes (1972), is amoral; one who has it may do good or evil with it and so "the king had to be of extraordinary excellence and quality . . . [and] depended for guidance on the presence within him, the "Divine Soul" which checked his divine will" (Moertono 1963:40). From his dual nature (*roroning tunggal*) stemmed the king's unique status as the embodiment of the divine in human form, the dynamic tension between sacred and profane in the royal person on which royal power derived.

In this sense the king was not just king (*ratu*) but priest (*pandhita*) preserving order within the kingdom by preserving order at the center and, ultimately, within himself, for a disturbance that affected the king would become palpable throughout the kingdom. The image of the king meditating in the quietness and isolation of his palace fits the care and circumspection with which his subjects of all ranks had to conduct themselves in the *kraton*, and especially in his presence. Audiences (*pasowanan*) were of great solemnity, and the careful arrangement of seating, status being directly proportional to indi-

---

10. The creation of such objects, particularly powerful *kris*, a kind of dagger, required supernatural power. These could only be forged after long periods of meditation and fasting by supernaturally endowed artisans who held the rank of *mpu* and were numbered among the most honored servants of the king.

32   Ethics, etiquette, and the exemplary center

viduals' proximity with the august presence, made it an iconic representation of the social order at large. The king's immobility, self-control, and silence marked his status as the unmoving center from which the motivating and preserving aura of power emanated. As preserver and sustainer, he ideally exercised power only indirectly in the kingdom, because direct action on his part might not only diffuse his power but have catastrophic effects. The doctrine of political noninterference was thus traditionally informed by elite understandings of the relation between royal domain and person of the king: the tranquillity of the latter determined the well-orderedness of the former.

In the person of the king, perhaps, one can see most clearly the traditional Javanese view of "the direct relationship between the state of a person's inner life and his capacity to control the environment" (Soedjatmoko, quoted in Anderson 1972:13). The doctrine of the exemplary center, and of king as paradigmatic representative of God, thus resonated throughout traditional society and especially among the traditional priyayi elite: persons at the center and, to use a phrase many priyayi (in the traditional sense) commonly used to explain the word priyayi to me, 'close to the king' (*cedhak ratu*).

In short, the king was more than a man among men, his *kraton* more than his residence, and those close to him more than his kin and retainers. His palace was the center of the center, a worldly image of the cosmic order, the main stage for the cult of glory that was celebrated by priyayi and had cultural resonances with virtually all forms of interpersonal conduct. This conception of kingship informed not just the rituals and strategies of statecraft, but also the high seriousness with which ritualized, stylistically shaped conduct was enacted and evaluated among celebrants of the cult of royal glory.

To convey very briefly some of the ways conduct served to distinguish the palace and priyayi from other places and persons, we can briefly consider prescribed relations between physical location and proper conduct prescribed for those who had occasion to enter the palace in the king's service. The term *kraton* can in fact be used in different contexts to refer to different physical areas. In the old days it could be used to speak of territory including the ends of the fields (*alun-alun*) that lay north and south of the palace where the army now drills, peddlers hawk wares from stalls, and children play soccer. To visit or leave the palace proper, one passed through seven thresh-

Ethics, etiquette, and the exemplary center

olds symbolizing the seven gates between the realm of mortals and *kahyangan* 'place of the deities'. One of the most important of these is the large door called *Brajanala* in the huge wall, about three hundred by four hundred eighty meters on a side and four meters high, which surrounds not just the palace, but a neighborhood (*kampung*) in which some ten thousand courtiers and elite lived around the turn of the century (van den Haspel 1985:61).

Within this precinct another inner wall gives onto a courtyard that is in turn walled off from the grounds of the palace proper, reached by a final door named *Sri Manganti*. This innermost royal precinct I call the "palace proper" was set off from all the others by explicit, conspicuous rules of conduct. As one official explained to me:

> If I am in the *alun-alun* and a servant comes from the king with a message, he tells me he is the king's messenger, I say "*Kawula*," (lit. 'servant') and then I make obeisance (*sembah*).[11] If I am standing outside of *Brajanala* or *Kemandhungan* and the messenger comes, it's just the same. But if I am inside *Sri Manganti* I say "*Kawula*," make obeisance, and then I squat down (*ndhodhok*) to hear the king's wishes.

These and other kinds of physical and linguistic self-lowering were behavioral, outward marks of inward awareness of place, used to acknowledge inferior status—here, to the king through his messenger surrogate, who animates his words—but also to show oneself a worthy celebrant of the cult of royal glory at the royal apex and center of the kingdom.

The limiting case of etiquette is naturally enough that adopted in the king's immediate presence, which verges on religious ritual in ways that illustrate the resonance between traditional priyayi concerns with maintaining a social order and acting in proper ways, observing *tata-krama* 'ordering of conduct'.

> When one is about to advance into the royal presence [*ngarsa dalem*] one must first take off one's *kris* ... then bow two times, then walk in a squatting position seven steps. Stop, make obeisance again, put the hands

---

11. I translate *sembah* as 'make obeisance', rather than 'bow', to underscore the differences between the motion described with the English word and the action as carried out by Javanese. It is described in Geertz 1960:58fn., and illustrated in Koentjaraningrat 1957:51. Geertz describes it in the context of marriage and the *slametan* cycle, but it seems to be generally recognized as a particularly priyayi gesture, expressive of rank distinction and fealty.

together in front of the body while hunching forward somewhat, then begin walking again. Take seven steps, stop again, make obeisance three times, wait for the space of about three breaths . . . and then begin walking again, pacing in time with one's breath, estimating the distance from the place where the king [or prince] is sitting. When about a step away, stop a little while, in order that the breathing can be ordered and quiet, while making deep obeisance. (Surakarta n.d.: 26–27)

To appear 'in the royal presence' (*ing ngarsa dalem*) is to be located in maximal proximity to the center of royal power, where fear and awe are the expected emotions, and etiquette (like that described in the lengthy passage partially quoted here) is at once a protection and guide.

Ethics of Elite Etiquette

Divorced from the political and cosmic significances of being "close to the king," one can easily see a kind of Victorianesque fussiness and preoccupation with form in the many particulars of priyayi etiquette. One may tend also to focus on the ways that complex, nuanced interactive rituals, difficult to master for those who did not grow up with them in courtly circles, were indirectly diacritic of priyayi elite community membership. But this sketchy cultural preface to an account of much more mundane forms of politesse may make it easier to understand why, at least for older priyayi still living in Surakarta, this view is misconceived. For them the proper ordering of conduct is not simply a matter of form and self-restraint, but of cultivating and maintaining an internal state and sense of composure through which one may act in accordance with one's place, and in full awareness of one's environment.

In prestigeful but potentially dangerous proximity with the king and high nobility, proper conduct was traditionally much more than a matter of social nicety. Considered with an eye to the traditional priyayi conception of court and king, the Javanese term closest to "etiquette," *tata-krama*, can be understood to signify not just what is conveyed by a gloss like 'the ordering of conduct', but to resonate with an ideology of kingship and society as something like 'the ethics of interaction'. This latter phrase comes closer to the moral tenor with which even the most mundane types of conduct could traditionally be evaluated and prescribed.

Ideally, conduct marked a reciprocal interactive attunement between persons, and minimally it provided a guide to properly ordered, safe conduct to help preserve internal equanimity in the face of uncertainty. Older priyayi explain etiquette through the moral significance of ordered conduct, the clues it provides to persons' natures, and the moral propriety of adopting humble or inferior postures, however conventional, in face-to-face interaction. Conventionalized humility, so ubiquitous in "polite" priyayi interaction and interactive social strategies, is particularly important here because it has shaped and helped transform the norms of linguistic etiquette and speech style usage that are described in later chapters.

TATA-KRAMA AND CONVENTIONAL HUMILITY

The term *tata-krama* (or *tata-krami*)[12] is composed of two lexemes. *Tata* means 'arrangement' or 'framework'; its active transitive verbal form *nata* means 'to put in order'. *Krama* here might be best translated as 'to take steps', taking that English phrase very broadly, and is also used to refer deferentially to the act or state of being married. *Tata-krama* signifies a concept like politesse as well as the quality of politeness in conduct. Seeing a young man who does not lower his head and body when entering a room where his elders are seated, an old priyayi may complain by saying 'his etiquette is lacking' (*tata-kramanipun kirang*, in polite Javanese). Such an action is *mboten tata-krama* 'not polite'.

In less extreme circumstances than those just described polite conduct may mark respect and deference and soften the sensible impact of one's physical and verbal actions on others. Polite conduct is generically *alus* 'refined', endowed with a "flatness of affect" (Geertz 1960:240) and significative indirectness that allows those attuned to their environment and others to read intent from the least obvious, most stylized forms of conduct. Such indirectness is encoded quite directly in certain parts of the speech style system discussed in Chapters 4 through 7. Refinement may make for conventionalized self-abnegation and a sort of extended obeisance in the presence of a su-

12. The alternation in sound shape exemplified by *krama* and *krami* is discussed in Chapter 7.

perior, but it can be at once looser and more reciprocal with familiars.

In the king's presence, as the passage cited previously indicates, it is impossible for most to point or even to raise their eyes. When dealing with unfamiliar others whose rank is somewhat higher or roughly equal to one's own, pointing might be permissible, but only in a properly subdued, muted manner, that is, with the right thumb, the part above the knuckle protruding from a fist. One may not have to squat in the presence of equals so as to keep the height of one's head below or at least approximately equal to theirs, but one must stand politely with the hands folded in front of one's genitals (*ngapurancang*). One may not have to sit on the floor in the presence of a superior who uses a chair, but when sitting in a chair it is best not to cross the legs, or if one must to rest one knee on the other, never in the broken four position. (Some told me that is more polite to place the right leg over the left.) One may not have to walk in a squatting position (*mlaku ndhodhok*) in the presence of persons who are seated, but one should make at least a token gesture of lowering one's head as one passes by, preferably "leading" with one's right hand and thumb in the manner described.

In all these ways conduct manifests awareness of place in two senses: first vis-a-vis the traditional noble and official hierarchies that are centered on the king and determinative of personal status, and second vis-a-vis those with whom one stands in a social and interactional relation in face-to-face conduct in a given setting. "To know one's place" is a phrase that for priyayi would carry no connotation of "not acting uppity," passively and perhaps resentfully accepting an inferior position to someone else. That one person's position is inferior is less important than the mutual awareness and acknowledgment of the asymmetry of status, and the mutual composure such awareness engenders. Some older priyayi related to me incidents in which persons they counted as their traditional superiors told them in the spirit of modernity that my narrators need not be overly polite and need not address those higher status persons in exalted language. These priyayi responded, they told me, in refined speech to say that it would not be appropriate or fitting (*pantes*) to act so familiarly; they felt more comfortable presenting themselves in a manner consonant with their self-perceived inferiority. It was as much their prerogative as their obligation to adopt an inferior's position.

Ethics, etiquette, and the exemplary center 37

Properly ordered conduct and "knowing one's place" traditionally go together in very literal ways when visiting a member of the traditional elite who still lives in a traditional Javanese house. Where host and visitor sit and how they interact are choreographed in ways that illustrate a tacit agreement—verbalized, perhaps, only for the benefit of a clumsy foreigner—for "placing" oneself in relation to someone else. In this careful physical orientation to others is a broadly similar concern with reciprocal maintenance of social harmony and maintenance of equilibrium. Two parts of the traditional priyayi house are the *pendhapa*, a large, often quite spacious, pavilionesque construction with open sides, and the *dalem*, the most basic part of the house, located behind the *pendhapa*. Here would be the closest equivalent to a Western living room, sleeping quarters for the master and mistress of the house, and a repository for *pusaka* (heirlooms). (*Dalem* is an honorific term discussed at length in Chapters 3 and 5.) All but the most intimate male friends are entertained in the *pendhapa*, while women are traditionally escorted to the *dalem*. In a *pendhapa* of any size there are several sets of guest furniture, each comprised of two or three chairs and a divan, grouped around a small table. The nicest of these sets, in some households upholstered and covered with plastic slipcovers, is closest to the door leading to the *dalem*.

Which set will be used, and who will sit where, was traditionally calculated in terms of relative status of guest and host. The higher the status of the guest, the closer to the *dalem* they sit. A guest who is considerably superior to the host will sit in the seat closest to and facing away from the *dalem*, appropriating the role of (figurative) head of the household he or she is actually visiting. If the host is of superior or roughly equal status with the guest—far more frequently the case, because it is typically the inferior's place to visit the superior, rather than the reverse—he or she will sit either closest to and with his or her back to the *dalem*, or in one of the seats intermediately distant, facing the guest on a parallel with the wall of the *dalem*.

Drinks and snacks—brought by a servant who usually approaches the table on his or her knees, so that his or her head will not be higher than those of the seated visitor and host—are consumed after at least one invitation to drink has been made by the host, and acknowledged but not acted upon by the guest. In relatively formal situations, in which persons are on their best behavior, this exchange may occur several times before any eating and drinking is done, often in precise if unconscious synchrony, choreographed so that guest and host, as one expression has it, "walk together."

HUMILITY, CONVENTIONAL AND OTHERWISE

Social conduct that serves to guard feelings is conventionally humble, described in Javanese as *andhap-asor*. The phrase is composed of two synonymous speech style variants that mean 'low, humble': *andhap*, from the polite (*basa*) vocabulary, and *asor*, its "ordinary" equivalent in the *ngoko* vocabulary. *Andhap-asor* conduct, which served to lower oneself while exalting others, was traditionally obligatory with superiors and usually appropriate with unfamiliar equals. Humility could be manifested in everything from physical self-lowering—in the presence of the king, entering a room where persons are seated, serving refreshments to one's master and guests—to verbal expression in which one engages in routinized self-effacement in both the styles and content of what one says.

Priyayi quite regularly prescribe and extol acts of self-lowering, however formulaic and empty of real humility: "those who act humbly are raised up in the end," as one proverb has it, and a real sense of moral superiority is sometimes evident in older priyayi's stories about occasions on which they acted in an *andhap-asor* manner in some difficult situation. To be *andhap-asor* is to put others first, to restrain oneself: "Don't go ahead or precede someone, at least not without proper hedging and apologies." At one meeting of a discussion group on mysticism I attended, the leader gestured to the plate of fried bananas prepared as snacks for guests as he uttered the multipurpose invitation *mangga*. One person picked up the plate, passed it to his neighbor, who offered it to the person next to him. That person in turn offered it to his neighbor on the other side. When the plate reached the leader, having changed hands four times with only one banana being taken, he chuckled and said to me "That's how the Javanese are: the plate goes all over the place, and no one takes anything."

It is properly *andhap-asor* to automatically turn aside a compliment, an act in which some priyayi are at their most peremptory. In reply to a remark "What a beautiful shirt" a Javanese with any breeding will respond "No, it's old," often in obvious contradiction with the facts. "I hear your son graduated from medical school" said one person to another. "Yes," was the reply, "now he can scratch for himself." (The verb 'to scratch', *cecèkèr*, is also used for birds.) The standard invitation to come or to stay for dinner is invariably hedged with a phrase meaning 'Just what there happens to be," even if the meal marks the end of the fasting month and has been in production for a week. Perhaps the most polite reply to a compliment is to turn it back on the complimenter with the simple utterance *pangèstunipun*, uttered elliptically in the sense of 'thanks to your blessings'. In this way one implies that in fact the wishes and prayers of the speech partner made (or will make) it come about, even if the addressee has no connection with it whatsoever.

In deferring to another's wishes—explicitly signaled, inferred, or simply guessed at—one engages in what is called *ngalah*. *Ngalah* is an active verb form derived from *kalah* 'lose', and can be glossed as 'to engage in the act of losing', or more idiomatically 'to give in'. As any Javanese will say, to *ngalah* is not at all the same thing as to *kalah*. It is to place another's desires or opinions above one's own voluntarily to preserve equanimity. A driver of a bus may mutter under his breath that a person on a bicycle who refuses to pull over to let the bus pass *ora gelem ngalah* ("isn't willing to give in"). I may go to someone's house to discuss linguistic etiquette but if they want to talk about philosophy, I *ngalah*. To put elders, superiors, and unfamiliar equals before oneself is highly valued, and Javanese may derive from such silent self-denial a feeling of moral properness and self-satisfaction which, however private, is quite real. Certainly they will not attempt to conceal their sense of propriety when they tell of occasions on which they have maintained their composure in the face of provocative or unseemly conduct by others who "don't know any better."

To control one's temper and remain silent (*meneng*) in the face of presumptuous or thoughtless conduct that deviates from what is proper, one old priyayi pointed out to me, is a way to *ngalah*.[13] To accept without comment someone's use of speech styles to oneself,

---

13. On the relation between self-denial in interaction and mystical practice, see Errington 1984.

even if one feels it is insufficiently refined (in ways dealt with later), is also to *ngalah*. Conversely, one may *ngalah* by "giving in" to what one senses or knows to be a speech partner's desires concerning one's etiquette usage in interaction with him or her, and by speaking to him or her in ways that are more elevated than is appropriate in one's own judgment. One elderly high noble priyayi told me of an uncle only a year his senior who spoke to him in "low" (*ngoko*) language and expected "high" (*basa*) language in return, thus marking his uncle's higher status. This usage was in my narrator's opinion not fitting, as he himself had achieved considerable status through services to the republic during and after the revolution. But if his uncle thought that descent was more important than service to society, said this gentleman, he himself would *ngalah* by accepting a condescending use of low ngoko Javanese in return for polite addressee-exalting *basa*, as his uncle desired.

The moral correctness attributed to self-sacrifice, communicative indirectness, and silent acceptance of others' wishes makes for highly conventionalized, routinized expressions of humility and indirectness, some of which can be read directly from linguistic etiquette and the structure of the speech styles. One may adopt humble forms of conduct not just out of real desire to convey respect, but to conform with what one perceives to be another's wishes. One may accept usage from someone not because one finds it proper, but because one does not wish to create open disagreement or ill feelings. We will see in Chapter 5 how this cultivated predisposition to "raise" others and "lower" oneself, which contributes strongly to feelings of role distance, has contributed also to change in the use of linguistic etiquette and of relatively salient linguistic mediators of social relations.

Strategic interaction and nonnormative uses of linguistic etiquette, some as obvious as they are natural, have had significant effects on the structures and uses of linguistic etiquette. Particular occasions of use are by their strategic nature difficult to observe or characterize as efficacious means to particular interactive ends, but are by the same token informed by the overarching, very general constitutive rules of all etiquette and *andhap-asor* behavior. Self-abasing, other-exalting conduct—in a single English word, flattery—may induce others to do something one wishes them to do or more generally predispose them favorably. At the same time such conduct is ethically proper. In Java-

Ethics, etiquette, and the exemplary center 41

nese culture, promotion of one's goals and effacement of one's self in interaction may go together in strategically efficacious and morally proper ways.

Effects of such culturally informed interactional strategies are important enough in the following chapters to deserve preliminary elaboration. One convenient way to do this is to explicate a Javanese aphorism about Javanese, cited to me by three older priyayi at different times, that conveys how it is that pleasing others may be to one's own advantage. It is really an extended pun on rules for Javanese orthography and names for orthographic characters, and for that reason is lost on most younger Javanese: *Wong Jawa, yèn ditaling-tarung isih mungel, yèn dipangku mati* ("If Javanese are opposed they fight, but if they're treated politely, they give in"). This translation conveys the import of the aphorism, whose literal meaning needs some contextualization.

Javanese orthography is syllabic, each "basic" consonantal character ordinarily representing one or more syllable initial consonants, a vowel, and perhaps a syllable-final consonant. In the absence of diacritics there is an "inherent" vowel /a/ which can be "killed"—that is, marked as not to be pronounced—if followed immediately with a symbol called the *pangku*. From the root *pangku* are derived verbs meaning 'hold/be held in the lap', and the symbol so named does indeed appear to hold the preceding consonant symbol in its "lap." Javanese people, like Javanese consonant symbols, "die"—i.e., remain quiet, pliable, and amenable to one's wishes—if they are "held in the lap," that is, are treated in very polite, refined ways.

A noninherent vowel is marked with diacritics added to consonant symbols, and among these is a pair of symbols called together *taling-tarung*, which stand on either side of the consonant symbol to mark the vowel /o/. They surround and fight with the consonant symbol, because the word *tarung* in fact means 'to fight'. But when surrounded by the *taling-tarung* a consonant symbol does not "die" (i.e., remain silent) but fights back and "still makes a noise;" so too Javanese, if overtly opposed or treated in ways they do not like, resist the wishes of others. One high-level political figure who advised me about my dealings with Javanese cited his own experience: when someone storms angrily into his office, he speaks softly and politely, and soon has them feeling a little bit embarrassed, quieted down, and willing to listen, at least if they were not totally obtuse ('don't have a face of woven bamboo', *rai gedhèk*).

An important part of flattery in Javanese is not just what one says but the speech style one uses to say it, and this aspect of verbal interaction is important in following chapters. There is a strong sense that superiors can be predisposed to one if treated very politely, and if one adapts to them the kinds of *andhap-asor* conduct, including speech style use, that invokes the diffuse, personalistic sorts of patron/client ties that may lead to advantages for oneself. One former high official in the preindependence royal government told me he preferred to speak Dutch in his office not just because it allowed him to avoid complex calculations of relative status (discussed in Chapter 3) obligatorily marked in Javanese linguistic etiquette, but because it prevented young job applicants from making him feel as if they were "his children," speaking very high language to him. Such was the feeling they could engender by addressing him with very exalted language, and being addressed with "low" language in return (as was only proper), that he also had to avoid them when they came to pay their respects in the evening at his house, where it would be considerably more difficult to avoid nonofficial interactive styles and accompanying role relations of patron to would-be client.[14]

If norms for proper conduct and guarding feelings in interaction can be obeyed while simultaneously engaging in self-serving interactive strategies, it is easy to see how the two might conspire to routinize cumulatively and devalue progressively the self-abasing or other-exalting import of speech style use. The pragmatic values (to introduce a term discussed in Chapter 4) of styles and style elements depend on both the particular and normative in use, which together affect the structure and function of the system as a whole.

Around the turn of the century the well-known priyayi pedagogue Padmasusastra addressed the matter more specifically and concretely in a didactic, illustrative dialogue. An older speaker complains that proper conduct is not understood (a sentiment older priyayi living in Surakarta now share) and gives as an example the way people make obeisance (give the *sembah*). Some people, Padmasusastra's character remarks, will *sembah* to a deputy cabinet minister but not to a min-

---

14. Dewey 1978:426–29 makes a similar point from a rather different perspective.

ister of full rank who has no portfolio (and so no access to political or economic favors). He goes on: "Isn't that just looking for one's own advantage . . . and isn't it really lowering the full cabinet minister?" (Padmasusastra 1896:35). So it is, and conducive likewise to a spread in use of this deferential nonlinguistic gesture to persons other than those of the highest status. To the degree such behavior spreads in use by those seeking their own ends by exalting others, it could be regularized in use to larger classes of persons of lower status.

If sensitive to and willing to guard another's equanimity with one's own conduct, one may be obliged to defer to their desires (*ngalah*) by speaking to them as they wish to be spoken to and spoken of—by using linguistic etiquette in ways that they, but not necessarily oneself, feel to be appropriate. A person may *ngalah* by accepting language that is in his or her estimation too "low" (like the gentleman who described interaction with his uncle) or, conversely, by giving language to an addressee which that person deems fitting, even if speaker finds it too "high." As Padmasusastra's elderly priyayi observes later in the same dialogue: "You can't talk to every notable in the proper way if you fall into error of hurting their feelings. So you must look first at who you're speaking to. If they are of an angry disposition . . . look for words which they want" (1896:36).

To avoid angering others is not just to one's advantage but is ethically proper, and may lead to use of words that would otherwise appear inappropriate and too "high" for that speech partner. When caught in this double bind—speak in accordance with people's status, but don't offend them with a style they feel is too low for them—Javanese often pay closer attention to the latter injunction than the former. As enduring cultural values normatively relevant to social interaction, humility and self-abnegation inform strategic interactive use of the speech style system by priyayi of different eras and generations, and they are likewise important to an account of the history of that system as means for morally proper ordering of one's presentation of self.

Priyayi in Surakarta Now

On January 31, 1985 the royal palace of Surakarta was destroyed by fire. No new city or politically potent exemplary center shall rise from its ashes; the *kraton* had become politically marginal by 1840 and impotent by World War II. The 1985 fire had less dramatic causes than that in Kartasura two hundred forty years earlier (starting it seems in antiquated electrical wiring) and made for dismaying front page news in national newspapers, but was in no sense a disaster comparable with that of its predecessor.[15] It is doubtful that it will be chronicled in classical Javanese meters like those that open this chapter.

That the seat of the royal government (the *kadipatèn*) was blown up by revolutionaries in the face of imminent Dutch occupation in 1946 might have been for some Javanese a *pralambang*, or secret sign of the future. There was never a need for a new one not because the prestige attached to government work has waned among priyayi or Javanese at large, but because that government is now Indonesian, geographically vast, and ethnically heterogeneous. Rising in rank nowadays still means getting closer to the center, but now that center is Jakarta, and young priyayi, like their parents, continue to look away from Surakarta. Priyayi I met in Surakarta during my research were mostly the young who were still in school, and the old who had retired from their careers in other cities or decided not to move after the end of the war.

Since the war the meaning of "priyayi," not unlike the English term "gentleman," has become attenuated, and now has less to do with noble descent and traditional official capacities than with one's deportment and occupation. An anecdote shows how rapid and recent this change in social categories is. One of my young informants, himself a priyayi in the traditional sense, told of a visit to an uncle who lived in a far suburb of Jakarta. His uncle had hired a new chauffeur and my narrator asked where the chauffeur was from, referring to him as a *priyantun* (the polite equivalent of priyayi). As he related the incident to me:

> My uncle was silent a moment, and then said that a chauffeur was not fittingly called a priyayi; 'person' (ngoko: *wong*, krama: *tiyang*) is fine. Well I just took it. But that's the problem, *mas* [referring to me]. For me it's

15. The president of the Republic pledged half his salary for six months towards the cost of rebuilding the palace, and a private organization based in Jakarta has been set up to raise funds to that end. The rebuilding will be no small challenge not only for technical reasons, because knowledge of traditional craftmanship is largely lost, but also for ritual reasons, because placating the powerful spirits around the palace site is a daunting prospect.

nothing, but as for my father and others of his generation, they're still very careful.

As criteria for membership in the class of priyayi become less precise and lose their implications of traditional class stratification, the younger traditional elite has experienced pervasive pressure to integrate with a new educated elite in a new urban society. As the size, cohesiveness, and distinctiveness of the Surakartan priyayi community diminish, the system of linguistic etiquette that they traditionally standardized has changed in many ways, as discussed in the following chapters and elsewhere (Errington 1985b).

Although traditional priyayi court circles are almost extinct and largely ignored by most contemporary Surakartans, the forms of linguistic etiquette still used by priyayi (in the traditional sense) on a day-to-day basis reflect the heritage of the traditional courtly elite, who were once recognized and emulated as standardizers of the language. To understand the evolution of priyayi linguistic etiquette and investigate differences in "proper" or "normal" usage in different eras and social circles, we need a linguistic picture of the recent and somewhat enigmatic past of this traditional courtly elite, together with an overview of the social hierarchies which informed verbal interaction in traditional priyayi society.

3

Status, Interaction, and Titles

Under the rule of Pakubuwana X between 1893 and 1939 Surakarta was at the height of its glory, if not its power, and it is difficult now to grasp or convey the importance of status as a factor in day-to-day interaction in the rarified atmosphere of the royal court. Working from written records and reports from older priyayi who knew that era, I sketch here some of the broadest status distinctions and their broadest interactional correlates in priyayi society. This picture is an oversimplification, if not a caricature, but in its oversimplicity helps to frame an account of speech styles and linguistic etiquette through its clear orientation to two related descriptive ends. The first goal is to describe broad patterns of traditional etiquette and status differentiation as older priyayi described them to me, and to contrast such traditional usage with etiquette use in Surakarta now. The second is to outline broad changes in rights to and uses of noble descent titles in such a way as to foreground longstanding interactive pressures that can be shown to have affected not just rights to titles but linguistic etiquette as a whole.

This account is most obviously incomplete in its neglect of official governmental hierarchies—their structures, changes in titles and statuses of office holders, and patterns of interaction adopted among nobles and royal office holders, members of elite groups that were never totally distinct. During the final era of the kingdom, when royal prerogatives were most restricted, the royal government approached the "hierarchical ideal" (Peacock 1975:173) in at least seventy distinct strata and substrata,[1] some titularly distinguished. A full account would cover two distinct sets of titles of office, explain complicated historical relations between terms that refer to official ranks as opposed to titles, and present a formal account of combinatory possibilities of title elements.[2] I avoid these topics and many details better presented elsewhere to focus on particulars that bear directly on speech styles and linguistic etiquette.

The concern with titles here would seem a bit quaint to many modern Surakartans and inadequately detailed to older priyayi whose accounts I summarize and present in partial ways. But titles are important for understanding the structure of traditional priyayi society and the shapes of traditional priyayi interaction, because they serve on the one hand as terms for status groups and status group members, and on the other as interactively significant means of reference and address to persons.[3] As linguistic marks of group membership, titles are a little like other trappings of nobility prescribed in treatises on court etiquette. They are linguistic badges of rank—like rights to wear certain patterns of *bathik* skirt, to be shaded by particular kinds of parasol, to be accompanied by particular numbers of servants, and

---

1. This information is based on a treatise authored at the behest of (or perhaps even by) Pakubuwana X some time before 1900, the *Serat Pranatan Adhel*, hereafter cited in the abbreviated form SPA. The date in the colophon is 1830 on the Javanese calendar, equivalent to A.D. 1900. By that time Pakubuwana X had been on the throne for seven years and was twenty-seven years old. Note that *adhel* is borrowed from the Dutch *adel* 'nobility'. The Dutch may well have provided the initial stimulus for such written codification.

2. I use an intuitive distinction between titles and title elements that could be developed on a formal basis. A complete account would also review and comment on a literature that is ambiguous, incomplete, and contradictory. See, for instance, Schrieke's comments (1957:185–90) and Rouffaer's comments (1921:608, 609 n.2) on Van Goens (1856), Rouffaer's comments (1921:613 n.2, 615 n.1) on van den Berg (1887, 1902), and Cohen Stuart's comments (1880:9–21) on McGillavry (1836) and Winter (1843, 1844, 1846, 1848). I do not consider problems of clarity and issues that are not crucial for present purposes, and rely primarily on information from consultants.

3. For the sake of brevity I sometimes use the phrases "address as," "be addressed with," and so on as abbreviations of "refer to addressee as" and "be referred to as addressee with."

so on—because they are contextually invariant signs of holders' places in a hierarchy of descent, relatively close to or distant from a king. This is one reason why priyayi naturally focus on title use to describe traditional social status differences bearing on conduct. But titles serve also serve along with kin terms, personal pronouns, and descriptive phrases as important linguistic mediators of social interaction in use to refer to and address persons. To use a title for a person is socially significant as an act informed by the same shared knowledge, tacit expectations, and communicative projects that shape interaction as a whole. This is why priyayi often responded to my general questions about etiquette usage by talking about titles.

Because titles' significances are anchored both in pansocial hierarchies and contextualized, dynamic interactive processes, changes in rights to and uses of titles show very clearly tensions between "official" linguistic use fixed by the ultimate prescriptive source, the king, and "actual" use implemented in contextually appropriate ways on a day-to-day basis. By sketching traditional priyayi status and interaction to highlight this dynamic interplay, we simultaneously broach the issue of normative and strategic linguistic etiquette and speech style use taken up in later chapters.

This double semantic/interactional focus on title use also helps to illustrate two correlative kinds of "fade out" of status as one moves from social strata "closer" to those "further" from the king, both informed by the ideology of kingship sketched in Chapter 2. On the one hand, the fineness of intragenerational and intergenerational title distinctions was relative to proximity with kings as sources of noble status through descent. There was a loss of elaborateness of titles, and so of fineness of intragenerational and intergenerational titular distinctions, as one moved "down" the noble hierarchy of descent and "further" from kings. On the other hand there was a kind of interactional status fadeout implicit in the degree to which status distinctions were more overtly and ubiquitously marked in interaction among those in higher social strata. In traditional priyayi society there appears to have been a pattern of stratified subgroup style variation (Brown and Gilman 1960) in the degree to which relatively fine status distinctions between unequals were presentationally marked.

I try to present my priyayi acquaintances' observations on and concerns for proper title use to convey something of their view of proper interaction and social organization more generally. I recount something of the common substance of their descriptions with the metapragmatic vocabulary to which they had common recourse, and I rehearse some of their talk about linguistic etiquette use. By foregrounding the key stylistic variants that they consistently mentioned, I try to provide a sense of their tacit assumptions about the connectedness of social status and interaction to linguistic etiquette and speech style use.

Speech Styles: An Operational Description

Every Javanese would agree that the basis of the *unggah-ungguh ing basa* is the difference between the lexicons and speech styles called *ngoko* and *basa*. These terms will be used here for different manners of speaking to persons—that is, for stylistically unitary modes of *address* rather than for the vocabularies that distinguish them (topics dealt with in Chapters 4 through 7). Ngoko is the "basic" language one thinks in, speaks to intimates and inferiors in, loses one's temper in; it is the most natural and spontaneous form of verbal of expression. Intonation, pitch, and stress in ngoko speech may change rapidly and strikingly, even in a single utterance, and morphophonemic processes create many glottal stops and a staccato effect largely absent in basa. Ngoko is spoken when one feels unrestrained, to people with whom one feels familiar (*akrab*), or to whom one is (or feels) superior.

Basa really counts here as a negatively defined term meaning "nonngoko speech," and covers several distinct styles that will be distinguished more specifically and technically in Chapter 4. Priyayi of different ages and backgrounds can use this very general term to refer to particular speech styles by tacitly presupposing various kinds of social knowledge about users and uses of basa I have discussed at some length elsewhere (Errington 1985:84–104). Basa is spoken to those with whom one feels reserved, whose sensibilities one is fearful of offending, whom one does not know well, or whom one feels to be worthy of respect and of higher status. By speaking basa one can acknowledge the addressee's worth (*aji*), and so honor (*ngajèni*) that addressee. Many basa variants on ngoko roots and affixes are phonologically lengthened, have more high vowels and dissimilated vowel patterns, and are conducive to refined, *alus* demeanors in which speech is smoothly modulated in pitch and stress, and permissive of frequent and lengthy pauses. As is the sensible feeling of basa speech, so also are the affective qualities of interaction in which it is appropriate.

Choices between ngoko or basa address styles can be said to be appropriate to or presuppose certain types of social relations between speech partners, and to be realized in patterns of speech style exchange that they interactively and reciprocally create. Put simply, and ignoring for present purposes style differences within basa repertoires, we can provisionally say that a speaker has a basic either/or choice between ngoko or basa address styles, which may be parts of one of three possible patterns of address style exchange. Reciprocal or symmetric exchange of ngoko marks mutual familiarity or intimacy, symmetric exchange of basa marks reserve or respect on both sides, and an asymmetric pattern of exchange serves to mark status inequality in which superior speaks ngoko and receives basa in return.

But even a minimal set of terminological distinctions for describing priyayi ways of talking about speech style use must include two classes of referential expressions for persons—personal pronouns and kin terms. To describe language use as ngoko or basa is often insufficient and sometimes unnecessary for priyayi, who will supplement or forgo them by alluding to patterns of personal pronoun or kin term use as crucial metonyms of speech style use and sometimes patterns of speech style exchange. The prominent place accorded to both types of usage here reflects priyayi concerns with these special mediators of social relations, and anticipates discussion in Chapters 4 and 5 of reasons why these metalinguistic descriptions are more enlightening than is immediately apparent.

The "ordinary" ngoko personal pronouns are *aku* (first person) and *kowé* (second person), but in ngoko speech one may use the second-person pronoun *panjenengan* along with honorific terms to mark regard for a nonetheless familiar or relatively inferior speech partner. This style is often called ngoko *alus* 'polished ngoko' by priyayi.[4] In

---

4. Now marginal in this style are the second person pronoun *sliramu* and *sliranè*.

basa speech priyayi traditionally chose between two pairs of personal pronouns, which will be cited here in the order first person/second person. Use of *kula/panjenengan* may mark a feeling of reserve toward an addressee who is roughly one's equal, or even of somewhat inferior status but not terribly familiar. Use of *dalem/nandalem* necessarily acknowledges an addressee's unequivocally higher status.

Title usage figured prominently in examples and descriptions of ways of marking esteem for persons, especially in address, provided by older priyayi. Like kin terms and proper names, titles are used vocatively (as is "Mom" in "Mom, can I borrow the car?"), and parenthetically ("Sure, Mom, I'll be careful") but also for reference to an addressee where in English one would use a second person pronoun ("Do Mom [you] have the keys?").[5] Priyayi also used titles rather than terms of rank[6] in their explanations of status distinctions that bear on conduct, but title use shows no simple correlation with speech style usage. Use of a title can convey the tone of an official exchange or mitigate a sense of speaker's superiority in use with ngoko by superior to inferior. It can accentuate the felt deference of basa given to a superior, contribute to a sense of decorum in reciprocal basa, or complement the intimacy of reciprocal ngoko. Usage could be further modulated in combinations of full and short forms of titles with and without names, themselves a highly nuancable means for mediating social relations.

The complexities of priyayi linguistic etiquette are out of all proportion to the information available about day-to-day usage even fifty years ago, and the Surakartan priyayi community is now so small and fragmented as to make it impossible to observe more than a small

---

5. Differences between vocative and referential uses of titles, kin terms, and names in Javanese are often signaled intonationally in ways that cannot be described here. Because Javanese is highly permissive of ellipsis, addressee is commonly identified as referent with a vocative or parenthetical, with no referring expression in following syntactic positions that would correspond to notional subject or object.

6. Terms of rank signify social classes and positions whose members and occupants may have rights to titles. The distinction is not always observed by Javanese or authors of some of the literature cited in note 2. English "Sir" is a title for persons of the rank of knight, as opposed to "count" and "doctor," which can be used to designate statusful classes as well as individual members of those classes.

fraction of the kinds of social situations and interaction reported to me and discussed here. Characterizations are based largely on usage that I observed, that priyayi volunteered, that I elicited by asking about individuals' usage, and that is described in a more or less overtly prescriptive literature dating from the late nineteenth century.[7] None of these sources is ideal. I was plagued by what Labov (1971a:113) calls the Observer's Paradox, although I like to think that I minimized the impact of my presence in several priyayi households by the amount of time I spent there and the kinds of relations I had with their members. Volunteered and elicited statements about how speakers and their kin and acquaintances speak or spoke to each other could not always be checked by observation. Priyayi relied heavily on notions of what was "usual" and normatively proper (*pantes*). They characterized general patterns of interaction between members of social classes as well as usage between particular individuals. Only by limited observation and cross-checking different priyayi statements made at different times could I guard against the possibility that reliable reports on particular usage between particular people might not be paradigmatic or hold for other apparently comparable situations. To guard against quasi-prescriptive distortions and speakers' simple incompetence as reporters of usage, I supplemented cross-checks and observations of use by asking a single person about a given sort of use more than once. In some cases, I was able to repeat such questions fourteen months after the first occasion on which usage was reported.

I adopted the strategy of only gradually trying to ease into more or less explicitly recognized "interview" situations in which I would take notes on the spot or use a tape recorder, and interesting remarks made early on in my acquaintances with some priyayi ocurred in casual conversation that I could only write down later. Some I did capture on tape or transcribe immediately, and I did observe remarks made to others (usually family members) in my presence in casual conversations centering on my interests. To replicate priyayi state-

---

7. The values and dangers of these sources are discussed in Errington 1985b:21–26. The works most important here are Padmasusastra's *Urap Sari* and *Serat Tata Cara*; the latter provides marvellously indirect yet precise prescriptions on the finely calibrated use of referring expressions for persons.

ments here verbatim and provide the lengthy remarks necessary to contextualize them—about the person providing information, their relation with person spoken of, their relation with me, and so on—is impractical for present purposes. A few readily accessible reports are included, although I more often rehearse the common substance of reports in the interest of expository clarity and conciseness.

My awareness of titles, kin terms, and personal pronouns as important parts of priyayi talk about talk developed only gradually, and at first from a practical need to understand priyayi answers to my broad, sometimes naive questions about use, questions usually of the form "How did (or do) you and your father/brother-in-law/secretary speak with each other?" Their answers contained numerous references to these elements, which I did not always understand, and as research progressed it became apparent that more specific questions framed in the technical vocabulary common in the literature were sometimes misunderstood or misconstrued. I soon found myself slipping into their idiom and focusing my questions on the same aspects of usage.

Despite enormous social and linguistic complexity in traditional linguistic interaction, the picture that has developed is relatively consistent and systematic, insofar as informants' statements about particular but broadly similar situations largely corroborate each other. They serve here together with information available in the literature as parts of a general picture of changing priyayi etiquette use.

Descent and the Traditional Noble Hierarchy

Descent from a kingly ancestor generally counted as the most important personal status attribute affecting conduct. Status relations between two persons depended on their respective degrees of descent from kings, and among those in at least the first two generations of descent, on birth order and the status of the biological mother. Calculation of relative status and proper conduct was more complicated for collaterally and affinally related nobles, two aspects of "who persons are to each other" discussed later. Noble status is calculated through the line of descent related or, as was traditionally more often the case, more closely related to a king: priyayi typically sought to marry their children (or as Javanese say 'take children-in-law' *pèk mantu*) from their own or higher social strata. So, for instance, offspring of a second-generation and a fourth-generation royal descendant (*wayah dalem* and *canggah dalem*, respectively) count as third-generation descendants (*buyut dalem*) of a royal ancestor regardless of which parent is mother and which father. One notable consequence is that a child may be of higher descent status than one of his or her parents.

One of my first, most striking impressions of the cohesiveness of what little remains of traditional priyayi circles in Surakarta was the quickness with which older priyayi elicited from me the names of other priyayi I knew, and the readiness and detail with which they informed me about how they were related to those persons. In fact all the nobility of south-central Java are part of an extended family descended from Sultan Agung through the lines of Pakubuwana (the kings or *Susuhunan* of Surakarta), Hamengkubuwana (the kings or *Sultan* of Yogyakarta) and the princely houses of Mangkunegara (in Surakarta) or Pakualam (in Yogyakarta). Although relations more distant than two degrees of collaterality are nowadays often spoken of with the vague phrase *taksih pamili* 'still family', older priyayi are still able and more than willing to provide explicit, detailed descriptions of what seemed to me tenuous kin relations with other members of the noble elite.

Table 1 shows how priyayi refer to individuals' descent statuses or genealogical distances from a king ancestor either with a term of descent in combination with the honorific *dalem*, glossable here as 'royal house' (but see Chapter 5), or by naming the number of generations "down" one is from a king, a custom that may have been as recently introduced as was the term *grad*, which was borrowed from Dutch[8] for this measure of descent status. The terms *putra* and *wayah* are of the honorific vocabulary used to refer to high status persons, discussed in Chapter 6, and are always used for first-generation and second-generation descendants of kings.

Each king is conceived to be a 'source' (*pancer*) of noble status, a

---

8. In Javanese the term *keturunan* 'descendant' can be used, a nominal form of the root *turun*, glossable as 'to descend' in a specifically genealogical sense, and more generally as 'fall'. The preference at least among my acquaintances seemed to be for generational terms for the first two grades, and for the number of the grade at more distant degrees of descent.

Table 1. Terms for Descent Generation circa 1900

Descent degree (grad)	Descent term	Collective designations	
1	putra (KI)[a] anak (K,Ng)[b]	para gusti	putra dalem
2	wayah (KI) putu (K,Ng)		
3	buyut	para ndara	sentana dalem
4	canggah		
5	warèng		
6	udheg-udheg		
7	gantung-siwur	wong cilik	
8	gropak molo		

[a] KI = *krama inggil*.
[b] K = *krama*; Ng = *ngoko*.

sociocentrically constituted point of reference for calculating individuals' degree of noble descent, memberships in noble status groups, and rights to noble prerogatives, including titles of descent.

Although phrases consisting of a descent term plus *dalem* can be used for each descent generation, there is another important division between *putra dalem*, who are first-generation descendants of kings, and *sentana dalem*, second-generation through fifth-generation descendants of kings. At the end of the century this entire noble group was called the *putra sentana dalem*, that is, first-generation through fifth-generation descendants of kings. Those further than five generations away from their *pancer* traditionally counted as commoners, or 'little people' (*wong cilik*), and as such fell outside the group to whom noble prerogatives or titles were accorded.

Two other commonly used collective expressions for nobility shown in Table 1 consist of the collective marker *para* plus a descent title: *gusti* or *ndara*, this latter a short form of the descent title *bendara* (SPA 5). At the turn of the century *gusti* was officially a title for just the subset of this group of *putra dalem* whose biological mothers were not concubines, an intragenerational status distinction among royal offspring discussed later. But *gusti* was then as now used in the collective designation *para gusti* for the entire group of royal offspring. Up until 1939 or so, *bendara* was a title element accorded just to young princes and princesses, but the historically related short form *ndara* was used in reference to and address of a far larger group of nobles, members of the second through fourth generations of descent sometimes collectively called *para ndara*. We will see that *ndara* has long been used to refer to and address persons with no official right to *bendara* as an individual title, and that this usage had effects on official rights to titles.

Written and spoken accounts indicate that there is a longstanding difference between referential meanings of these terms as titular badges of individuals' descent statuses and as designations for collectivities of individuals who comprise a descent group. This skewing is symptomatic in turn of longstanding differences and tensions between royally prescribed rights to and everday uses of titles, and between official and unofficial but acceptable or even obligatory use. The phrases *para gusti* and *para ndara*, it turns out, might be better said to have once had meanings like 'the ones who are referred to and addressed with the titles *gusti/ndara*', rather than 'the ones who bear or have official rights to the titles *gusti/ndara*'. This symptom of longstanding differences between the everyday and official use of titles has correlates in patterns of use that have affected titles more broadly over the last century or so.

THE KING'S HOUSEHOLD

Given the traditional exemplariness of the king and his household it is not surprising that priyayi acquaintances often answered my general exploratory questions about traditionally proper language use by telling me what they knew of the way the king, his wives, and his children spoke with each other on a day-to-day basis. By the same token, it is expositorily useful to start with usage within this very highest group because it shows most clearly and categorically patterns of etiquette and title use replicated in less elaborated, often more flexible ways within lower noble and official strata.

The royal domain had shrunk considerably by the middle of the nineteenth century but the royal family had not. Pakubuwana IX, for instance, had thirty wives who bore him fifty-eight children; his son

Status, interaction, and titles 57

who became Pakubuwana X had forty wives and sixty children. The group of royal wives was itself stratified, at least one member serving as *garwa dalem*[9] (also called the *garwa padmi*), best translated into English as 'queen', because a *garwa dalem* was designated mother of the crown prince and other highest status royal offspring. But kings could have more than one *garwa dalem*—Pakubuwana X, for instance, had two—one of whom was then further designated *pramaiswari* and accompanied the king on state and ritual occasions. If there was only one *garwa dalem*, she was also *pramaiswari*. Candidates for the rank of *garwa dalem* were qualified with a few notable exceptions by their own high descent status. One of Pakubuwana X's *garwa dalem* was a daughter of the Sultan of Yogyakarta and his *pramaiswari*, the other a princess of the house of Mangkunegara. Comparability of rank was an important criterion in choice of "first" spouse among the higher noble elite, and traditionally was (and to some extent still is) in the hands of the parents.[10]

Women in the second and much larger group of royal wives were referred to variously as *priyantun dalem*, 'royal priyayi',[11] *garwa ampil*, *garwa ampéyan*, or simply as *ampéyan* or *selir*. These latter two terms were used generically to describe the second wife, including the king's. All can be translated as 'concubine'.[12] *Priyantun dalem*

---

9. *Garwa* is an honorific with an "ordinary" ngoko equivalent *bojo* and a polite, nonhonorific krama equivalent *sémah*.

10. Status concerns are one reason marriage to cousins is still to a certain extent considered preferable in priyayi circles (see Koentjaraningrat 1957:55). During the relatively stable period in the middle of the nineteenth century, members of competing noble houses were, so to speak, driven into the arms of their erstwhile enemies.

11. *Priyantun* is the basa equivalent of the ngoko *priyayi*. This use of the term fits the etymology of *priyayi* from the phrase *para yayi*, 'all the (royal) younger siblings'. Javanese wives typically address their husbands as 'elder male sibling' and receive a term meaning 'younger sibling', on which more in Chapter 5. Use of the term *priyayi* in these two distinct ways suggests the king's superordinate status in two sorts of metaphoric elder sibling/younger sibling role relationships: as head of the noble/official elite on one hand, and as husband to wives on the other. Stereotyped gender relations are used quite explicitly in some treatises on statecraft as ideal images of the master/servant relationship.

12. There is in some nonnoble circles a manner of distinguishing "first wife" from "concubine" as *garwa ngajeng* 'front wife' from *garwa wingking*

were further divided into the *priyantun nèm* 'young priyayi' and the *priyantun sepuh* 'old priyayi'. Concubines' places in these groups accorded with their descent status, the amount of time they had been a concubine, and the king's own wishes. Physical age was a secondary factor, and descent was only occasionally crucial.[13]

The full title of the Susuhunan of Surakarta was *Susuhunan Pakubuwana Sénapati Ingalaga Ngabdurahman Sajidin Panatagama*, the last element of which means literally 'arranger (orderer) of religion', and indicates his status not only as a Muslim but head of Islam within the kingdom. So it was that he could interpret Islamic law limiting a man to four wives in such a way as to permit himself an unlimited number of concubines. His delegated religious official, the *penghulu*, was empowered to place wives in and remove them from the group of "actual" wives as they became pregnant and delivered his children. Only when carrying a royal child was a concubine necessarily recognized as a wife of the king, and only the *garwa dalem* was always a member of that group of four.

All the king's wives lived within the walls of the palace in the *keputrèn* 'place of the females' along with their numerous servants and royal offspring. These quarters, located next to the king's own chambers, were forbidden to all males save the king and his prepubescent sons. The wives along with servants and children formed a large group; according to one of my older informants who was a regular visitor to the palace in the 1920s there were forty rooms for the family itself, and one hundred or more for the servants. The *pramaiswari* as titular head of the *keputrèn* delegated her authority to a group of female servants who actually formed a branch of the palace government headed by a female cabinet-level officer. When young princes reached puberty, they were circumcised, given their adult titles and names, and moved to housing specially arranged for them outside the palace proper. Daughters lived in the *keputrèn* until they were married, and returned there if their husbands predeceased them.

'wife from the back'. Although most of my priyayi informants consider this somewhat vulgar and improper, it is used extensively in the *Serat Pranatan Adhel* and other older texts.

13. This was reportedly the case for some of Pakubuwana IX's *selir*, for instance, who were grandchildren of kings and immediately placed among the *priyantun sepuh*.

Status, interaction, and titles 59

All sons and daughters of the king by his wives were called *putra dalem* 'royal offspring'[14] but it did sometimes happen that the king fathered a child outside of wedlock, and chose for one reason or other not to make the mother a *selir*. Such children, called *putra ciritan*, had a different status. The word *ciritan* refers literally to a small bit of diarrhea that inadvertently slips from the anus, but in this context alludes to the royal seed that "slipped out" and bore fruit in the womb of a woman not married to the king. In these cases arrangements were made to find the woman a husband and, if necessary, a job, house, and allowance to go with the wife-to-be. That such an arrangement might be acceptable and even desirable for the (as it were) precuckolded husband indicates something about the status of the king: raising an illegitimate prince or princess—whose pedigree, it seems, was rarely a great secret—was a source of prestige and good fortune.

THE KING'S CHILDREN: *PUTRA DALEM*

Around the turn of the century the king's children could be referred to collectively as *para gusti*, but the title *gusti* was prescriptively accorded just to offspring of the king's first wife (*garwa dalem*). Table 2 indicates schematically how rights to *gusti* and *bendara*, as parts of official titles combined with *radèn mas/ayu*, were diacritic of the statuses of *putra dalem* over and against other nobility, and diacritic of status of title holder's mother.[15] These titles were held by princes before their circumcisions and princesses before their marriages.

Upon acceding to their adult titles, *putra dalem* were further distinguished by rights to titles. The eldest male child from the *garwa dalem* was raised to the office of crown prince with the exalted title *Kanjeng Gusti Pangéran Adipati Anom Sudibya Raja Narendra ing Mataram*, often abbreviated in reference to *adipati anom* (as in Table 2). He was the only one of the *putra dalem* who necessarily held an

---

14. According to one old former official, there was an official distinction between *putra dalem*, who were offspring of the queen, and *putra jengandika*, who were offspring of concubines. No one else ever used or reported use of this latter term to me. *Jengandika* is discussed in Chapter 5.

15. For the sake of orthographic convenience I deviate from the common practice of representing titles and title elements in Latin orthography with capital initial letters.

Table 2. Titles of Descent circa 1900

Male

Grad	By pramaiswari eldest	By pramaiswari others	By selir	Everyday usage
1 (young) (adult)	gusti radèn mas / kangjeng gusti pangéran adipati anom ...	kangjeng gusti pangéran arya	bendara radèn mas / bendara kangjeng pangéran arya	gusti
2 (young) (adult)	radèn mas / kangjeng pangéran arya	radèn mas		ndara dèn mas
3, 4	radèn mas			ndara mas
5	radèn			dèn
6, 7, ... (commoners)	mas			

Female

Grad	By pramaiswari	By selir	Everyday usage
1 (young) (adult)	gusti radèn ajeng / gusti radèn ayu	bendara radèn ajeng / bendara radèn ayu	gusti
2 (young) (adult)	radèn ajeng / radèn ayu		ndara dèn ajeng / ndara dèn ayu
3 (young) 4 (adult)	radèn ajeng / radèn ayu		ndara ajeng / ndara ayu
5 (young) (adult)	radèn roro / radèn nganten		dèn
6, 7, ... (commoners)			

official post, for he was traditionally regarded as the head of the group of all *putra sentana* (i.e., descendants of kings down through the fourth generation). He was the head of his own *kadipatèn*, the branch of the palace government (as opposed to that of the realm at large) responsible for organizing the *putra sentana* for frequent, elaborate court ceremonies.

His younger male siblings by *garwa dalem* had the adult title *gusti pangéran arya*, and like him were princes (*pangéran*).[16] At these very highest levels of nobility, status differences between siblings keying to birth order were further marked by what can operationally be called proper names: princes by the *garwa padmi* had the names Mangkubumi, Buminata, and Purbaya, in that order, while the eldest male from a concubine had the name Ngabéhi.[17] On marriage female offspring from a *garwa dalem* held the title *gusti kangjeng ratu*, and the eldest had the name *Sekar Kedhaton* 'flower of the palace' before marriage, and afterwards *Pembayun* an honorific meaning 'breast'. Daughters of concubines had the title *bendara radèn ajeng* before marriage, after which they were *bendara radèn ayu*, save for the eldest who had the title *kangjeng ratu alit*. Women's titles were often modified if they married "up" the noble or official hierarchy or if they held offices in the palace administration.

A *garwa dalem* was jural mother to the king's children, *priyantun dalem* their surrogate carriers. (*Ampil*, part of the designation for concubines *garwa ampil*, is an honorific root glossable as 'carry the possession of an honored person while walking behind him or her.') Differences in biological mothers' statuses were likewise reflected in linguistic etiquette. *Putra dalem* referred to and addressed a *garwa*

16. McGillavry's 1836 account makes no mention of *kangjeng* in princely titles, but van den Berg (1887:101) and later accounts do. It would fit the larger pattern of status elaboration through rights to titles being sketched here if this reflects the official institution of *kangjeng* as a princely title in the late nineteenth century.

17. It could be argued that just because of this obligatory, conventional link between personal status and referential term, these and other terms for male offspring of concubines—*Arya, Tumenggung, Panji, Rongga, Demang*, and others granted as the king wished—are really titles accorded to members of social classes of one. The latter three in fact are identical in sound shape with now defunct terms of official rank, while *Tumenggung* and *Ngabéhi* are identical with title elements still in use. *Ngabéhi* is historically a petrified form derived from *kabèh* 'all', which can be glossed here as 'he who is over all'.

dalem in exalted *basa* with the pronouns *dalem/nandalem* and addressed her as *ibu*, the high honorific kin term glossable as 'mother' (in usage before the revolution discussed in Chapter 5). *Priyantun dalem* were addressed as *mbok*,[18] a term listed in most dictionaries as a ngoko word, but better treated in traditional usage as the ordinary word for 'mother' used by commoners and all but the highest ranking priyayi.

Reports by three older priyayi whose court functions put them in contact with the king's family in the 1930's indicate that asymmetric exchange of ngoko and basa was the rule rather than the exception between kings' young children and wives. *Putra dalem* used elaborate basa to the first wife with honorific pronouns *dalem/nandalem*, and received ngoko with the pronouns *aku/kowé* in return. With concubines they might exchange basa, but only with the less exalted pronouns *kula/panjenengan*, and always in return for *dalem/nandalem*. This usage keyed to both descent status and kin relation: a prince or princess was almost always superior in descent status to a concubine but not to a *garwa dalem*, who was effectively if not actually a *putra dalem* herself. Descent status being equal, the kin relation presupposed the use of ngoko from mother to child in return for the highest possible language. If descent status, physical age, personal esteem, or some other factor contraindicated kin relation, as with concubines, basa was exchanged but with personal pronominal diacritics of the relatively more important descent status difference.

Within the group of young royal siblings and half-siblings exchange was also asymmetric, keying to birth order regardless of status of biological mothers: younger *putra dalem* are reported to have spoken basa with pronouns *dalem/nandalem* to their elder siblings, and received ngoko with *aku/kowé* in return. A difference of days in birth (quite possible for half-siblings) was sufficient to determine asymmetry of the status relation. As one put it, "If it's me who's younger [as hypothetical prince], I [give] *dalem-dalem* and they [give] *kowé* [in ngoko]." Padmasusastra (1896:148) has the king's eldest son by a concubine use ngoko to address a younger sibling by a concubine in return for basa with the second-person pronoun *panjenengandalem*, the "full," formal variant on *nandalem*. (The difference is discussed in Chapter 5.) According to older priyayi the ritually confirmed

---

18. At present *priyantun dalem* are reportedly called *bibi*.

Status, interaction, and titles 63

crown prince who later became Pakubuwana XI could give ngoko with *aku/kowé* to all his siblings, regardless of physical age, and receive basa with *dalem/nandalem*.[19] Asymmetric exchange of personal pronouns if not basa seems to have been an omnipresent feature of such interaction; Padmasusastra (1896:149) has an example of the crown prince giving his eldest male sibling by a concubine basa with the kin term *kangmas* 'elder male sibling' (see Chapter 5) and receives basa with the still more exalted titular phrase *kangjeng gusti*, a short form of the crown prince's title. An older priyayi to whom I showed this example noted that use of title rather than kin term unambiguously marked the elder sibling's regard for junior's higher descent status. Use of the corresponding term for younger sibling would be referentially accurate but woefully inappropriate.

Status relations could change quickly and dramatically within the upper noble strata. As crown prince, for instance, the future Pakubuwana XI is reported to have spoken basa with *dalem/nandalem* to his father's younger male siblings and received ngoko in return. But as king he gave them basa with *kula/panjenengan*, and received basa with *dalem/nandalem*. Pakubuwana X, on the other hand, stopped speaking basa to all but two older siblings of his father upon acceding to the throne. Pakubuwana XII, present head of the line, is reported to engage in usage with his father's siblings that, my older priyayi acquaintances all agreed, would have been impossible even fifty years ago: he exchanges *dalem* and basa with them symmetrically, a pattern often alluded to as *dalem-daleman* 'to address each other with *dalem*'.

In these maximally exemplary and intensely status conscious social circles the skewing of prescribed and everyday title use is quite clear in the case of *gusti*. In ordinary interaction (what Javanese commonly call *padinan* in ngoko and *padintenan* in basa),[20] the title

19. It should be restated that these are the most general "rules of usage," which may have (had) exceptions. They are reliable at least to the extent that three older priyayi in frequent contact with the king's own family independently provided such characterizations of use. Day-to-day usage depended on the personal inclination of the crown prince in relation to the person in question.
20. These terms are from the ngoko/krama roots *dina/dinten* 'day', and can be translated as 'everyday usage'.

gusti was used by almost everyone of lower rank in reference to and address of all *putra dalem*, regardless of the status of the biological mother. Concubines and servants in the palace, for instance, were reported by older priyayi to address and refer to their own and other concubines' children regularly as *gusti*, despite the fact that those addressees and referents were not biological descendants of the *garwa dalem*, as speakers well knew. In their hypothetical examples of usage to *putra dalem* by servants, concubines, and low officials, older priyayi made common and conspicuous parenthetical use of *gusti*, which they accompanied with the *sembah*, or bow, which normatively accompanied such acts of address.[21] The appropriateness of the situation for such ostensibly incorrect use depended on the relative officialness of the context, and the social status of referent in relation to speaker and addressee (if referent and addressee were distinct). A single example from a palace official of forty years' experience must suffice:

> If the king [Pakubuwana X] asked his attendant "Who's that child over there?"—he had many children, and sometimes didn't remember them all—then the answer had to be complete: "That is your child *bendara radèn mas* so-and-so" or if female, "*bendara radèn ayu.*" Not "*gusti* so-and-so." But if a servant spoke to that child, so for instance, the same attendant reported to the royal child, she'd say "*Gusti*, please come over here." Like that. "You've been summoned by your father."

Such unofficial use was tacitly but in a very real sense obligatory, because inferiors could abstain from ostensibly "incorrect" usage only at the risk of being regarded as unknowledgeable, boorish, or worse, as *digsura*—haughty and unwilling to act in a properly humble, *andhap-asor* manner. This is an example of much more widespread contrasts between official and everyday title use, which priyayi explain (at least to an inquisitive foreigner) by recourse to the de facto conventionality of such use and the ethical value of being humble sketched in Chapter 2: it is better to go along with what people want and expect, even if you know that it is wrong. In this as in many other respects the king's family was exemplary of broader, sometimes less apparent differences between prescribed rights to and actual uses of other titles and honorific kin terms.

21. Opening parentheticals often consist of a title or kin term with the hesitation particle *anu*, a little like "Well, Sir/Ma'am/Dad..."

LOWER NOBILITY: *SENTANA DALEM*

Status distinctions within the king's family were replicated less elaborately and marked less overtly in lower elite strata with respect to rights to titles and patterns of interaction. A prince might have more than one *padmi* and stood to his own offspring (*wayah dalem*, grandchildren of the king) and his wives as his father stood to himself, his siblings, and mother(s). Similarly asymmetric patterns of speech style exchange were keyed to similar status distinctions. Most notable were differences in interaction reported between children of princes and their biological mothers, to whom they were not necessarily much superior in descent status. It was apparently not uncommon for a concubine to be a middling status descendant of a king—of the third generation or fourth generation (*buyut* or *canggah*)—and the difference in descent status between biological mother and child could then be far less determinative of respectful and deferential demeanor by parent to child.

The mother of one of my older acquaintances, a grandson of Pakubuwana X, was a fifth-generation descendant of the Sultan of Yogyakarta (*warèng dalem*). The difference in their respective descent statuses was counterbalanced by the kin relation between them, so that their language use to each other was, as this priyayi put it, "both basa, but it wasn't necessary to use *dalem, kula/panjenengan* was sufficient." Such symmetric exchange of personal pronouns and speech styles seems to have been relatively rare in higher elite strata in the early part of the century. Had the difference in their descent statuses been that between a *putra dalem* and *wayah dalem*, said this noble, or had he been a biological offspring of his father's first wife, this woman would have been *dalem/nandalem* or *kula/panjenengan* to him, that is, she would have addressed him with one of those pairs of pronouns in basa and probably received ngoko. This older priyayi's remark that both he and his mother were *dalem/nandalem* to their husband and father (respectively) implied that they received ngoko in return.

The ways that statuses of children of "first" wives and concubines were distinguished in princely families—along with rights to offices, titles, and privilege—broadly paralleled distinctions in the king's family and lower noble families. Throughout priyayi society there was potential for a marked tension between siblings at lower levels of descent. "The relation between children of a *padmi* and those of a *selir* is in general not of a friendly nature. The first-mentioned have many more rights . . . " (Adatrechtbundels 1931:191). I was told that children of prince's concubines ordinarily spoke basa to children of first wives, with *dalem/nandalem* or *kula/panjenengan* if there was an appreciable difference in age or some compensatory difference in official status.

At the same time there was a kind of fadeout of intragenerational status distinctions marked in rights to titles. Like the crown prince, the eldest male child by the first wife traditionally acceded to an adult title identical to or closely resembling his father's, *kangjeng pangéran arya*, and he succeeded his father, as the crown prince did the king, as *pangéran sentana* 'prince among the *sentana*', not as a *pangéran putra*. He was a twig, as it were, from his father's branch, and a secondary reference point for reckoning descent at lower levels in the noble hierarchy.[22] Priyayi still refer to princely lines by suffixing the prince's name with *-an* to derive a form translatable as "that of X," or "house of X" (in the sense of lineage). A noble may volunteer for instance that she is *wayah dalem saking Purwakusuman* "grandchild to a king from the line of Purwakusuma" [the prince's name] in which case Purwakusuma is also her father, the descent line (*trah*) is *trah Purwakusuman*, and speaker presumes knowledge of another priyayi about the identity of Purwakusuma's father and grandfather.

No other title distinctions marked status differences among *wayah dalem*, who traditionally shared with nobility of the third and fourth generations the titles *radèn mas* for men, *radèn ajeng* for unmarried

22. According to van den Berg's account (1887), taken over by van den Haspel (1985:69–72), titular distinctions distinguishing eldest male child by first wife from other descendants existed at the third and fourth levels of descent as well, "pulling" descendants of a *pangéran sentana* "up" a notch, at least titularly, in relation to other nobility. Space precludes an extensive discussion of this and other sources, but according to my own informants this was not the case at least as early as the 1920s. The title elements *arya* and *panji* attributed by van den Berg to nobility in this pattern are accorded just to male nobility who also have official duties within the palace, serving in the group of royal servants (*abdi dalem*) known as *riya nginggil* and *riya ngandhap*.

women, and *radèn ayu* for married women.[23] As Table 1 shows, lower nobility can also be spoken of with a phrase derived from descent title elements. This group was sometimes referred to by older priyayi as *dènmasan* 'the *dèn mas* group'. Like "sinking status" in Bali (Geertz 1980:26–33, see also Lansing 1983:37–41) and "declining descent" in Thailand (Haas 1951), differences in noble status faded out along with official titular diacritics of status "further" away from the king.

But in traditional everyday interaction there was an ubiquitous, socially crucial pattern of title usage that distinguished grandchildren of kings from lower nobility. This distinction involved the short form of a descent title officially accorded just to young princes and princesses, *bendara*. Before 1930 or so children of a prince, regardless of their mothers' statuses, had no right to *bendara* in their adult titles. But these and lower status priyayi readily confirm that *ndara*, a short form of *bendara*, was an important means of address and reference not just for *wayah dalem* but *sentana dalem* down through the fourth generation of descent, the *dènmasan*. As shown in Table 1, *ndara* was used in the collective designation *para ndara* to designate the entire class of lower nobility, and was also in use as a term of address in more restricted ways discussed later.

The group of second-generation through fourth-generation descendants of kings shared certain rights, notable among them the right to receive obeisance (the *sembah*) from and to be addressed with *dalem/ nandalem* by fifth-generation nobility—'little priyayi' (*priyayi cilik*) with rights just to the single title *radèn*—and all nonnobles.[24] Priyayi used the term *ndara* in this collective sense to refer to general concepts and institutions of nobility. Two explained peculiarities of and motivations for linguistic and titular use by alluding to the *rasa*

23. In what follows, for brevity's sake, I ignore the use of *ajeng*, which parallels exactly use of *mas* and *ayu*.
24. Two of my informants insisted that rights to be addressed with *dalem/ nandalem* were restricted to second-generation and third-generation descendants, but four others described examples of speech usage for the entire class of *sentana dalem*. Where lower nobility received the *sembah* just at the opening and ending of interaction, princes and princesses received it at the beginning and end of each occasion of speech by a marked inferior.

ndara—roughly, 'feeling of nobility'—shared by priyayi in the old days. One priyayi reported to me an inquiry made to him by an old prince concerning another's claim to the title *radèn mas* as "What is the source of his *ndara*ness?" (*Ndarané saka ndi?*).

All things being equal, interaction among members of different generations within this noble group were similarly patterned: individuals of lower-descent status gave *dalem/nandalem* or *kula/panjenengan* with basa in return for ngoko. Among third-generation and fourth-generation descendants, official rights to and everday uses of titles in address and reference were rather different. As shown in table 2, *wayah dalem* were regularly addressed and referred to with *ndara* plus a short form of their full descent title, that is, as *ndara dèn mas/ayu*. (The first syllable of this four syllable unit is reduced by quite regular processes discussed in Chapter 5.)

Now *dèn* reportedly served as an important diacritic of descent status in these complex terms of reference and address and, according to my two most articulate informants, was tacitly recognized to be appropriate for reference and address to grandchildren of kings, but not third-generation and fourth-generation nobles (i.e., *buyut* and *canggah*) who were simply *ndara mas/ayu*. One older priyayi denied that this was the case, and two others said they didn't remember any such difference. But late nineteenth-century texts exemplify what older priyayi reported to me as common usage during the 1920s and 1930s: uses of *ndara* and *bendara* are quite different, and there is a skewing between "official" referential and everyday use of both terms. Different appropriate uses of the short colloquial and full official forms of titles are symptomatic of broader differences between everyday and official use discussed later.

In and below the lowest level of titled nobility—fifth-generation descendants (*warèng dalem*) with rights to the simplest title, *radèn*—there were similar discrepancies between prescriptively correct and situationally appropriate uses. Textual evidence from the end of the nineteenth century corroborates older priyayi observations that before changes (discussed later) were made in official rights to titles, *radèn* was used by and for persons of lower descent and other status-seeking commoners who had no prescriptive right to any title of descent. Padmasusastra (1896:166) has one priyayi make a revealing remark to another: *"Dèn béhi,* I'm rather amazed when I reflect on rich people these days making use of the hierarchy of titles however they want. A man and a women as soon as they're married call themselves *radèn* and *radèn nganten*."[25] Male members of this aspiring class of commoners had rights to no more than the title *mas*, which presupposed no royal descent status at all, but it appears that they were able to escape censure with their implicit claims to noble descent. Prescriptive rights to and tacit understandings about uses of *radèn*, like titles of higher nobility, were skewed among (would-be) elite members in such a way that everyday use of *ndara* contrasted significantly with everday use of *radèn*. Padmasusastra's observation and covert, conservative prescription is symptomatic of the same skewed relationship between prescribed and actual title use already encountered.

Seniority, Status, and Etiquette Use

This sketch of speech style use is oversimple not just because the terms employed in it are so general, but because it relies heavily on examples of use that are taken to be representative with all other things being equal. Such circumstances were rare, however, not just because of interactionally relevant official status differences, but also because of two types of interactively relevant kin relations and attendant genealogical and affinal seniority. These intrinsically relational factors combined with relative descent status, the history of a social relationship, and other considerations to affect the interactional styles in different contexts. Affinal and collateral seniority were mentioned so often by priyayi to explain the use they reported, and I observed, that they must be mentioned here.

The Javanese words *tuwa* (in ngoko) and *sepuh* (in basa) can be glossed as 'old' to refer to length of individuals' lives measured in cycles of time units, but also as 'senior' to refer to various sorts of status relations. As one elderly priyayi explained to me there are

25. *Dèn béhi* is a shortened form of a complex title consisting of the descent title *radèn* and office title *ngabéhi*, accorded to mid-level officials, which will not be discussed at any length here. The original Javanese: *Dèn béhi, aku rada gumun ngrasakaké wong sugih ing jaman saiki, athik nganggo unggah-ungguh ajenengan sakkarepé dhéwé, lanang wadon yèn wis omah-omah mesthi jeneng radèn nganten.* . . .

"three kinds of old: old in rank (*sepuh lungguh*), old in knowledge (*sepuh kawruh*, and old in age (*sepuh tuwuh*)." There is also a principle of genealogical seniority, called in Javanese the *awu* relation, through which an asymmetric descent or sibling relationship between two ancestor kin is superimposed, as it were, on their collaterally related descendants.[26] Among priyayi, relative seniority in *awu* was directly relevant to the calculation of status and properly ordered conduct, linguistic and otherwise.

Status relations between nobles of different descent generations from a single kingly ancestor are relatively simple to calculate. But as a source of noble status (*pancer*), each king is descended from kingly forebears who are definers of descent status not just of that king but other, lesser nobles as well. Status relations between nobility who trace their lines back to different *pancer* are complicated by a double focus on shared and different royal ancestors, that is, the seniority relations of different *pancer* to each other as well as descent statuses of individuals from their respective *pancer*. It often happens that an *awu* seniority relation between two nobles contradicts the difference in their status as noble descendants, and has varying effects on their etiquette usage.

A convenient example of such complex status relations was provided by an elderly grandson (*wayah dalem*) of Pakubuwana X who told me of his relation with a twenty-year-old son of the present king, Pakubuwana XII. As descendants of kings, the latter *putra dalem* is of markedly higher status than the *wayah dalem*. But as collaterally related kin, the *wayah dalem* is genealogically senior or older in *awu* because his *pancer*, Pakubuwana X, was father to the prince's *pancer*. He is thus a generation closer to their shared kingly ancestor, and this *awu* seniority, together with the marked difference in age of these two nobles, mitigates the effect of the descent status difference

---

26. There is curiously little discussion of *awu* in the literature. Koentjaraningrat (1957:68) briefly mentions the effect of the *awu* relation on kin term use, and the term is defined in Gericke and Roorda (1901). Among consanguineals the principle applies trivially, because a person is older than his siblings not just physically but also in terms of relative proximity to shared ancestors. Although such relations are never characterized in terms of *awu*, speakers agreed to my suggestion that this would be counted as an application of the same principle.

Status, interaction, and titles 71

on the ways they interact with each other. Their pattern of linguistic interaction is emblematic of other broad changes in etiquette use over the last fifty years or so: they exchange basa symmetrically with the personal pronouns *dalem/nandalem*, and thus are *dalem-daleman* 'to be *dalem* to each other/address each other as *dalem*'. Fifty years ago this pattern of use would have been anomalous if not impossible for reasons to be discussed.

Calculation of interactively relevant descent status and *awu* relations is much simpler when differences in descent vis-a-vis different king-ancestors clearly outweigh genealogical seniority of one of those king-ancestors to the other. One king may be a fourth-generation descendant (*canggah dalem*) of his great-great-grandfather and as such "junior" in *awu* to any third generation descendant (*buyut dalem*) of that same king-ancestor. But the *buyut dalem* is obviously of far lower descent status, and the etiquette pattern to be adopted is quite clearly asymmetric. As the priyayi who responded to my question about etiquette use in such a relation said: "Of course the king gives *aku/kowé* [i.e., ngoko] and gets *dalem-dalem* [i.e., exalted basa]," as he simultaneously modeled for me the bow (*sembah*) with which the *buyut* would accompany the opening and closing of his every utterance to the king.

Awu seniority between kin of a single noble generation who share a king-ancestor is a function of the birth order of the two siblings at the head of their respective descent lines. So a grandchild of a king is superior to another grandchild of the same king insofar as the former's parent is the elder of the two ancestor siblings or half-siblings. Thus, birth order of the sibling-ancestors is superimposed on their descendants to determine seniority in *awu*. *Awu* relations traditionally governed kin term use in address and reference, and it is not uncommon for priyayi who are fifty and sixty years old to address adolescent "cousins" or "parents" with kin terms (discussed in Chapter 6) meaning 'elder sibling' or 'parent', and receive 'younger sibling' or 'child' in return. Traditionally such usage was accompanied in higher priyayi circles by more or less overtly asymmetric patterns of etiquette use—if not exchange of ngoko for basa, then asymmetric exchange of personal pronouns—because to address someone as elder kin is traditionally to accord them high enough status to require use of basa and, perhaps, to be addressed in ngoko.

This traditional correlation only became clear to me over the course of round-about elicitation sessions with several elderly priyayi. One provided an example of the effect of *awu* seniority on his interaction with a much younger collaterally related woman by saying he addressed here as *mbakyu* 'elder female sibling'. He stopped with this, regarding his statement as complete, and only when I asked for further clarification did he continue that he used *dalem* to her, so presupposing further knowledge on my part that use of *dalem* entailed use of basa to her in exchange for ngoko. This interchange between me [JE] and my consultant [PT] is a good example of priyayi tacit assumptions about the connectedness between linguistic conduct and status relations that informs their metapragmatic statements.

JE: And what sort of language did you use [to this woman]? (*Lajeng basanipun?*)
PT: Well of course *mbakyu*. (*Inggih mbakyu.*)
JE: Krama [a basa style] or ngoko? (*Krama menapa ngoko?*)
PT: Well, of course *dalem-dalem*. (*Inggih dalem-dalem.*)

Younger speakers these days are not particularly sensitive to *awu* seniority, nor as likely as their parents and grandparents to modulate their kin term or etiquette use in accordance with *awu* relations. A sixteen-year-old daughter of the gentleman just quoted, who I happened to observe address an agemate as 'mother' (*ibu*) and receive 'child' (*anak*) in return, was unable to explain to me why she did so, answering my question merely by saying (with a little embarrassment) that she just did what her parents had told her was proper (*pantes*).

Relations between affines (called in Javanese *ipéan*) determine another kind of seniority that can complicate etiquette use: one stands to one's spouse's kin in the same relation as one's spouse, irrespective of physical age. Examples commonly used to illustrate this principle were of proper interaction with one's spouse's siblings. To mark one's relation to a spouse's younger siblings as elder sibling, one addresses them with a kin term meaning 'younger sibling' and receives a term meaning 'elder sibling' (*kangmas* for males, and *mbakyu* for females, both discussed in Chapter 5). Traditionally one adopted correspondingly asymmetric patterns of etiquette. (The referential terms for these affines are *kangmas ipé* and *mbakyu ipé*.) A forty-year-old man who married the third youngest of four siblings would stand as affinal younger brother to his wife's (say) twenty-four-year-old elder sister, and several contradictory types of status criteria—physical age, descent status, and affinal seniority—could make for problematic choices of etiquette usage in general, and speech style usage in particular.

Older priyayi seem to find these complexities at least as diverting as they are onerous. One invited me to consider the following improbable but by no means impossible situation: suppose a man *A* and his younger sister *B* married (respectively) a younger sister *C* and her elder brother *D*. How would the in-laws address and speak to each other? Person *A* as spouse of *C* would be younger sibling to *D*, who as spouse of *B* would be younger sibling to *A*. My informant speculated that all things being equal, blood relations would take precedence over affinal relations between siblings. Another example: Pakubuwana X took as son-in-law a *wayah dalem* to whom he married his third eldest child. Before the wedding that *wayah dalem* was of lesser status than any of the *putra dalem*. As husband to a princess, however, he came to stand as elder brother to his wife's younger siblings. The priyayi who told me of this case said that those siblings were obliged to address him as *kangmas* (elder sibling) with the personal pronouns *dalem/nandalem*. Although he as elder brother would be within his rights to give ngoko to them, he gave them basa with *kula/panjenengan*.

Group Styles and Change in Priyayi Interaction

Priyayi were fond of pointing out to me how contradictory personal and relational attributes could make the task of deciding on a proper demeanor as complex as actually using the speech styles in proper manner: what's hard, they said, is the application (*trap-trapan*). Complicated as social relations were between members of the traditional elite, older priyayi evinced little sense that these complex considerations were particularly obtrusive in the shaping of interaction. I was party to older priyayi talk about their and others' kin relations and descent status on several occasions which suggested, as one insightful Dutch-educated priyayi noted, the way Westerners make small talk about the weather—a favored topic for sometimes desultory and rarely inappropriate conversation.

But these calculations and patterns of etiquette are most strikingly complex just in the upper strata of traditional priyayi society, and this sketch focuses on status and interaction within those strata to emphasize the high elite perspective on social relations and conduct. Examples of speech style use just presented illustrate interactively relevant, finely drawn differences between persons—different mother, different age, different degree of descent, and so on—that were more important determinants of etiquette use and interactional style than what those elite members shared: one or both parents, generation of descent, kin group, and so on. More or less asymmetric exchanges of kin terms, personal pronouns, and speech styles were the rule rather than the exception, and physical age was rarely the only or even necessarily the primary consideration for choosing an interactive style.

As important to an understanding of traditional linguistic etiquette use is some sense of variation in its use across social strata. Taken collectively, reports by middle- and lower-ranking priyayi on their own and others' everyday usage bear out a general observation: just as titular marks of status differences "faded out" further from the king, so too did behavioral and specifically linguistic marks of status difference in conduct become less overt between kin. There is evidence of broad intragenerational and cross-strata contrasts between what Brown and Gilman (1960:269) call "group styles": criteria for choosing between speech styles shifted from social differences to similarities as stylistic marking of differences became less elaborate.[27] (Changes in group styles of priyayi basa usage are discussed in Errington 1985b.)

In high elite circles relatively obvious asymmetric ngoko-for-basa patterns of speech style use marked relatively finely drawn status distinctions. Further down the hierarchy among fairly close family members—husband and wife, child and parent, siblings, close collaterals—there was a kind of fadeout of linguistic marks of social difference. Within four old-fashioned noble families below the level of *buyut dalem* with which I was acquainted, asymmetric exchange of basa and ngoko was regarded as obligatory only between the male head of the household and the children, but not between children and wives of any status.

27. Bax (1975) makes similar observations on rural versus urban usage of ngoko and basa.

Use of basa by lower elite children to mothers was apparently once acceptable but much less common than use of ngoko *alus*, with the second person pronoun *panjenengan* and honorifics in return for plain ngoko. The possibility of basa use by child to mother in a commoner family struck older priyayi to whom I suggested it as pretentious. As one said, "If they are not priyayi, why would they act like priyayi?" (*Dudu priyayi, kok mriyayèni?*) For an elder sibling to give a younger sibling ngoko in return for basa among the low nobility might be unseemly, according to one priyayi, because they were after all 'little priyayi' (*priyayi cilik*).[28] Use of polite ngoko containing polite personal pronouns and honorifics was generally adequate to mark respect for a commoner or low-ranking priyayi father, and sufficient for elder siblings to whom, as we have seen, nobles of the first and second generation of royal descent often gave basa with *dalem* and received ngoko.

When asked if they spoke basa to elder siblings or their mothers, four older low-ranking priyayi responded with surprise that to do so would be to act like a 'high priyayi' (*priyayi luhur*), and to leave oneself open to accusations of trying to climb socially. Both patterns are, as one fourth-generation, mid-level official put it, *ningrat sanget*, 'very *ningrat*'. *Ningrat* is a name element emblematic of high descent status[29] used by lower priyayi and commoners to identify (and set themselves off from) the highest '*ningrat* circles' (*kalangan ningrat*) associated with the most elaborate and rigid implementation of linguistic etiquette. This same priyayi reported that his father's elder sibling required his younger children to give their elder siblings basa, which they do, he noted with some amusement, to this day. Among higher nobility it still happens that younger siblings (one of my acquaintance was seventeen years old) give basa to older siblings (in this case forty-five years old) of their own choice.

These few examples of contrasting etiquette usage illustrate not

28. The ways priyayi of different noble and official classes use these designations vary in interesting sociocentric ways that cannot be discussed at length here.

29. Very precise relations existed between elite name elements and official and descent statuses of their holders. *Ningrat* for instance was accorded to holders of cabinet level positions with jurisidiction internal to the *negara*, and to certain *wayah dalem*. See Errington 1985b:87–92.

just how self-presentational style marked social difference lower in the hierarchy less overtly, but how obligations to adopt certain patterns of respect and deference became looser. Intrafamily usage was increasingly prescribed by the head of the household or, indeed, simply adopted by individuals as they wished. Less self-consciously exemplary and more personally shaped, asymmetries of etiquette use tended to fade out like the status differences they marked, and left more room for relative intimacy and respect as factors in the shaping of self-presentation.

Over the last fifty years such self-determined, generally less traditional status oriented usage has spread through much of what remains of the upper strata of priyayi society in Surakarta. Younger persons of traditionally high status no longer share or feel terribly constrained by attitudes towards status and conduct they call 'old-fashioned' (*kolot*), 'feudal' (*feodal*), and 'the way of the *ndara*' (*cara ndara-ndara*). Those of their parents who do not share this self-consciously forward-looking flexibility in interaction are increasingly unable to prescribe use by their children to any save themselves. One elderly *wayah dalem*, for instance, told me that he was given basa by his younger half-brother with whom he felt close just because it was their father's wish. But nowadays he cannot induce his youngest seventeen-year-old daughter to give her thirty-five-year-old half-brother basa. Similarly, a father may train his daughter to address a genealogically senior agemate as "mother," but is not able to induce her to give that agemate basa in return for ngoko. As he said to me, "It's not fitting (*pantes*) anymore." His half-amused, half-concerned comment that these days children are not concerned with etiquette is true insofar as younger priyayi adopt patterns of etiquette use with non-priyayi and priyayi alike that are keyed more to relative social distance or intimacy than to relative status.

The use of linguistic etiquette by the younger prince and older royal grandchild that illustrates the effect of genealogical seniority on interaction is also evidence of such change. Fifty years ago this pattern would have been anomalous, if not impossible. Older informants (including the elder of this pair) said that reciprocal use of *dalem* and *nandalem* along with basa speech styles was impossible in the old days because no two priyayi were of exactly equal status, and among high priyayi differences in status always presupposed some difference, however muted, in etiquette usage. Older priyayi to whom I recounted this case said that at the very least the *wayah dalem* would have acknowledged lower descent status by giving *dalem/nandalem* with basa, and might receive *kula/panjenengan* with basa from the prince to acknowledge physical and genealogical seniority.

As the sociopolitical primacy of priyayi has been vitiated along with the traditional ideology of kingship, younger priyayi have gradually become part of a larger heterogeneous urban elite, and are losing the ideology of obligatory interactional marking of status inequality. There is an ongoing shift to broader ranges of symmetric patterns of speech style exchange similar to those used among non-priyayi, which I have discussed at length elsewhere (Errington 1985b). Even members of the very highest traditional social strata are less frequently using asymmetric patterns of linguistic etiquette to mark unequal status relations, and are shifting instead to increasingly symmetric usage to mark mutually mitigating status differences.

This broad shift in attitudes toward and uses of linguistic etiquette is related to broader changes in the ways priyayi, in the traditional sense of the term, place themselves in relation to the palace in contemporary Surakarta. In the following chapters, some linguistic correlates of the ongoing integration of the traditional elite into a larger urban educated class will be considered as they relate to intergenerational variation in use of these same interactionally important linguistic elements: speech styles, kin terms, and personal pronouns.

Changes in Rights to Titles

The examples already given of differences between titles' official meanings as linguistic terms signifying social structural positions, and as contextually construed expressions of respect and deference in interaction, are worth briefly reconsidering in light of changes in rights to titles that were royally decreed by Pakubuwana X and his son Pakubuwana XI. A comparison of prescribed rights to titles before about 1930, schematized in Table 2, with prescribed title rights in 1940, presented in Table 3, suggests the pervasive influence of nonprescribed title use on the referential values of titles: prescriptive rights at the later date generally correspond to actual everyday uses before (and to an extent after) 1930. It would be oversimplistic to say

Table 3. Titles of Descent after 1939

Male

Grad	By pramaiswari eldest	others	By selir	Everyday usage
1 (young) (adult)	kangjeng gusti pangéran adipati anom	gusti radèn mas kangjeng gusti pangéran arya	(kangjeng) gusti pangéran arya	gusti
2 (young) (adult)	bendara pangéran arya	radèn mas bendara radèn mas		ndara dèn mas
3 4	radèn mas			ndara mas
5	radèn			dèn mas
6,7,...	radèn			dèn

Female

Grad		Everyday usage
1 (young) (adult)	gusti radèn ajeng gusti radèn ayu	gusti
2 (young) (adult)	bendara radèn ajeng radèn ayu	ndara dèn ajeng ndara dèn ayu
3 (young) 4 (adult)	radèn ajeng radèn ayu	ndara ajeng ndara ayu
5 (young) (adult)	radèn roro radèn nganten	dèn ajeng dèn ayu
6,7,...	radèn	dèn

Status, interaction, and titles 79

that the kings simply ratified fait accompli by royal decree, because economic and political factors may have figured in their decisions, but this remarkable correspondence suggests such a longstanding dynamic relation with analogues in use of certain speech style vocabularies.[30] These changes can be interpreted as symptoms of the tension between the two and as a kind of royal post hoc ratification of actual usage.

It is easiest to proceed stratificationally rather than chronologically, again moving from the top to the bottom of the descent status hierarchy. According to older informants, Pakubuwana XI gave all princes and princesses official rights to the title *gusti*, regardless of status of their mothers, shortly after succeeding his father.[31] This ratification of a longstanding pattern of actual usage is perhaps attributable in part to his own prior status as son of a concubine, addressed and referred to as *gusti* while still a prince in the manner described by the priyayi quoted earlier. The fact that he himself had no offspring by a *garwa dalem* may also have been part of the reason he titularly "raised" his children, but similar circumstances earlier in the history of the kingdom occasioned no such changes in official rights to titles.

The tension between unofficial and prescriptive rights was not resolved by this change, it seems, because there is evidence of continuing differences between the two: nonprescriptive usage of *gusti* has shifted down a notch, as it were, in the noble hierarchy. It was not reported to me—perhaps because it is less widespread in today's smaller traditional priyayi community—but I did observe an occasion of use of *gusti* to refer to a grandchild of a king (*wayah dalem*), which would clearly have been incorrect usage under any circumstances fifty years ago.

During a casual visit to the house of an older priyayi who still lives within the walls around the palace compound, I was joined in conversation by my host's wife's younger sister, who referred to her own child in address of our common host as *ti Ping*. Later, my host ex-

---

30. Under Pakubuwana XII these changes are continuing, if anything at an accelerated pace.
31. Unfortunately, I have been unable to find any archival or library sources that indicate exactly when this or other relevant decrees (*pranatan dalem*) were issued.

plained to me that although this woman is of low descent status, she married a prince and her child is therefore a royal grandchild with the title *bendara radèn ajeng* (discussed later). But members of the prince's household use *gusti* to address and refer to (*nyebut*)[32] this woman's daughter. *Ti* it turns out is a shortened form of *gusti*, used nowadays in combination with names. (Ping is a childhood nickname.) My host went on to say that such use of *gusti* for people who are not even *putra dalem* shows how the title is "chasing" *bendara* down the hierarchy, its value "falling" as nonnormative use continues and spreads. "Titles are like money," he perceptively added (in Indonesian) "and their values are still falling" (*nilainya turun.*)

Table 3 also shows how the title element *bendara*, which under Pakubuwana X was prescriptively the right of young *putra dalem*, has since been officially accorded to *wayah dalem*, the highest class of nobles to have been earlier referred to and addressed as *ndara*.[33] At the same time, *ndara* has become inappropriate in use to refer and address *wayah dalem*. I learned this when I once naively used a combination of *ndara* plus the name for a *wayah dalem*. I was corrected with uncharacteristic firmness by my host, this gentleman's nephew's wife, who said that I should call him *kangjeng*, a title now officially accorded just to *putra dalem*, and which the *wayah dalem* in question does not prescriptively hold. When I asked about proper use of *ndara*, she said that it is best used for *buyut dalem* (i.e., those now a generation lower than holders of the title *bendara*) and lower. Her prescriptive statement reflects the ongoing displacement and devaluation of *ndara*, like *bendara*, in everday use.

In fact, *ndara* is so commonly used these days outside of priyayi circles altogether, by people who hold the title *radèn* (discussed later) or who have no noble ancestry at all, that it hardly counts as a priyayi title. It has been widely appropriated by commoners, more so, it seems than was *radèn* at the turn of the century. Some servants are required to refer to and address the commoner heads of their house-

32. The verb *nyebut* (from *sebut*) I translate as 'refer', but it could also be translated as 'mention'.

33. I myself knew no *wayah dalem* with this title, because my acquaintances of such high descent status were all either *pangéran sentana* with the title *bendara pangéran arya* or had been accorded a more exalted, combined title of nobility and office *kangjeng radèn mas arya*.

holds as *ndara kakung* 'the male [honorific] *ndara*' and *ndara putri* 'the female [honorific] *ndara*'. Nowadays vocative and parenthetical uses of *ndara* hardly count as title use among speakers who have little sense of its connection to the full title element or the traditional elite hierarchy. More progressive Javanese (many themselves priyayi in the traditional sense) find such usage old fashioned and snobbish, what they are fond of calling *feodal* and sometimes dismiss, along with the whole complex of traditional courtly etiquette, as *cara ndara-ndara*. For them the shortened title element is not just a devalued descent marker but an emblem of an attenuated, anachronistic elite milieu.

Ndara is still used by old-fashioned priyayi in larger title expressions, and they are careful to distinguish these expressions, given in Table 3, from isolated use of *ndara* in referential or vocative use, which is typical, they say, of commoners. As recently as the 1930s and 1940s a great deal hinged interactionally on the difference between use of *ndara*, *ndara dèn mas/ayu*, and *ndara mas/ayu*. As Table 2 shows, *ndara dèn mas/ayu* was for reference and address of *wayah dalem*, whereas *ndara mas/ayu* was for the next two lower generations of persons, with official rights to the same titles *radèn mas/ayu*. So everyday use traditionally marked noble status distinctions that did not carry over to official rights to titles.

Ndara mas/ayu fell out of use for reasons having to do with changes in official rights to other elements of the descent title system and need to be considered first. At least as early as the turn of the century, nonnoble, well-to-do Surakartans like those described by Padmasusastra in the passage cited earlier were appropriating the title *radèn*, and by 1920 the cohesiveness of the traditional noble and official hierarchy was being eroded as its members gradually became less of a literati and more of an intelligentsia.[34] Around this time Pakubuwana X changed rights to descent titles in a symbolically potent move, as one older priyayi explained it to me, to "keep his base from narrowing": he decreed that anyone who could produce two witnesses willing to testify that he or she was descended from a king of Java, in his or any other royal line, would be granted the title *radèn*.

34. For a brief discussion see Errington 1985b: 39–62. Linguistic etiquette was a target of political reform that a group called *Jawa Dipa* attempted to institute by doing away with basa address styles. See Bonneff 1981.

Of the three traditional royal prerogatives (Rouffaer 1921:607) two—control of appanages and trade—had fallen from kings' hands, and consequently Pakubuwana X had recourse to the last, which was the awarding of titles.

To prevent the titular conflation of this potentially vast new titled group of "little priyayi" with his own fifth-generation nobility, who had previously held sole prescriptive right to *radèn*, Pakubuwana X accorded these latter *canggah dalem* the additional title element *mas* and *ayu*, so allowing them the element formerly diacritic of second-generation, third-generation, and fourth-generation nobility designated the *dènmasan*. This expansion of rights to titles also had indirect effects on use of the low title element *mas*, which are discussed in some detail in Chapter 5.

This expansion of rights to *radèn mas/ayu* did not please older members of the nonprincely nobility, the *para ndara* with prior right to those titles. Three older acquaintances who reported this residual discontent to me agreed that there was a kind of unofficial rear-guard response in everyday title usage. Second-generation and third-generation nobility felt, as one priyayi put it, as if "yesterday [the fifth-generation nobility] were *radèn*, now they're *ndara*?! Hold on a second." Around 1930 newly raised fifth-generation descent nobles began to be spoken of and referred to by their noble superiors in everyday usage as *dèn mas/ayu*, not *ndara mas/ayu* because, in the words of one older priyayi, the new nobility were "not really *ndara*" (*dudu ndara tenan*). These new *radèn mas/ayu* unsurprisingly rejected this unofficial titular holdover of a formerly prescriptive title distinction, as evidenced by the fact that over the next decade or so—my informants identified the Japanese occupation in 1940 as a *terminus ad quem*—they came to be commonly spoken of and addressed, like third-generation and fourth-generation descendants, as *ndara mas/ayu*. Everyday usage thus furthered the expansion of rights to titles (and, indirectly, their devaluation), which was already officially sanctioned. Official change would have conflated the group of royal grandchildren (*wayah dalem*) with nobles down to the fifth generation (*canggah dalem*) had *wayah dalem* not been given rights to the title *bendara*. Here too, then, official use came to fit with everyday use as the change in one element of the official system inevitably affected all the others.

Undetailed as this account of a subtle, complex set of social and linguistic changes is, it testifies to the social manipulability of titles as linguistic mediators of face-to-face interaction, and to the dynamic relation between interactional uses and officially prescribed meanings of titles as designators of noble groups and diacritics of social status. Changes in prescriptive and everyday norms for title use have a special place in this account as a convenient entree to joined issues in priyayi social and linguistic change encountered in later chapters. As parts of systems of semantically meaningful terms definable by recourse to pansocial hierarchies, titles are oppositively related markers of status distinctions that bear on conduct. Changes in rights to and uses of titles are clear for the same reason that priyayi were so sensitive to their interactional importance: there is an overt link between their semantic content and social significances. In interaction informed by overriding norms of other-exalting, self-lowering conduct, the skewing of titles' prescribed referential values and everyday uses made for a dynamic relation such that the official referential meanings on which interactionally appropriate uses were parasitic made for changes in de facto normative uses, ratified post hoc by royal decree as changes in their semantic values.

The trend in title use in the increasingly isolated and weakened elite hierarchy is clear, and was summed up by the priyayi remark on title inflation cited previously. If economic inflation occurs when too much money chases too few goods, this social symbolic inflation accelerated as more and grander titles were keyed to fewer politically and socioeconomically real status differences. As elements of both systems became officially available to larger classes of people, they were also devalued as markers of elite status.

Don Alhambra, Grand Inquisitor in a very different kingdom,[35] observed of a realm whose entire populace was promoted that "when every one is somebody, then no one's anybody." The final celebration of the cult of royal glory in latter day Surakarta certainly cost the priyayi elite something of their social and titular claims to being somebody. This sketch of priyayi status, interaction, and priyayi title change serves, if nothing else, as a preliminary encounter with basic issues in the following chapters on the speech style system: the effect

35. In W. S. Gilbert and Arthur Sullivan, *The Gondoliers*, act II.

of recent social change on social interaction, dynamic relations between normative and strategic use of certain kinds of terms for persons, and speakers' focused concerns with and observations on appropriate linguistic interaction. This sketch of the speech styles as one aspect of etiquette yields a general picture of speech style use and introduces some general notions about the social and linguistic forces that have shaped linguistic etiquette.

4

Basic Classifications

Priyayi descriptions of speech style use like those cited in Chapter 3 contrast strikingly in their simplicity with terminologically elaborate accounts of speech style structure in the literature. Obvious differences between the two do not mean that speakers' accounts are woefully incomplete or that scholarly analyses are overwrought and redundant. They are symptomatic rather of the fact that native speakers tacitly presuppose knowledge of speech style structure like that described in the literature when they describe linguistic interaction and speech style use. This chapter provides an organizational overview of the basic structure of the speech style vocabularies and introduces metalinguistic terms that are used in the following chapters, as elsewhere in the literature, to describe them. More importantly, it introduces traditional classifications in such a way as to make room for something like a speaker's point of view on use that can be linked, in turn, to speech style use as a dynamic mediator of social interaction.

This account subsumes and moves beyond much of the traditional literature in two general ways. First, it proceeds from previously unnoted correlative distinctions between the contrasting structural properties, social significances, and referential significances of classes of speech style elements. These are adduced with a pair of simple, crosscutting distinctions between objects and modes of lexical reference, which yield an intuitively plausible classification of style elements and suggest something about relative interactional importance of speech elements both inside and outside the speech style system. They also reflect on interactive social pressures that have affected the structure and normative uses of the speech style system. The expository strategy is to emphasize broad linguistic and semiotic contrasts that are implicit both in native speakers' views of linguistic etiquette use and in linguists' descriptions of speech style structure. These contrasts will be elaborated in Chapters 5, 6, and 7 to consider the changing structures and uses of speech style vocabularies and linguistic etiquette as a whole.

All but the most recent descriptions portray the speech styles as a system in the Saussurean sense of the term. Focusing on structured paradigmatic stylistic oppositions between sets of grammatically and semantically comparable speech segments which combine in patterned syntagmatically coherent relations, these accounts unproblematically assume that the system transparently incorporates lexical and grammatical categories of the basic code. Speech styles are in this respect treated as a parasystem or interrelated set of subsystems superimposed on the linguistic code. Knowledge of such structure was taken for granted by native speakers, for instance, when they described speech style use to me in the ways presented in Chapter 3. They simply assumed patterned relations between parts of stylistically distinct sentential wholes in order to focus on what linguists have tended to neglect: the fit of speech style and linguistic etiquette use with contexts, and especially status relations between persons in interaction, broadly sketched in Chapter 3. Their concern with appropriate implementation coincides naturally with their descriptive focus on elements of the system that are structurally and interactively crucial markers of deference, intimacy, and respect.

Like linguists, native speakers conceptualize speech style use normatively by presuming stable, conventional part/whole relations between speech styles, and aspects of social relations between speech partners as well as context in general. Although this account is similarly code-oriented, it is not static, because it goes beyond much of the literature to explore the fit between changes in speech style use (together with other interactionally important vocabularies) and broad norms of interaction already sketched in Chapters 2 and 3. Like interactionally oriented descriptions provided by native speakers, this account deals with broadly "appropriate" use but explicates patterned change over time in what has counted as normatively "appropriate" for priyayi and commoners of different eras. Unlike de-

Basic classifications 87

scriptions that gloss over broad correlations between speech style structure and semantic significances of speech style elements, this work is primarily concerned with ways that interpenetrating stylistic and referential significance have informed strategic speech style use and in turn have cumulatively affected speech style structure.

To deal with the effect of use on structure is to bridge the gap between code-oriented and interactional points of view on linguistic etiquette, and assumes a very broad distinction between two interpenetrating symbolic significances intrinsic to speech as interaction, and so to speech style use as linguistic etiquette. There is, on the one hand, the specifically linguistic or *semantic* significance of speech, the kind of representativeness that is a distinctive semiotic property of use of language systems. On the other hand, there is the broadly interactive, contextually situated social or *pragmatic* significance of speech (and speech styles) as enacted, conventional conduct, which is the specifically linguistic face of emergent, other-oriented interaction. This semiotic dichotomy between semantic and pragmatic significances of speech can be explicated by recasting traditional structural analyses and recontextualizing native speaker's observations broadly enough to motivate a sociolinguistic account of speech style structure, use, and change.

A good starting point is the word basa, introduced in Chapter 3 as a metalinguistic term frequently used by native speakers. Basa is not widely used in the literature, perhaps because it is ambiguous between several analytically distinguishable senses which native speakers tacitly assume in different contexts. The broadest sense of basa can be glossed simply as 'language' or *langue* in the Saussurean sense—the English language is *basa Inggris*, Javanese is *basa Jawa*—and can be opposed to two narrower senses having to do just with the speech styles. Basa in some contexts of use is glossable more narrowly as 'non-ngoko [Javanese] morpheme' or 'non-ngoko speech style'. So a person may say *Kok nganggo basa?!* "How is that he is speaking basa?" to express surprise that a young boy in a television drama addresses his father in polite language.

As these two glosses indicate, basa is ambiguous also between a paradigmatic sense to refer to (classes of) non-ngoko morphemes, and a syntagmatic sense to refer to combinations of non-ngoko morphemes in larger speech styles. This syntagmatic/paradigmatic ambiguity extends to transitive causative forms of the word, suffixed with -*aké*, which may mean 'put into words, express in language', but also 'to find/make into equivalent non-ngoko language' as in the sentence *Omah yèn dibasakaké dalem*, "The word 'house' (*omah*) when made basa is *dalem*." In yet another sense discussed in Chapter 6, *mbasakaké* serves to describe a special, strategic kind of use of honorific basa lexemes. As a term for non-ngoko morphemes, basa is used for speech elements whose pragmatic significances may be tied either to their use in acts of *address*, speaking *to* a speech partner who may or may not be a referent in speech; or to acts of *reference and predication*, speaking *of* persons—identifying them and characterizing their states, attributes, and actions—whether or not they are present for or partners to occasions of use.

Acts of address style use are linguistic aspects of demeanor in mutually monitored interaction with a speech partner, and in the literature basa address styles and their constituent elements are usually called *krama* and *madya*. Uhlenbeck (1978:315) has pointed out that these words, like basa and ngoko, are similarly ambiguous between a paradigmatic sense to refer to stylistically opposed morphemes, and a syntagmatic sense to refer to structurally unitary address styles comprised of such elements.

> One may say that one speaks in or uses *krama, madya,* or *ngoko,* or that a sentence is in *krama, madya,* or *ngoko.* In that case the term refers to the speech style chosen by the speakers. But one may also say of a word or a grammatical element that it is *krama, madya,* or *ngoko.* . . . The ambiguity of the Javanese terminology reflects the important fact that a complete description of the Javanese forms of respect requires attention not only to their paradigmatic aspect, that is, to the lexical morphological relations between the various items involved, but also to their syntagmatic aspect, that is, to their cooccurrence in the sentence. This need has not always been recognized in the existing literature. (Uhlenbeck 1978:301)

Acts of reference to and predication of persons may be endowed with another kind of pragmatic significance because the speech style system includes a set of basa lexemes that can be called most generally *honorifics*. These are lexemes whose social-significative or pragmatic functions are mapped onto their semantic functions:

> [They are] words and forms which—regardless of the level [i.e., ngoko, madya, krama] being used—refer to body parts, possessions, affairs, and mental states of persons who in the speaker's opinion are of higher rank

than he, or for one reason or another, he places at a higher rank . . . (Walbeehm 1896:13).

Honorific terms differ from ngoko, madya, and krama terms structurally because they can be used in any address style, semantically because their membership is (crudely put) restricted to the domain of persons, and pragmatically because their social significative function as markers of deference is keyed to the identity of objects of linguistic reference. Because the term basa refers to all types of non-ngoko lexemes, it is indefinite with respect to the krama/honorific distinction. In the example of the use of *basakaké* cited previously, *dalem*, the honorific equivalent of *omah*, was cited, but its krama equivalent *griya* could have been just as validly used.

The simple set of examples in Figure 1 helps to develop this terminological overview of the speech styles, although they exemplify neither all the stylistic distinctions to be discussed nor the full repertoire of any Javanese speaker, priyayi or otherwise. They illustrate correlative structural and functional properties of different sets of speech style vocabularies commonly noted in the literature, but also make clear some tacitly assumed semiotic and semantic properties of classes of speech style elements.

Address Styles: Ngoko, Krama, Madya

Sentences 1 through 4 in Figure 1 all count as basa because they contain non-ngoko components classifiable as krama and madya: sentences 1 and 2 are krama, sentences 3 and 4 are madya, whereas sentences 5 and 6 are ngoko, because of stylistic oppositions between the sentences' component elements. These elements are selected from two-member ngoko/krama sets (column 4), three-member ngoko/krama/madya sets (columns 1 and 5), and the very complex set of second-person pronouns (column 2). Elements selected from these sets combine according to co-occurrence constraints which ensure that they are stylistically well-formed.

Walbeehm noted (1896:4) that it is misleading to say that ngoko designates a speech style or a speech style vocabulary (in Dutch *taalsoort*) if one thereby imputes to ngoko address styles and their component elements the same status as basa morphemes and styles. Ngoko is not speech style but the language proper, on which elabo-

Figure 1. Semiotic/linguistic speech style structure

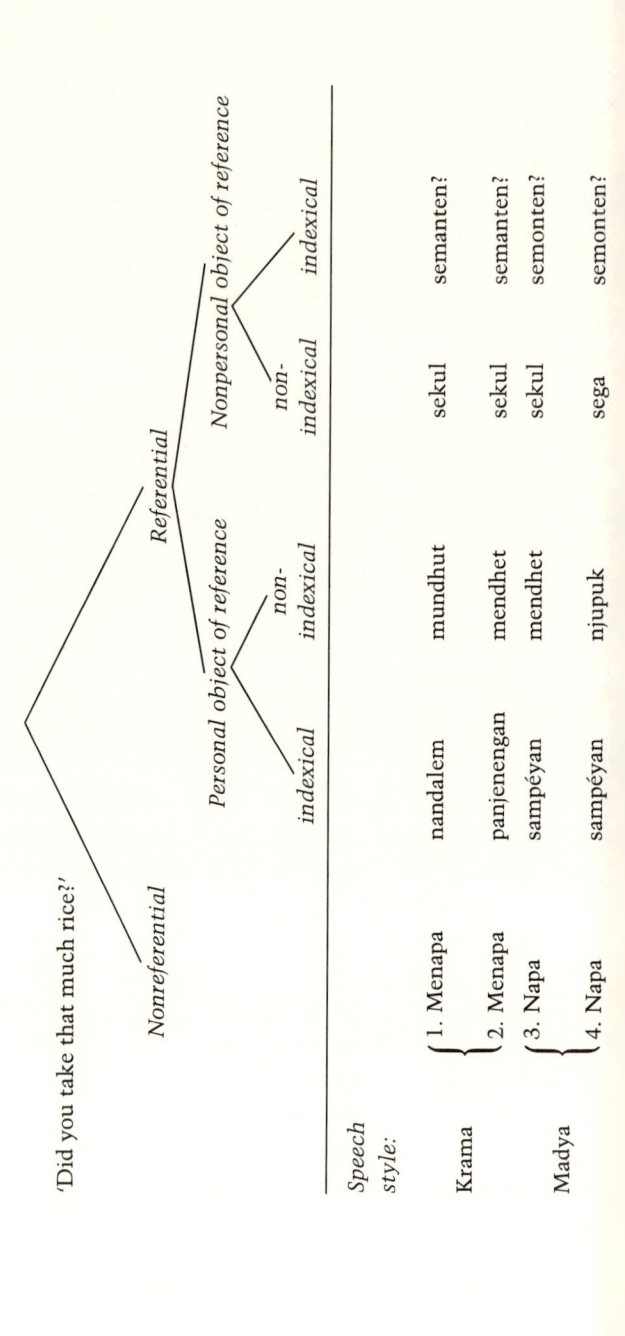

'Did you take that much rice?'

		Referential			
	Nonreferential	Personal object of reference		Nonpersonal object of reference	
		indexical	non-indexical	non-indexical	indexical

Speech style:

Krama
{ 1. Menapa — nandalem — mundhut — sekul — semanten?
{ 2. Menapa — panjenengan — mendhet — sekul — semanten?

Madya
{ 3. Napa — sampéyan — mendhet — sekul — semonten?
{ 4. Napa — sampéyan — njupuk — sega — semonten?

Ngoko	5. Apa 6. Apa	sliramu	mundhut	sega	semono?
Gloss:	QUESTION MARKER	kowé 2ND PERSON PRONOUN	njupuk TAKE	sega RICE	semono? THAT MUCH
Pragmatic function on axis of:	ADDRESS	ADDRESS & REFERENCE	ADDRESS OR REFERENCE	ADDRESS	ADDRESS
Set structure:	krama madya ngoko	krama inggil krama madya ngoko	krama inggil krama ngoko	krama ngoko	krama madya ngoko

rated sets of stylistic oppositions and repertoires are superimposed. There is practically no basa morpheme without a ngoko equivalent,[1] but most words of the ordinary language do not have basa alternants and so do not really count as ngoko per se. Speakers sometimes allude to the intrinsically oppositional value of the speech styles when they say that lexemes that do not stand in an oppositive stylistic relation and thus have no place in the style system "are both ngoko and basa."

The ngoko/krama opposition is sometimes called the basis of the speech styles (as Padmasusastra 1896:2 put it, *bakuning basa*) because krama is by far the largest basa vocabulary and most paradigmatic speech style sets have at least a krama member. Walbeehm (1896:29) lists 579 obligatory and 104 optional krama forms. This terminological distinction is discussed in Chapter 7. Members of the largest class of paradigmatic sets in the system are comprised of single krama alternants (like *sekul* 'cooked rice' in column 4 of Figure 1) in dyadic opposition to "basic" ngoko forms (like *sega*).

Krama variants are unrestricted in their referential range and grammatical function just because there is no intrinsic relation between their semantic and pragmatic functions. The relative open-endedness of the krama class has made it susceptible to expansion through extensions of analogical sound patterns, a linguistic response to social pressures discussed in Chapter 7. But there is a rough, useful correlation between the range of ngoko/krama oppositions and relative frequency of use: on the whole, morphemes in this class of paradigmatic sets have higher text frequencies than those that are not, and ngoko elements that are more frequently used are relatively more likely to have krama alternants. Uhlenbeck has pointed out (1978:284) that the semantic range of the krama lexicon involves relatively basic concepts not unlike those signified by the vocabulary of Basic English, and although this correlation is very rough—there are krama alternants for the ngoko words meaning 'north' and 'eat', for instance, but not for ngoko words glossable as 'south' and 'drink'—it is quite useful in discussing the honorific vocabulary in Chapter 6. But this correlation is really contingent with respect to the interplay between semantic and pragmatic significances of speech style elements.

1. Honorifics that do not alternate transparently with ngoko lexemes are discussed in Chapter 6.

Figure 2. Patterns of ngoko and krama address style exchange

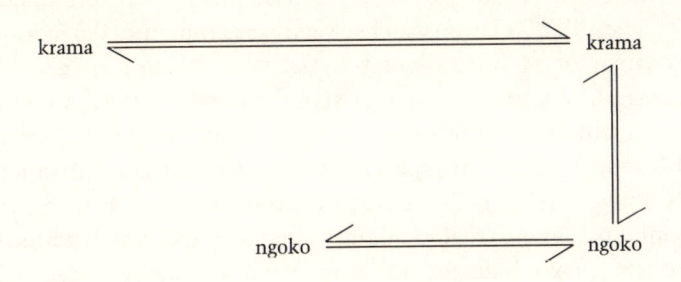

```
krama  ⇄ ─────────────────────→  krama
                                   ↑↓
                                   ↓↑
ngoko  ⇄ ─────────────────────→  ngoko
```

The basic address style opposition is often described in the literature as being between speech like sentence 6 of Figure 1, which consists entirely of ngoko morphemes, and speech like sentence 2, which consists entirely of krama alternants to those morphemes. These structurally unitary address styles, like their elements, can be thought of as dyadically opposed and usable in one of the three patterns of exchange schematized in Figure 2, which straightforwardly transposes Brown and Gilman's (1960) analysis of social "semantics" of personal pronoun exchange in Western European languages.

Occasions of ngoko and krama address style use can be said to mediate social relations between speech partners as do the "pronouns of power and solidarity" because of their structural unity as styles used in patterns of exchange. Rules of syntagmatic patterning dictate that choice of the ngoko word meaning 'take' (*njupuk* in sentence 6, column 3 of Figure 1) entails use of the ngoko word for 'rice' (*sega* in column 4), and correspondingly that *sekul*, the krama alternant to *sega*, must co-occur with *mendhet*, the krama alternant to ngoko *njupuk*. (The converse is not true for reasons that will become clear when honorific terms are discussed later.) Implementation and interpretation of speech style use depends in the first place on this general principle of structural unity. Any combination of the stylistic elements of sentences 1 and 5 other than just those presented here would be structurally ill-formed and so pragmatically uninterpretable in virtually any situation.

As unitary address styles, ngoko and krama have social significances like those of *tu* and *vous* in French, *du* and *sie* in German, and other T and V forms, as Brown and Gilman call them, insofar as those significances are realized in asymmetric or symmetric patterns of exchange. Use of a ngoko speech style, or T form, presupposes either a "familiar" relationship between speech partners in symmetric exchange, or addressee's inferior status in asymmetric exchange for krama, or V form. That social significances of address style use are only realized in patterns of exchange is an obvious but crucial fact, because it means that speech style usage is intrinsically a reciprocally shaped and negotiated part of interaction. In effect there are two contexts for construal of address style use, and two dynamically related wholes of which any occasion or token of address style use is part: *in presentia* it is part of a contemporaneous and coexperienced environment, and *in absentia* it is part of a pattern of exchange in dialogue that is realized through consecutive social acts, preceding and following, by speech partners exchanging roles as speaker and addressee.

Thus realized in mutually constructed patterns of exchange, pragmatic significances of address style use can not be unilaterally enacted by or assigned to one speech partner by the other, a point priyayi made to me when they emphasized the relation of mutual dependence and reciprocal attunement between speech partners that is necessary for smooth interaction (see Chapter 2). The point is clear from cases of failed interaction, in which conflicting views on and evaluations of personal and relative status prevent successful negotiation of a mutually acceptable pattern of exchange. This is the moral of one low-ranking, well-educated priyayi's story about his progressive youth in the 1930s:

> In Yogyakarta the Sultan always respected his servants and people. Outside of the palace he spoke basa to anyone he met. But in Surakarta the nobility maintained the old ways. Sometimes a prince or royal grandchild [*wayah dalem*] would be out in this neighborhood on horseback, and stop to ask me [in ngoko] "Where's so-and-so's house?" [*Omahé si anu nèng ndi?*] like that. For me the prince was no one special; if the Sultan of Yogya could speak basa to me, why shouldn't a prince in Solo? So I'd answer [in ngoko]: "Over there, it's close." [*Nèng kono, cedhak kok.*] The prince didn't like that, but I wasn't going to give in to him.

A cat can look at a king, and as early as the beginning of this century low-ranking priyayi could reciprocate low style of usage with impunity, withholding symbolic acknowledgment of speech partner's superior status by giving what he got.[2]

Paradigmatic sets that contain madya elements also contain krama elements together with which they make distinctive contributions to the referential significance of utterances. Elements of these three member sets also have the highest frequencies of use of any class of speech style variants, higher even than elements of ngoko/krama sets. Tripartite ngoko/madya/krama oppositions exist only within the small, closed classes of morphosyntactic and deictic morphemes, and none are found in any large, open-ended lexical class. Poedjosoedarmo (n.d.) has suggested, and I have argued elsewhere (1985b:135–45) that many distinctively madya forms probably originated as fast-speech elisions and reductions of frequently used "full" krama forms.

Members of some of these sets modify, conjoin, or demarcate larger syntactic units: a few bound morphemes, auxiliary aspect markers, relative clause and topic markers, conjunctions, negative particles, prepositions, and so on. Others consist of interrogative, indefinite, and relative pronouns that likewise serve significative functions as parts of larger grammatical wholes. An example in Figure 1 is the paradigmatic set in column 1, consisting of *menapa* (krama)/*napa* (madya)/*apa* (ngoko), which mark these examples as yes/no questions but, in other syntactic environments, can serve as conjunctions, indefinite head nouns of relative clauses, and related functions.

Although madya forms are generally distinct in sound shape from their ngoko and krama equivalents, a few are also obligatory in ngoko or krama styles and so on distributional grounds best treated as members of two classes (Errington 1985b:121–35). The morphosyntactic apparatus of the language is only partially elaborated for krama and madya styles, as the active verb marker (*N*-)[3] prefixed to all roots

---

2. I have the sense that priyayi, at least, tend to privilege what they will receive over what they give in cases where usage is unclear; that is, they are more willing to give some style they feel is inappropriate in order to receive what they feel is appropriate. Some priyayi explained that you sometimes have to give basa to lower-class people to make sure you don't get ngoko back, apparently an insufferable circumstance for older elite members.

3. N serves to transcribe homorganic nasals in this and a few other prefixes phonetically realized in the following ways: m/___p,w,b; n/___t,j,d; ny/___c; ng/___k,g,vowel. For more information see index of Javanese words.

meaning 'take' in column 3 illustrates. But all indexically referential ngoko elements have madya and krama alternants with which they share meanings characterizable only with recourse to aspects of contexts and acts of use. These duplex structures (Jakobson 1971:130–47) anchor use to context through conventionally encoded contextual feature types that are presupposed in contexts for occasions of use of indexical elements to contribute to referential meaning. They include aspect markers, personal pronouns (like those in column 2) and demonstrative pronouns like *semanten* (krama), *semonten* (madya), and *semono* (ngoko), meaning 'that much' in column 5.

Although there are less than fifty morphemes diacritic of madya address styles like sentences 3 and 4, their availability makes for considerable structural complexity in address style repertoires and pragmatic ambiguity in address style use. The obvious gloss for *madya* 'middle' correctly suggests that this vocabulary and the address styles it distinguishes can be thought of as intermediate on a continuum of polish or politeness between "low" (or crude, *kasar*) ngoko and "high" (or refined, *alus*) krama. This is true first because the distinctively madya inventory is so small, and because speakers make frequent use of non-madya lexemes in madya speech, often choosing between members of two-way ngoko/krama oppositions. To refer to cooked rice in a madya speech style, for instance, one chooses between the ngoko *sega* and krama *sekul* as in column 4 of Figure 1, this choice between members of the two-way opposition making also for a choice between the madya substyles often called *madyangoko* (like sentence 4) and *madyakrama* (like sentence 3) in the literature.

So there are really two types of oppositions between classes of stylistic variants that are diacritic of address styles, two types of "linked conjugates" (Geertz 1960:253) and syntagmatic patternings of vocabularies that are diacritic of more or less refined ways of speaking to others. Elements of ngoko/krama and ngoko/madya/krama oppositions serve to distinguish speech styles in different ways, are subject to different co-occurrence constraints, and also contribute in different ways to semantico-referential significances of speech. Figure 3 schematizes the structural asymmetry between members of these two types of sets: knowledge of a given choice between members of tripartite ngoko/madya/krama sets (at least, where madya elements

Figure 3. Syntagmatic patterning between three- and two-member sets

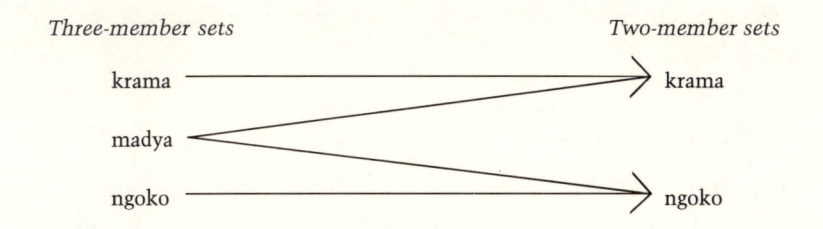

```
Three-member sets                    Two-member sets
    krama ─────────────────────────⟶ krama
    madya ◀──────────────
                         ───────────⟶
    ngoko ─────────────────────────⟶ ngoko
```

are phonologically distinct) allows one to predict more about choice between two-member ngoko/krama sets than in the converse case.

Complexities of madya and krama use stem in part from differences in distribution of control of these two basa address styles in the speech community at large, discussed at length elsewhere together with patterns of change in syntagmatic structures of priyayi address style repertoires (Errington 1985b:89–107). I bypass that issue here to focus on the interplay of pragmatic and semantic symbolism in speech style structure, use, and change in speech style vocabulary membership. In Chapter 7 some unobvious ways that differences in structures of krama and madya address styles make krama address styles intrinsically more polished (*alus*) than madya are discussed in relation to other interactive significances of speech.

To distinguish between ngoko, madya, and krama address styles and style elements is nothing new, but there are analytically important semantic correlates to those distinctions previously unnoted in the literature. First, we can distinguish between morphemes (and paradigmatic sets of morphemes) that do and do not have referential significance (columns 2–5 vs. column 1 in Figure 1). Among those which have referential significance we can further distinguish between those whose *mode* of reference is either nonindexical (columns 3 and 4) or indexical (columns 2 and 5). Three member paradigmatic sets that contain madya members fall either into nonreferential or indexically referential classes, and paradigmatic sets of each type have in turn different set-internal structures not apparent in these examples but discussed in Chapter 7.

98   Basic classifications

This catalog of speech style vocabularies and sketch of their correlative structural elaboration and semantic content can be extended to classes of paradigmatic sets that contain honorific basa lexemes, and especially the small but interactively important class of personal pronouns.

Honorific Lexemes

The term "honorific" is used here for the entire group of basa lexemes that somehow serve to mark deference for persons they are used to identify, most often called *krama inggil* 'high krama' in the literature (as in the passage from Walbeehm quoted previously).[4] All honorifics' stylistic significances involve statuses of persons they serve to speak *of*, and so are tied directly to the semantic content they share with their nonhonorific alternants in the semantic domain of person. But unlike nonhonorifics, their social significances in use are keyed to the axis of reference and are fundamentally skewed with the social significance of use of ngoko/(madya)/krama styles and style elements on the axis of address.

The krama lexeme *inggil* rather than its ngoko equivalent *dhuwur* 'high', 'tall', is always used in this idiomatic metalinguistic term.[5] The term "honorific" is used here to avoid a systematic ambiguity between two senses of krama inggil as it is commonly used by authors and sometimes by native speakers. There is another metalinguis-

---

4. That Walbeehm and some others have further classified the honorific vocabulary as a subset of krama has few implications for the larger analysis. One of the several oversimplifications in Figure 1 is that honorifics are not used to speak of an addressee to whom one uses madya; the complexities of this situation stem from the several social significances of madya usage touched on in Chapters 5 and 7 and discussed in Errington 1985b:155–56.

5. Some authors (e. g., Padmasusastra 1896:20) and most native speakers extend the paradigmatic/syntagmatic ambiguity of ngoko, madya, and krama to the term krama inggil as well. In fact the "highness" of words and utterances that speakers call krama inggil may be of two distinct sorts, and some speakers call the "highest" (i.e., most refined) basa morpheme in a given set of leveled alternants the "highest" basa equivalent, whether or not such a morpheme has honorific import. These terminological uses and ambiguities are discussed in Errington 1985b:84–89, 92–98.

tic term, krama andhap, common in the literature but hardly known to native speakers, to which krama inggil stands as unmarked to marked member of a semantic opposition. In its narrower meaning (its minus interpretation) krama inggil refers to just those honorifics that mark relatively high status of an individual they serve to identify or characterize directly, independently of any relation between that person and another. (This awkward characterization suffices in lieu of discussion in Chapter 6.) An example in column 3 of Figure 1 is the active transitive form of the krama inggil verb root *pundhut* 'take, acquire': use of *mundhut* rather than *njupuk* (ngoko) or *mendhet* (krama) marks speakers' deference or respect for the person spoken of, who in examples 1–6 but by no means all cases is addressee.

Krama andhap is opposed to this narrower sense of krama inggil as a cover term for a small class of honorifics that serve to mark an asymmetric status relation between someone spoken of as an inferior in some type of transitory coordinate relation to a superior. An example that could be substituted for *mundhut* in examples 1–6 would be *nyuwun* 'request' (active transitive form of *suwun*, discussed at length in Chapter 6), which would mark relatively lower status of the person as agent of the act of requesting (here, addressee) in relation to relatively higher status of person who is recipient/addressee of that act (unspecified in these sentences). The term krama andhap— containing another krama lexeme *andhap* (ngoko *asor* 'low, short') frozen in a metalinguistic phrase—alludes to the relatively "low" status of referent in relation to some higher status other.

Because the term krama inggil is commonly used in a broader, zero interpretation as a cover term for all honorifics, including members of the krama andhap vocabulary, there is enough potential for pernicious ambiguity in technical discussion to justify using the English term "honorific" and sometimes "deferential" here for krama inggil's broader sense, and reserving krama inggil in its narrow sense or minus interpretation as a designation for the larger proper subset of honorifics that are not members of the krama andhap vocabulary.

The coincident semantic and pragmatic functions of krama inggil honorifics articulate with norms for humble, *andhap-asor* conduct discussed in Chapter 2 in a very specific, virtually categorical rule of use: krama inggil honorifics are not used for self-reference. Use of krama inggil for reference to either speech partner normatively marks high status of that referent in relation to the other partner, ordinarily presupposed likewise as reference point for status comparison. To make oneself an object of honorific reference is to mark oneself as worthy of speech partner's deference, an act that is rude and arrogant (*digsura*) in the mouths of all save the very highest nobility, and these days in the most traditional of contexts. This point is of practical importance for a study of changing membership of the krama inggil vocabulary in Chapter 6. Conversely, one does not predicate actions of others of which one is recipient with krama andhap, which is tantamount to marking oneself as that person's superior.

To say that the uses of honorifics have social significances subsistent on their semantico-referential significances and that they function pragmatically on the axis of reference rather than address, is to say also that encoded ngoko/(madya)/krama oppositions are skewed fundamentally with encoded nonhonorific/honorific oppositions. The difference between non-basa/basa modes of address, and nonhonorific/honorific modes of reference, is easy enough to overlook (compare Geertz 1960:253 and Uhlenbeck 1978:309) and basic enough to speech style structure to deserve illustration through speakers' own understandings of use.

Speakers' descriptions of possible appropriate uses of sentences 7–9 are useful in this regard because these three sentences, marked as madya by *mpun* 'already' (ngoko equivalent *wis*, krama *sampun*) and *dèrèng* (ngoko *durung*, krama *dèrèng*), differ just through alternations between members of the paradigmatic set of terms that share the sense glossable as 'go out': ngoko *mangkat* in 7 (madyangoko), krama *késah* in 8 (madyakrama), and krama inggil *tindak* in 9 (simply madya). The subject noun phrase *Har* is a short form of a male name not stylistically elaborated in the system.[6] This verb was chosen to provide speakers with examples that cannot be construed as referential of either speech partner. These examples thus allow for a

---

6. But it is unusual that a person referred to with a short form of a name without title like this should also be referred to honorifically, a point taken up in the next chapter.

direct comparison of differences in social significances of use of ngoko/krama as opposed to honorific lexemes.

7. Har	mpun	mangkat,	dèrèng? (MADYANGOKO)
8. Har	mpun	késah,	dèrèng? (MADYAKRAMA)
9. Har	mpun	tindak,	dèrèng? (MADYA)
PROPER NAME	ALREADY	GO OUT	NOT YET

Has Har left yet?

Speakers regularly contrasted sentences 7 and 8 by saying something about differences in intimacy or formality conveyed by each about the relation between speech partners, so assuming either a relatively formal reciprocal exchange pattern of madyakrama (sentence 8) or relatively intimate madyangoko (sentence 7). Use of *késah* for Har, they said, indicated nothing about Har's status in relation to anyone; it just showed that the speaker wanted to be polite to the speech partner. On the other hand, speakers consistently contrasted use of 7 and 8 over and against 9 by specifying in the last case that Har, a third-person referent, was worthy of the respect marked by honorific usage. They then naturally shifted their attention from the ngoko/ krama opposition between patterns of address style exchange to the nonhonorific/ honorific opposition between modes of reference to an individual.

Examples of potentially honorific use to third persons show this functional skewing clearly, but social significances of acts of honorific reference to speech partners are complicated by the distinct statuses of such persons as both referents in and parties to the act of speech exchange. Broadly speaking, asymmetric or unilateral use of honorifics for a speech partner in any address style presupposes an asymmetry in social status between speech partners, whereas symmetric or reciprocal exchange presupposes comparability if not equality of status. Use of honorifics for addressee may thus complement or supplement the marking of social relations in patterns of address style use. Asymmetric patterns of ngoko and krama address style exchange are ordinarily keyed to differences in status between speech partners, and the lower status person, who gives krama and receives ngoko, will ordinarily use honorifics for reference to an addressee. The speech partner may or may not return honorifics in

102   Basic classifications

ngoko (as in sentence 5 in Figure 2) to mitigate the linguistic marks of the status difference[7] presupposed by the asymmetric pattern of address styles. Symmetrically exchanged honorifics in symmetrically exchanged krama may heighten the sense of mutual regard or social distance accruing to a relation between speech partners, whereas asymmetric exchange of honorifics with symmetric krama address style use may mark the higher status of one partner in comparison with an unfamiliar speech partner.

From an interactional or contextual perspective speech partners are privileged attribute-bearing individuals and objects of potentially honorific reference because they are coparticipants in and cocreators of the dynamic pattern of speech style exchange that mediates the social relation. The crucial distinction between objects of honorific reference who are and are not speech partners has a reflex in received terminological distinctions between ngoko address styles in which honorifics do and do not appear for reference to addressee. The former has been given a distinct name in the literature, *antyabasa*, and is commonly (but not exclusively) called *ngoko alus* ('refined ngoko') by native speakers.[8] Krama address style usage together with honorific reference to speech participants is sometimes called *mudhakrama* in the literature, as opposed to *kramantara*, which contains no honorifics used for addressee. The absence of analogous terminological differences for styles in which honorifics are and are not used in krama for reference to a non-speech partner testifies to addressee's privileged position as both referent and participant in linguistic interaction.

There are just two honorifics for which the functional distinction between speech partner and non-speech partner as objects of refer-

---

7. This style of use was favored, for instance, by many older priyayi when addressing me.

8. Another variant sometimes called *basaantya* in the literature is described as allowing for the use of krama lexemes as surrogate krama inggil, but is now rarely used in contemporary Surakarta. It is worth noting, though, that the range of ngoko morphemes said to appear obligatorily in *basaantya*, and for which krama alternants are specifically described as not being substitutable, overlaps largely with the range of ngoko morphemes which also have obligatory madya equivalents. Compare Padmasusastra 1896:21 with Poedjosoedarmo 1968a:15, both discussed in Errington 1985b:71–75, and Poedjosoedarmo et al. 1979:9.

ence is irrelevant, and for which the distinction between pragmatic function on the axis of reference and address is therefore also irrelevant. These are honorific personal pronouns *dalem* (first person) and *nandalem* (second person), whose social significances are always keyed to the status relation between the speech participants by whom, of whom, and to whom they are used, and who together exhaust their referential range. Presupposing their referents as occupants of reciprocally defined, interchangeable roles of speech partners, personal pronouns[9] are unique referring expressions for interactionally privileged objects of and parties to possibly honorific reference. Unlike other honorifics, but like all deictics, honorific and nonhonorific personal pronouns are indexically referential, anchored referentially in the *hic et nunc* of face-to-face interaction.

Before discussing this special pair of honorifics and the paradigmatic sets that contain them, it is worth noting that paradigmatic sets of terms like those in columns 2 and 3 of Figure 1 have structures distinct from all others, and that this structural difference correlates with their common semantic domain, that of person, over and against all others. We can thus draw a distinction between *objects* of reference, personal and otherwise, which cross-cuts the distinction between *modes* of reference of sets of elements which are indexical and non-indexical. These distinctions have no precedent in the literature, especially with respect to the classificatorily unique place thus accorded to the tiny class of paradigmatic sets of personal pronouns, just two in number. But the semantic domain of person extends well beyond personal pronouns to other terms important in social interaction, and so extends beyond the speech styles to linguistic etiquette in general. The sketches of rapid change in title use in Chapter 3, and in personal pronoun and kin term use in Chapter 5, both reflect the expository usefulness of this distinction for an integrated account of the speech styles as parts of linguistic etiquette.

9. For present purposes I treat what are commonly called third-person pronouns, indexical elements referential of non-speech participants, as negatively and residually defined elements (Benveniste 1971:217—22) that can be ignored in most of what follows. As Uhlenbeck has pointed out, third-person pronoun paradigms are not terribly elaborate in the speech style system, and are little used in Javanese.

Personal Pronouns

Complex as the received classificatory terminology is, it fails to uniquely identify each member of the paradigmatic sets of personal pronouns, which are the most elaborate and finely differentiated speech style vocabularies. Only in paradigmatic sets of personal pronouns are there both madya elements (speaker *kula*, addressee *sampéyan*) and honorific alternants (speaker *dalem*, addressee *nandalem*), and this unique paradigmatic complexity has syntagmatic correlates in the exceptional specificity of co-occurrence restrictions on personal pronoun use in ngoko, madya, or krama address styles, with or without krama inggil for reference to addressee.

The priyayi second person pronoun repertoire is in fact larger than Figure 1 indicates because of fast-speech forms that are considered in Chapter 5. One such form is *panjenengandalem*, originally the "full" form of which *nandalem* was a fast-speech variant, discussed in Chapter 5. Nonpronominal honorifics can be combined with all styles of address (ngoko, madya, or krama), but honorific second-person pronouns cannot. There are really two honorific second-person pronouns: *sliramu*, which is only used in ngoko with honorifics for addressee (as in sentence 5), and *nandalem* (or *panjenengan*, though Figure 1 fails to exhibit this fact), which is used always in krama address styles with honorifics for reference to addressee. *Panjenengan*, on the other hand, can be used in krama speech with or without honorifics for reference to addressee and, for that matter, in ngoko (like *sliramu*) with honorifics for reference to addressee. So the schematization of priyayi repertoires in Figure 1 misleadingly suggests that *nandalem* counts as krama inggil, *panjenengan* as krama, *sampéyan* as madya, and *kowé* as ngoko. This point is taken up in the next chapter.

A major shortcoming of received descriptions is their failure to account systematically for these unique set-internal and combinatory complexities which native speakers, but not analysts, exploit when they use personal pronouns as a convenient metapragmatic terminology. Priyayi uses of *nandalem* and the first-person pronoun *dalem*, for instance, go together always and only with krama address style and honorific reference to addressee. Personal pronouns that stand in one-to-one relations with styles—ngoko or basa, with or without honorifics—can be used as a descriptive terminology that is in fact more precise than explicitly metalinguistic terms like ngoko, madya, and krama, which refer just to styles of address, not reference, to speech partner.

Presupposing in use of speech partners as referents, personal pronouns have pragmatic functions in the speech styles complementary to their indexically referential functions, which are bound existentially to face-to-face speech exchange through tokens of pronoun use. Personal pronouns are referential of speech participants qua speech participants, and their referential meanings are presupposing of and subsistent on the intrinsically reciprocal and exchangable social roles of speaker and addressee. There is a broad parallelism, then, between the social "meanings" of address style and honorific use for reference to speech partners, and the linguistic "meanings" of personal pronouns: both are realized in and construed as parts of patterns of exchange created by persons who adopt the intersubjective, reciprocal roles of speaker (speech and speech style chooser) and addressee (speech and speech style recipient).

In this respect, it is worth noting that some personal pronouns stand or have stood not just in one-to-one relations with an address style and honorific use for addressee, but with larger patterns of exchange of address styles and perhaps honorifics between speech partners. At one time, the first-person pronoun *dalem* and second-person pronoun *nandalem* were used by priyayi just to absolute superiors, in krama with honorifics, in return for ngoko with or without honorifics. To specify use of one personal pronoun was thus to specify not just an entire speech style, but a broader interactive pattern of which it was part. This is one reason why speakers' descriptions reported in Chapter 3 are in fact not just concise but also descriptively adequate from their point of view on what counts as relatively important in linguistic etiquette.

Speech Style Use, Change, and Pragmatic Salience

This classificatory approach to the speech styles does not diverge from received analyses so much as it builds on them, explicating tacit assumptions about the system's linguistic-significative (semantic) and social-significative (pragmatic) properties. This recasting and

106   Basic classifications

generalizing of correlative structural, semantic, and pragmatic differences within the speech style system informs the code-oriented view which is explored and extended in the following chapters. Having set out the common substance of descriptions of speech style structure, we need to reconsider use of the speech style system as broadly conventional yet contextually grounded in its semantic and pragmatic significances.

We have seen how the system is structured through patterned combinations of basa variants that alternate as parts of stylistic overlays on the "basic" ngoko code. Traditional descriptions catalog the system-internal paradigmatic and syntagmatic relations sketched here as one face of what can be called with Saussure (1966:110–14) the value (*valeur*) of the system's elements: relations of stylistic opposition between semantically and grammatically comparable members of paradigmatic sets. These system-internal relations are partially constitutive of pragmatic significances of style elements' use, because styles are oppositively defined. But the social representativeness of style use, what selections between those opposed system elements stand for, have been described normatively by identifying recurring features of contexts in which uses of styles are deemed more or less appropriate. This is the other, essentially contextual face of their value, and what they represent: a judgment on the nature of contexts and speech partner relations of which speech style uses are part. Knowledge of the speech styles is knowledge of system structure but also of situation types in which different speech levels are understood by speakers to be appropriately used, the types of interactional wholes of which they are appropriate parts.

Descriptions of normative relations of style type to context type can be drawn from the literature and elicited from native speakers, but are in principle at a constant and significant remove from actual occasions of face-to-face interaction and tokens of speech style use, which mediate that interaction to show "who you are to me, who I am to you." That is why, as priyayi said to me, what's hard about using the speech levels is not their structure (e.g., knowing that *sekul* is the krama of *sega*) but their application (*trap-trapan*) in particular interaction with particular people. Put more technically, shared knowledge of conventions of use must always be assimilated to knowledge of the code-contingent, *hic et nunc* of interaction by gauging message content, presence of bystanders, the location of interaction, enduring biographical relations, and a huge variety of variably relevant information that eludes normative descriptions of pragmatic value.

In other terms, as Silverstein (1976) has pointed out, the significances of stylistic variation like that in Javanese are essentially indexical insofar as occasions of style use, linguistic parts of larger social wholes, conventionally presuppose certain features in contexts of use. Such indexical interactional representativeness is therefore of a semiotic type with the indexically referential significances of demonstrative and personal pronouns, tense markers, and other deictic elements of linguistic codes that encode referential meaning characterizable only through types of context features presupposed in contexts of use for acts of reference to be achieved. A Javanese speech style's meaning is indexical insofar as tokens of its use conventionally presuppose recurring features of social contexts like those sketched here: a status relation between speaker and addressee or referent and so on. In this respect Javanese can be said to encode in unusually elaborate manner an interactively, indexically significant stylistic system that is superimposed on the underlying code.

But the significances of speech style use are not exhausted by or wholly describable through tokens' relations to stable, independently observable features of contexts of occasions of use. Their significances as mediators of social relations are intrinsically interactional, intersubjective, and emergent in crucially negotiated, reciprocally realized exchange. Their meanings are not just decoded but interpreted as parts of the social wholes that they both presuppose and serve to create in ongoing interaction. In that significance, arising at the juncture of convention and interaction, lies the possibility of relatively creative or strategic manipulation of normative pragmatic values that may reciprocally affect normative use.

Code-oriented descriptions focus on normative pragmatic value, and tend to marginalize strategic use as subsistent or parasitic on shared norms. Only with a broadly ethnographic case-study approach could I adequately present and interpret examples of assumedly strategic speech style use and develop a notion of strategy specific enough to identify such cases but broad enough to generalize to diverse uses of speech styles as linguistic means to diverse social ends.

Examples like those provided by Wolff and Poedjosoedarmo (1982:69–89) could be presented as linguistic and cultural texts illustrative of strategic exploitation of encoded pragmatic value: to frame reported speech, reassign speech participant roles, play on status relations ironically, strengthen messages rhetorically, renegotiate relative status and intimacy, and so on.

I do not develop such a notion of strategy here, although any account of strategic use of Javanese would presuppose much of the information and approach presented here. But this account of structural change and the interactive dynamics of code and interaction allows for and in fact requires a fairly specific notion of strategic use. Because the speech styles' significances are neither wholly conventional nor artifacts of preexisting social relations, there is a dynamic relation between shared conventional knowledge (code) and interactive implementation (use) such that convention not only informs but is reciprocally transformed by use. So changes in the structure and pragmatic values of speech style elements can only be dealt with as symptoms of and clues to recurring patterns of strategic interactive use, the dynamic interplay between encoded system and interpreted interaction.

To the extent that this account deals with both the causes and effects of variation and change in linguistic etiquette, it moves beyond code-oriented descriptions to relations between code, use, and user, the interplay between the referential and social indexical significances of speech style use. What counts as strategic linguistic interaction can be illustrated, as much as defined, with the kinds of title use presented and discussed in Chapter 3, and examples of use of kin terms and personal pronouns in Chapter 5. What can fairly be called strategies of other-exalting, self-abasing linguistic etiquette use are clear in the histories of all these terms for persons, especially titles, because their social significances are a direct function of their prescribed referential meanings. One reason for sketching title use was to anticipate the problem of change in the speech style system taken up in the next chapter, and to broach one aspect of the code/use dynamic in creative and strategic use.

To address this dynamic of structure and use is to introduce an instrumental, user-oriented perspective on speech, the same user-oriented perspective that was introduced together with priyayi descriptions of speech style use in Chapter 3. These show how priyayi report on and perceive use of personal pronouns and kin terms as relatively conspicuous elements of the speech style system. In this chapter we have seen some structural reasons why personal pronouns should be special metapragmatic means for describing as well as engaging in speech style use: to describe use of the system by describing use of members of finely differentiated (hence, expressively nuanced) sets is to name the stylistic whole through structured relations between its parts.

People's conceptualizations of verbal interaction on one hand, and the structural differentiation of classes of paradigmatic sets in the speech style system on the other, suggest that different elements of the speech style system are useful means both for describing and strategically engaging in linguistic interaction. This contrast can be encapsulated in the notion of *relative pragmatic salience*, which is extended in following chapters to different vocabularies' susceptibilities to strategic use, as read from change in system structure and norms for use. Structural mutability and change in elements' normative pragmatic values can be taken as another aspect of the relation between subjective awarenesses of linguistic means to particular interactive ends and knowledge of shared social norms that elude traditional descriptions. As linguistic change has been argued to provide a window on linguistic competence (Kiparsky 1968:174), so can change in pragmatic values of speech style elements be thought of as a window on one aspect of priyayi speakers' communicative competences: their awarenesses and uses of speech as mediators of face-to-face interaction and modes of self-presentation.

One advantage of a semiotic distinction between semantically and pragmatically indexical significances of speech, and a semantic distinction between modes and objects of reference of speech style elements, is that together they allow for a natural, unitary treatment of speech styles as parts of linguistic etiquette. One advantage of a focus on the semiotic interplay between indexical and nonindexical significative modes of speech style elements is that it allows for a unified account of the different parts of normative verbal interaction, inside and outside the speech styles, that count for priyayi as more or less polished (*alus*) and crude (*kasar*) elements of interactive demeanor. These simple distinctions are taken up and extended in the following chapters to elaborate not only the peculiarities of the speech style vocabularies, but also the semiotic fit between speech style use and linguistic etiquette, a special part of face-to-face conduct.

5

Terms for Persons

From an interactional viewpoint, more may depend on acts that somehow identify persons, especially speech partners, than on any other aspect of linguistic style, and such acts are performed with personal pronouns, titles, proper names, kin terms, and combinations of these three. Linguistic etiquette subsumes the speech styles in large part because personal pronouns and kin terms, terms for persons elaborated within the speech style system, are only parts of larger interactively important repertoires. Acts of vocative use, parenthetical use, and reference to persons can be nuanced in interactionally strategic ways too complex to be dealt with fully here, and all four kinds of expressions can be considered from the analytic perspective developed in Chapter 4 and the sketch of title use and change in Chapter 3. To develop a picture of the integral fit between speech styles and linguistic etiquette, we can compare these expressions' modes and objects of reference and correlative availability for stylistically nuancable occasions of vocative and parenthetical use.

Terms in the semantic domain of "person" can be compared through attributes of those who are referential objects of and perhaps parties to occasions of their use, how their semantic content serves in use to identify persons or to secure uptake with them (to use Goffman's phrase) in linguistic interaction. Uses of simple expressions of each type in ngoko sentences like 1–4 (marked as such by *mengko* 'later') illustrate a basic contrast between the referential definiteness of personal pronouns (1) and proper names (2) on the one hand, and indefiniteness of kin terms (3) and titles (4) on the other.

112   Terms for persons

1. Panjenengan	mengko	tindak.	(second person pronoun)
2. Hartono	mengko	lunga.	(proper name)
3. Bapak	mengko	tindak.	(kin term)
4. Gusti	mengko	tindak.	(noble title)
	LATER	GO OUT	

Definite terms like *panjenengan* and *Hartono* serve in referential use to pick out particular individuals as denotata, whereas use of indefinite terms like *bapak* and *gusti* may (but not must) serve to denote individual, nonunique members of some class or collectivity. All of these sentences could be used to speak of addressee, and only sentence 1 must be so used. The distinction between indefinite and definite expressions bears on linguistic etiquette because kin terms and titles (at least among priyayi) are commonly used in relatively polite (refined, *alus*) acts of reference to individuals. Sentences like 3 and 4, for instance, are construable as referential either of speaker, addressee, or some non-speech partner, each conveying different evaluations of relations between speech partners and referents. Uses of personal pronouns and proper names, on the other hand, always identify some particular denotatum and do so in relatively direct manner.

Use of a proper name denotes just its bearer as an enduring, context-independent, intrinsically individual attribute. Referential uses of proper names depend neither on acquaintance with the identity of a preestablished speech partner, as do personal pronouns, nor do they signify traits shared by individuals, as do kin terms and titles. To refer to someone by name alone, an act called *njangkar* in Javanese, presupposes familiarity with and perhaps superiority to referent on the part of the speaker. Use of a simple proper name is normatively appropriate to young agemates, by parent to and about the parent's own child, and for reference to others in similarly intimate and perhaps inferior relations to speaker. To such persons names can be further used vocatively to secure uptake with a would-be speech partner, and parenthetically to identify a person who is a speech partner and may or may not be object of reference in an utterance.

The sense of intimacy conveyed in use of a simple proper name is virtually always inconsistent with the esteem conveyed by use of a krama inggil predicate like *tindak*,[1] and so sentence 2 is more ac-

---

1. It is more usual also to *njangkar* to an addressee with a short form of a name, in this case perhaps "Har." Alternations between short and full forms

ceptable with nonhonorific ngoko *lunga*. Such connections between acts of reference to persons with expressions inside and outside the speech style system—honorific or nonhonorific on the one hand, use or nonuse of proper name on the other—are structural reflexes of the basic fit between their social significative functions, which inform linguistic etiquette use in general and speech style use in particular.

Personal pronouns are other definite expressions that pick out persons as denotata through their shifting interactional attributes as speech partners, preestablished parties to use of pronominal tokens in the *hic et nunc* of intersubjective, occasional speech role relations. Their indexical character has a correlate in that, unlike all these other terms for persons, personal pronouns by their nature cannot be used vocatively, that is, to secure uptake of just the subjective, occasional social relation that pronominal use presupposes.[2] We will see, though, that some *basa* first person pronouns can be used as special response formulas by an inferior to a superior's vocative summons as a kind of indexical self-identifying signal that uptake has been secured. A less obvious structural correlate is that personal pronouns are uniquely ineligible to combine with kin terms, titles, and names in more complex referring expressions.

Kin terms and titles may be used in expressions referential of indefinitely large groups or classes of trait-sharing individuals or, construed with crucial recourse to information not necessarily copresent with an act of reference, as referential of particular individuals. A correlate of their shared significative nature is their usability, unlike proper names and personal pronouns, in predicate expressions to characterize individuals' traits ("He has become a father," "You are a *gusti*," and so on). In sentences like 3 and 4, uses of titles and kin terms are construed as denotative of some particular person through an interpretive step involving knowledge about an occasion of use that is shared by speech partners and extrinsic to the message. This construal of use of indefinite expressions for particular persons—"Which *gusti*? Which *bapak*?"—lends these acts a referential indi-

---

of names, as well as nicknames, make for further variation in use of proper names.

2. From this viewpoint, vocative uses of pronouns like "Hey you!" are really marginal, because they are ostensibly intended to secure uptake which use of the pronoun presupposes. Successful use may depend on the target of vocative use being the sole person in earshot, and aware of that fact.

rectness in comparison with use of proper names and personal pronouns. This may be one reason why indefinite terms are felt to be relatively polite means for reference to speech partners.

A crucial distinction must be drawn between uses of kin terms and titles for reference to persons, and their vocative and parenthetical uses to identify a would-be or already established speech partner who may or may not be referent. This distinction is important for an account of krama inggil kin terms that do not (or once did not) serve in vocative or parenthetical expressions, or in reference to speech partners. Vocative uses need to be set off here also because contextually dependent, indexically direct acts are loci for interactively significant stylistic elaboration quite distinct from that within the speech style system.

Besides these four types of terms, we need to consider yet another group of expressions that are used in distinctively figurative, idiomatic ways to identify persons—ways that are not totally transparent with respect to their semantic content or morphosyntactic characteristics. Use of these terms in isolation correspondingly requires a kind of double construal, recognized first as acts of reference to an individual person, and second as referential of some particular individual by recourse to collateral information, such as that which informs use of kin terms and titles. These terms have all been usable as independent expressions, but have also combined in complex referential expressions with kin terms, titles, and personal pronouns.[3] They need to be considered here together with personal pronouns in particular not just because of textual evidence that they have been most commonly combined with personal pronouns, but more importantly because they have themselves repeatedly evolved into new personal pronouns at the "top" of stylistic paradigms in use among speakers at the "top" of the social hierarchy.

It is difficult to make sense of these changes without considering the interplay between knowledge of code and context that allows for successful acts of reference to individuals with indefinite expressions, because there have been changes in the functions of these terms for persons from one of these categories to another. Figurative

3. That they are not so used with simple proper names is a function of the social anomaly accruing to juxtaposed deferential figurative use and intimate proper name use.

expressions have repeatedly been assimilated to personal pronoun repertoires, a title has been transformed into a kin term, and all these kinds of terms have undergone pragmatic devaluation as the result of recurring patterns of strategic other-exalting, self-abasing speech style use.

Personal Pronouns and Figurative Expressions

A century and a half of remarkably rapid change in priyayi personal pronoun repertoires can be outlined with a heuristic distinction between three sociohistorical periods, patterns of use, and generations of users. The earliest of these periods, from around 1850 to around 1920 and called "traditional" here, is known from texts written as early as the 1830s and from older living priyayi speakers' recollections of how people of their parents' and grandparents' generations spoke. The second period and type of usage, called "conservative," is characteristic of priyayi still fairly close to what remain of palace social circles, most but not all of whom were more than fifty years old, a few as old as eighty, at the time of the research. What I observed of conservative usage largely confirms reports on use that they provided, some cited and discussed in Chapter 3. The last pattern of usage, called "modern," is characteristic of younger priyayi born since the end of World War II, none older than thirty-five, who are no longer closely connected with the palace and have integrated in various ways into a larger, more heterogeneous urban educated class. Note that the terms traditional, conservative, and modern are used as convenient semitechnical labels for patterns of usage that do not correspond in any straightforward way with broader social attitudes.[4]

Changes in structures and uses of personal pronoun paradigms across these three periods, schematized in Table 4, are obvious structural evidence of personal pronouns' pragmatic salience and mutability in comparison with the different address styles with which they have normatively combined at different times. These shifts in pragmatic value can only be explained as results of recurring, strategic use with the cumulative effect of expanding the range of referents by whom, to whom, and of whom these personal pronouns were

4. This statement and these sociohistorical distinctions are elaborated more carefully to different descriptive ends in Errington 1985b.

116   Terms for persons

Table 4. Overview of Priyayi Non-ngoko Personal Pronoun Usage

Address of:	high noble superiors	other superiors/ approximate equals	inferiors
With the speech style:	krama with honorifics for addressee	krama with or without honorifics for addressee	krama or madya no honorifics for addressee

For reference to:

Traditional usage

| Speaker | kawula/(abdidalem) kula | kula | kula |
| Addressee | (panjenengan) sampéyan, (panjenengan (dalem)) + title or kin term | (panjenengan) sampéyan | sampéyan, samang, ndika(?) |

Conservative usage

| Speaker | abdidalem/(a)dalem | dalem/kula | kula |
| Addressee | panjenengandalem, nandalem | panjenengan | panjenengan/ sampéyan |

Modern usage

| Speaker | (a)dalem | dalem | kula |
| Addressee | panjenengan, nandalem[a] | panjenengan | (pe)njenengan, sampéyan |

[a] Marginal for most modern priyayi speakers.

used. This progressive revaluation (or, from the priyayi viewpoint, devaluation) has been accompanied by a repeated assimilation of formerly indefinite, figurative expressions into personal pronoun repertoires. An account of personal pronoun change is also an account of personal pronouns' special mediational significances in acts of reference to speech partners, by speech partners, and as speech partners, interactionally privileged objects of reference.

Shifts of figurative expressions from nonindexical to indexical modes of reference have accompanied shifts in the motivation of their deferential expressiveness from referential content to stylistic opposition as new members of speech style paradigms endowed with systematic pragmatic value. These shifts in social expressiveness came about through an automatization of referential meaning and loss of figurative expressions' semantic transparency vis-a-vis their components. These transformations deserve special attention, both as responses to and continuations of patterns of use of pragmatically salient speech style elements and as interactively motivated structural shifts from semantically to oppositively and stylistically motivated politeness.

FIRST-PERSON PRONOUNS

At the turn of this century priyayi first-person pronoun repertoires were comparatively simple. They consisted of *aku*, the passive clitic *tak-*, and possessive suffix *-ku* in ngoko, and of *kula* and *kawula*, usable in all morphosyntactic environments in *basa*. *Kula* is related historically and at the turn of the century was opposed stylistically to *kawula*, which still appears in the phrase *kawula dalem* as a designation for low level officials.[5] *Kawula* was traditionally used for self-reference in a highly circumscribed range of situations: by servants to the king (SUS 29),[6] to kings' children (SUS 50) and, according to informants, to the highest officials. There are also examples in the literature of a prince (*kangjeng gusti pangéran*) giving *kawula* to the king (SUS 140) and to an elder brother (SUS 145). Padmasusastra (SUS 29) explicitly distinguishes one type of usage with exalted persons that did not require self-reference with *kawula*—in response to a summons (*pangundang*) when, as is the still the case between servant and master in Java, the inferior responds immediately with a term that can be treated as a *basa* first-person pronoun. At least as recently as the turn of the century this term was *kula*, which served as a functional complement and response to vocative usage signaling that uptake has been secured. It may be that short, pronominal forms of the "full," originally nonindexical word *kawula* first came into use in just this way. This pattern would parallel the apparent evolution of pronominal *dalem*, discussed later.

The sense of *kawula* was thus ambiguous between an indexical self-referential expression and an indefinite term usable for individ-

---

5. These were officials lower than the fourth stratum of the bureaucratic hierarchy.
6. For ease of reference, the abbreviation SUS is used for *Serat Urap Sari* (Padmasusastra 1896), and STC for *Serat Tata Cara* (Padmasusastra 1907).

uals and a class of individuals, speech partner(s) or not, who were members of the lower class of royal servants known collectively as *kawula dalem*.[7] Use of the English phrase "your servant" is analogously construable either as idiomatic act of indirect, polite self-reference, or as act of reference to some non-speech partner, depending on the construed identity of the referent in discourse and social context. *Kula* has never served as an informal alternant to nonindexical *kawula*, for instance in a necessarily nonpronominal phrase like *kula dalem,[8] but only as a first-person pronoun, a shortened form that came to stand in stylistic alternation to the older "full" form.

Kula was traditionally used by members of so many social strata, in such a wide range of contexts, to such a broad range of addressees, that its appropriate use is best characterized negatively: as a term of self reference in address of anyone to whom one spoke basa and did not use *kawula*. The opposition between *kawula* and *kula* at the turn of the century was less between formal (literary) and informal (casual) variants—one finds *kula*, for instance, in otherwise flowery, formal letters (e.g., STC 25)—than between a highly deferential variant used only with krama and honorifics to the most exalted of addressees, and a polite variant used to equals and even inferiors in krama or madya without honorifics.

This broad appropriateness of *kula* may have been a factor in the development of the newer first-person pronoun *dalem*, which is now quite common. Indexical *dalem* evolved from the nonindexical, indefinitely referential term *abdi dalem*, which designated upper level royal servants as opposed to *kawula dalem*. *Abdi* is the krama andhap of ngoko *batur* 'servant', whereas *dalem*, discussed in Chapters 2 and 3, is the krama inggil of *omah* 'house'. At least as early as the turn of the century the phrase *abdi dalem* was being used to heighten deferentiality of acts of self-reference in basa as a prefatory allusion to referent's figurative or literal status vis-a-vis the addressee. Examples from older texts suggest that *abdi dalem* was prefatorily combined not just with the first-person pronoun *kula* (never, apparently, with *kawula*) but with other expressions referential of both

7. In most contexts, use of *kawula* for a non-speech participant will be signaled by the presence of some noun phrase marker, usually a deictic or genitive/nominalizing suffix. The important point here, however, is that there are contexts in which double construability is possible.

8. The asterisk here and elsewhere indicates an unacceptable form.

speech partners and non-speech partners, for instance, in the phrase *abdi dalem anak kula*, glossable as 'the servant (krama andhap) of the house (krama inggil) [who is] my child' (STC 162).[9]

But nonindexical prefatory use of *abdi dalem* has long since given way to a more restricted, indexically referential use to refer just to the speaker. Consequently it has displaced *kula* stylistically in the speech styled system, and evolved into a semantically and syntactically distinct term that will be represented here as *abdidalem* 'first-person pronoun', a single referential unit. Older priyayi reports indicate that at least as early as the 1920s *abdidalem* was being used for self-reference, independently of the kinds of referential material to which it had previously been appended—that is, not in expressions glossable as something like 'the humble servant(s) of the honored house X', where X represents some term for a person, but '[speaker], servant of the honored house', where [speaker] represents the person who, as speaker, is the agent and presupposed object of the act of reference. An occasion of such use would have been at some point potentially ambiguous between an act of indexical self-reference and an indefinite act of classificatory reference to a member of that class who might be speaker, addressee, or anyone else. Its use for self-reference at this point was polite not just by virtue of its semantic content, or its incipient pragmatic value in the speech style system, but its intrinsic semantic indefiniteness and concomitant indirectness, requiring construal as a figurative expression.

Once it became an automatized element of a paradigmatic set whose politeness was motivated by its stylistic opposition to other elements, *abdidalem* became subject to regular fast-speech processes that modified its phonetic form, which was no longer transparent with respect to the original semantic content of its component lexemes. Elided fast-speech alternants, *adalem* and *dalem*, were reported in use as derivative variants by conservative speakers when they were children, and which they consistently allied with the "full" (*jangkep*) *abdidalem*. This reduction and multiplication of variants appears to parallel the evolution of the short pronominal form *kula* from *kawula*.

---

9. The expression is used to refer to speaker's actual son to qualify the status of referent as princely addressee's figurative (and in fact, prospective) servant.

Written records allow no more than a rough guess as to just when this innovation may have occurred. The earliest examples of use of *abdidalem* and *adalem* I have found date from 1912 and 1913,[10] but by 1931 both were obviously widespread enough to lead one priyayi to propose in print that pronominal self-referential *dalem* be replaced with *kula* (Sastrawirya 1931:35). This accords with the recollections of half a dozen older priyayi who told me that by 1930 it was a common and de facto obligatory form of self-reference in speech to descendants of kings at the second grade (*wayah dalem*) and lower, and to officials of the rank of cabinet minister (*bupati*) and higher. According to one official of the house of Mangkunegara, that prince issued an edict (*pranatan*) in the 1930s restricting the use of *dalem* as first-person pronoun in address of the prince, his children, and grandchildren, in a vain attempt to legislate use.

However rare pronominal *dalem* may have been in traditional and conservative courtly circles, it is heard quite commonly in contemporary Surakarta by and to priyayi and non-priyayi alike. Ongoing strategic use has hardly been forestalled by explicit regulations, and continues to widen the ranges of social situations in which stylistically self-abasing self-reference is possible or even normative. Use of *dalem* by commoners to commoners has come about as an appropriation and emulation of elite usage, making it less characteristic of elite use than generally polite use, which hardly involves traditional status attributes.

The upshot is that there are now two honorific words in Javanese, one krama inggil, the other krama andhap, which share a sound shape. One is the older nonpronominal krama inggil honorific *dalem* 'honored house'; the other a new short pronominal krama andhap form that has evolved from *abdidalem* and is used almost always in krama with honorifics for reference to addressee, most often in asymmetric exchange.

Pronominal *dalem* is most widely used (not just in Surakarta but

10. The first is in a published and obviously fabricated conversation between a servant (*abdi dalem*) of prince Mangkunegara and a cabinet minister (*bupati*) of the Sultan of Yogyakarta (Soeradipoera 1913:65–66). The second is in a letter from one Sastrasaputra to G. A. J. Hazeu, dated 1912 (KITLV, H1083). It is unclear whether Sastrasaputra was from Surakarta, and so dangerous to infer that this usage was already extant in Surakarta, or if so, in what contexts.

elsewhere in Java) in response to and so as a kind of functional complement to vocative summons by a superior, pronounced then with a distinctive low-pitch to mid-pitch intonation and lengthened second syllable. Some non-priyayi use pronominal *dalem* only this way, reporting (correctly, so far as I was able to observe) that they use *kula* in other syntactic environments and pragmatic contexts. Now the parallel functional complementarity of *dalem* and *kula* in contemporary Surakarta, and of *kula* and *kawula* in traditional Surakarta, suggests that the leading edge of pronominal *dalem*'s spread in the community, as perhaps of *kula* before it, was as a signal to superior that uptake had been secured with the individual uttering its token. If this is the case, then an indexically significant use of an otherwise nonindexically referential expression served as a point of transition in its mode of reference, and marked the beginning of its entry into the the personal pronoun paradigm.

Variation in conservative and modern priyayi use of pronominal *dalem* shows how its normative pragmatic value is still changing.[11] More than one young priyayi told me that although they are teased by friends and relatives from Jakarta for sounding unctuous and self-abasing when they use *dalem*, with Surakartan priyayi it is virtually obligatory, and not unappreciated by older Surakartans with pretensions to priyayi status. I learned this lesson the hard way when I moved to Surakarta after a year in Yogyakarta, where I gave *kula* to everyone to whom I spoke basa. Through various indirect lines of communication I found that some older Surakartan priyayi, not all of high status, were disinclined to speak Javanese with me because I did not give them *dalem*.

Older priyayi consistently (and sometimes resentfully) called my attention to pronominal *dalem*'s rapid spread since the end of the revolution, and provided for my benefit examples of its use that they found unfitting. The half dozen who were most careful to take my linguistic education in hand all cited use of *dalem* as a 'common mistake' (*salah kaprah*) which I should avoid. The following admonition is typical.

11. Although use of *dalem* is hardly universal in Central Java, Keeler's characterization (1984:13) of it as "too obsequious" usage typical of East Java does not hold for Surakarta where it is obligatory among high status priyayi and common among other educated speakers. An example of how such les-

Nak Joe,[12] you shouldn't use *dalem* to just anybody. Take a look, see what the situation is first. If you're dealing with an older person who's of the nobility, *dalem* is fine. But if you're dealing with an ordinary person [here he mentioned two mutual acquaintances of low-to-middling noble descent] you should use *kula*. They're nobles, but only low nobles.

This conservative priyayi knew he was prescribing use of pronominal *dalem* in a far narrower range than that adopted by many younger priyayi, including his own children. But parents are sometimes hard put to govern their children's usage, which is at least as strongly affected by what they hear among educated non-priyayi agemates who count as their peers. One great-grandson of a king who was mentioned in the prescription just quoted as someone to whom I should not use *dalem* himself complained to me that *dalem* should just be used to high nobility (*para luhur*) and not to himself. He had not forgotten this remark several weeks later when we were both party to his twenty-five-year-old son's act of self-reference with *dalem* in basa to him, which he spontaneously observed later was a sign of the times: even priyayi are 'carried along' (*katut*) by the speech of people who don't know better. Why, his children ask him, should they use *kula* to their noble father when their commoner friends use *dalem* to their parents? This gentleman's neighbors are indeed training their children to use *dalem* in response to summons from their parents and whenever they are on their best linguistic behavior.

Modern priyayi who are aware of varying standards for use of *dalem* in the community can be quite frank about its strategic usefulness as a means to nonlinguistic social ends. One told me how he managed to predispose a non-priyayi bureaucrat at his university to help him by adopting a very humble attitude, and concluded his story with the cynical remark "Everyone likes to be *dalem*ed" (*seneng didalem-dalemi*). This is a good example of overtly strategic use of linguistic etiquette, and of the manipulability of highly salient pronominal speech style elements in 'humble' (*andhap-asor*) behavior intended to achieve particular goals.

In just three or four generations, then, pronominal *abdidalem* has evolved from a figuratively to an indexically construed term of self-

---

sons are taught is given in Chapter 6. Keeler also reports use of *dalem* in response to a vocative more widespread than other uses.

12. *Nak* is a short form of *anak* 'child', discussed later.

reference that is oppositionally rather than semantically motivated in its politeness and, as an automatized unit, has developed fast-speech short forms, displacing *kula* as generally polite *basa* usage. That pronominal *dalem* is now syntactically and semantically distinct from the non-indexical krama inggil honorific *dalem* 'honored house' is clear from the existence of an idiomatic construction that serves to disambiguate possessive phrases in which each appears. Nonindexical *dalem*, stable in referential meaning and pragmatic value as a term outside the domain of person, has long been used in the kinds of possessive constructions mentioned in Chapter 3 (*putra dalem*, etc.) for possessions and attributes of honored referents. That such usage is referentially indefinite allows for strategically allusive use; the wife of a middling rank priyayi may request the blessings of the widow of a high official for her newborn child, for instance, with the phrase *pandonga dalem* 'the prayers of the royal house' and then refer to her own child, the addressee's classificatory grandchild, as *wayah dalem* 'grandchild of the (honored) house'(STC 283). Such allusive, elliptical reference promotes or foregrounds the grandparent/grandchild relation and effaces the mother(speaker)/child relation because self-reference with krama inggil honorifics is never appropriate in interaction with a superior.

But the growth of indexical *dalem* as short pronominal form of *abdidalem* has led to a convergence between self-lowering and other-exalting possessive constructions. Pronominal *dalem*, like *kula*, can be used as a basa alternant to the ngoko possessive suffix *-ku* in constructions of the form *X dalem* 'my X' in self-reference. Uses of such possessive constructions with lexemes undifferentiated in the speech style system, and having no honorific alternant—for instance, *kanca* 'friend' in *kanca dalem*—are therefore potentially construable as meaning 'my friend' or 'friend of the honored house' (i.e., addressee or some non-speech partner).

Conservative priyayi avoid this ambiguity of *dalem* in self-referential expressions by adding the impersonal genitive/nominal markers *-é/-ipun* (ngoko/krama) to lexemes referential of attribute or thing possessed. For these speakers the phrase *kanca dalem* means only 'friend of the honored house' or 'your house', whereas *kancané dalem* (ngoko) and *kancanipun dalem* (krama) mean only 'my friend'. Modern priyayi and non-priyayi speakers make no such diacritic use of *-é/-ipun*, and in their speech indexical *dalem* has just the same

124   Terms for persons

syntactic characteristics as *kula*. It is thus becoming regularized as a personal pronoun.

This example shows how the pragmatic salience of personal pronouns and the ways their strategic uses by priyayi and appropriation by non-priyayi have made for striking, rapid structural change in the speech style system.

SECOND-PERSON PRONOUNS

The single most striking feature of traditional normative etiquette for priyayi living in Surakarta now would be second-person pronoun usage. As late as the turn of the century, *sampéyan* and its fast-speech variants *samang* and *mang* (a passive form) were normatively used in krama, with or without honorifics, to refer to addressees who today would be addressed as *panjenengan*, a form then used hardly at all as an independent pronominal form. Nowadays priyayi hardly use *sampéyan*, and only in madya speech styles to address low status commoners who cannot reciprocate full krama. Use of *sampéyan* is rather condescending, not at all intimate, and counts for conservative priyayi as appropriate in use "down" the social hierarchy and "out" of their social group (Errington 1985b:102–05).

Examples of priyayi use of *sampéyan* common in older texts—wife to husband, child to father, junior/inferior to senior/superior in general—are thus anomalous by present standards. Use of *sampéyan* by priyayi in contemporary Surakarta is much more like traditional use of another second-person pronoun, *ndika*, which was then associated with uneducated non-priyayi villagers as is *sampéyan* now. *Ndika* was not commonly used by priyayi at the turn of the century and is now virtually obsolete, even if priyayi recognize and identify it as 'village talk' *krama désa*.[13]

The history of *ndika* parallels that of pronominal *dalem*, *sampéyan*, and *panjenengan*, discussed later. According to a grammar written by deGroot not long before he died in 1829, *dika* was used to intimate equals or inferiors in familiar basa styles (1843:115–16) as a colloquial fast-speech alternant to *ijengandika*, at the time apparently in wider use than *sampéyan*, with which it alternated in *basa* usage, to all save the most exalted speech partners. *(I)jengandika*,

13. On the ambiguities of this native metalinguistic term, see Errington 1985b:121–32. Nowadays *ndika* is at best marginal in village use as well.

segmentable and glossable as 'foot over there'[14] was thus colloquialized as was *abdidalem*, and its colloquialized short form was later displaced in polite usage by *sampéyan*, discussed later. There has since been a double shift in the structure of the second-person pronoun paradigm and pragmatic values of its members. *Sampéyan*, once used in all *basa* address styles, has been devalued and assimilated to the specifically madya inventory, while *ndika* has fallen out of use everywhere save in highly ritualized palace events.[15] *Sampéyan*'s devaluation occurred in concert with the introduction of a new pronoun *panjenengan* through a broadly parallel process.

At least as old as the available records is use of *sampéyan* as a krama inggil honorific glossable (like *jeng*) as 'foot, leg' (krama: *suku*, ngoko: *sikil*) for speaking deferentially of honored persons' bodies. It has also served figuratively to speak of persons as social entities through a *pars pro toto* trope with a long, honorable history in Javanese. An occasion of such figurative use is construable as an act of reference to a person as social entity by two related interpretations. First, it fits the limiting case of proper deferential conduct described in Chapter 2, which requires that one lower one's eyes to avoid beholding a respected person's face, and so address one's words and gaze alike to the addressee's prescriptively visible part, the foot (Roorda 1843:137). Secondly, use of a word meaning 'foot' can be construed in light of a vertical conception of status and linguistic etiquette (Errington 1985b:92–98) as figuratively placing addressee's foot (lowest part) as high as speaker's head (highest part). Conservative priyayi offered this sort of interpretation for *Ingkang Sinuhun*, which can be literally glossed as 'that which is held up', and for *sampéyan dalem*, 'foot of the royal house', phrases that are used for the king.[16]

14. This gloss is adopted from Gericke and Roorda 1901, where it is segmented into *jeng*, an archaic word meaning 'foot' and *dika*, derived from *rika*, archaic distal deictic locative (see Chapter 7). One priyayi linked the first element etymologically to krama *ngajeng* (ngoko: *ngarep*) 'in front, before'.

15. By the beginning of this century, its only use was in the register appropriately spoken by high officials in official royal audience (*basa kedhaton*; see Errington 1982). Striking evidence of this devaluation is a reported occasion of use of *ndika* in madya by the prime minister to a lower official (SUS 1895:35) to which Padmasusastra adds a highly un-Javanese footnote indicating that he had himself observed such usage. His care to justify the example suggests it was unusual and, presumably, on its way to extinction.

16. Conservative priyayi, perhaps prescriptively inspired, told me that it

126   Terms for persons

Statuses of persons who one might refer to and address with *sampéyan dalem* were thus much higher than of those one might address as *sampéyan*, and differences between normative uses of both pronouns were thus roughly analogous to differences between normative uses of *kawula* and *kula*. For all but the very highest elite, *sampéyan dalem* was traditionally too honorific, and *sampéyan* together with *kula* was used with basa to most superior, some equal, and even some marginally inferior addressees. Uses of both second-person pronouns could be elaborated with prefatory expressions of respect like titles of descent discussed in Chapter 3 or kin terms discussed later, but also with lexical material that, like *abdidalem* in use for self-reference, augmented the linguistic marking of speaker's deference for the addressee/referent.

The most common such term was *panjenengan*, a nominal derived from the root *jeneng* with the circumfix *paN- -an*. *Jeneng* is a ngoko noun that can be glossed as 'name'[17] (krama: *nami*, krama inggil: *asma*) but historically was glossable as 'to stand', or 'position, place' (Gericke and Roorda 1901). From *jeneng* are also derived honorific verbal forms *jumeneng* (with the archaic active verb infix *-um-*) 'to act as/in the capacity of', always said of persons of high official or noble status, and *jumenengaké* (causative affix *-aké* in ngoko) 'to install/be installed in (high) office', or 'to cause/be caused to take on/act in the capacity of'. *Njenengi*, an active transitive form glossable as 'to witness something (in one's official capacity)' serves as an honorific basa alternant to *ndedegi*. Each of these polymorphemic forms signifies a state or activity connected with high official and noble status.

Panjenengan is an abstract noun that can be glossed somewhat awkwardly either as 'functionship' or 'worthiness (by virtue of official status)' or alternately (following Gericke in a note to deGroot 1843:117–18) as 'place of standing', or figuratively, 'the feet'. The first sort of gloss recalls English nominal forms derived with the affix '-ship' from lexemes referential of official or noble statuses. Like

---

was really wrong to use *sampéyan dalem* for anyone other than the king or perhaps the crown prince, but older texts provide examples of such use for other princes. *Nandalem* is reportedly in everyday use in address of the king.

17. In other contexts it can be glossed as 'title' and so overlaps in meaning with another root, *aran*, in ways that cannot be discussed here.

them, *panjenengan* could be used to refer to capacities (as in "Who holds the judgeship?") or to refer to individuals through their statusful social capacities, *pars pro toto* relationships between prestigious social attribute and person (compare "your/his lordship"). As a prefatory honorific expression *panjenengan* was glossable as something like 'the worthiness of X', and by making acts of reference to persons interpretively derivative of acts of reference to their attributes, *panjenengan* lent an indirect, allusive quality to acts of reference.

Nowadays *panjenengan* is a second-person pronoun commonly used by priyayi and non-priyayi, as *sampéyan* once was, to those of some status who may or may not be one's superiors, with or without honorifics. The shape of this change as it is inferrable from older texts parallels the evolution of the first-person pronoun *dalem* in interesting ways. In the early nineteenth century *panjenengan* was used in complex referential expressions like *panjenengan sampéyan* and *panjenengan dalem* for those of the very highest statuses (de-Groot 1843:117). Later texts contain numerous examples of honorific possessive constructions containing *panjenengan* in use for reference to nonaddressee, including speaker, for instance with the krama nominalizing/genitive suffix *-ipun* (ngoko: *-é*) in *panjenenganipun Sinuhun Pakubuwana*, idiomatically glossable as '(His) majesty Sinuhun Pakubuwana', and with the genitive affix *ning* in *panjenenganing ratu*, glossable as 'majesty of the king' (Winter 1848: 232). *Panjenengan* functions syntactically in the phrase *panjenengan dalem*, 'worthiness of the royal house' as does *abdi* in *abdi dalem*, and *panjenengan dalem* was often used for reference to the king in discourse in which his identity as referent was already established (Winter 1848:82). *Panjenengan sampéyan*, functionally and structurally analogous to *abdidalem kula*, was an elaborated honorific form of reference to speech partner consisting of an indefinite term appended prefatorily to a preexisting personal pronoun.

By the end of the century appropriate use of *panjenengan* had become narrower and more highly codified in stylistic opposition to other terms. Padmasusastra (SUS 21–28) explicitly distinguishes between the pragmatic values of *panjenengan dalem*, appropriate for reference to and perhaps address of high ranking noble officials, and *panjenenganipun* for high officials not of noble status. No examples with *panjenengan dalem*, *panjenengan*, or *panjenenganipun* are forthcoming in later texts for reference to the king, but *panjenengan* with and without *dalem* or *-ipun* was commonly combined with titles—*panjenengan dalem kangjeng* (SUS 35) for a prince, *panjenengan dalem kyai lurah* and *panjenenganipun kyai lurah* (SUS 21) for a prime minister[18]—and kin terms as in *panjenenganipun bapak* 'father' (STC 54), and *panjenenganipun ingkang rayi* 'younger sibling' (STC 149). Padmasusastra also provides one conversation (STC 122) in which *panjenengan kangjeng* and *panjenengan dalem kangjeng* alternate in use for reference to a princely speech partner, and another in which use of *panjenengan dalem* serves to refer to the king (*panjenengan dalem Ingkang Sinuhun* SUS 229).

In these contexts *panjenengan dalem* was not an indexically referential expression but either a prefatory part of a complex referential expression for non-speech partner, or an independent referring expression for persons (addressee or not) preestablished as topics in previous discourse. In this respect use of *panjenengan dalem*, like *abdi dalem*, made for acts of reference that were both honorific and indirect. *Panjenengan sampéyan* conveyed added respect when used, for instance, by a prince's servant to an official of middling rank (STC 119), but also expressed formality in use to address persons collectively at social gatherings (STC 81) or in written invitations (STC 168). By the end of the century *panjenengan sampéyan*'s former deferential expressiveness as an alternant to *sampéyan* appropriately used, for instance, to princely addressees (deGroot 1843:114) had diminished considerably. Speakers in Padmasusastra's *Serat Tata Cara* switch between *panjenengan sampéyan* and *sampéyan* in a single conversation, and even within a single utterance, for reference to addressees of higher but not the highest status.

Panjenengan seems to have come into use as an independent term for reference to addressee about the turn of the century, occurring just a few times (by my count, seven) among several hundred occasions of use of pronominal reference to addressee in the *Serat Tata Cara*. Dangerous as it is to read too much into written sources, two characteristics common to occasions of use in that work are worth noting. First, all these uses of *panjenengan* are put in the mouths of non-priyayi or extremely low-ranking priyayi in address of their superiors, inviting the conjecture that the innovation occurred in

---

18. The highest officials were regularly addressed and referred to with what at the time were relatively low-ranking official titles like *lurah*; for brief discussion, see Errington 1982.

speech by inferior to superior as a new sort of humble (*andhap-asor*) act. Second, most of these occasions of use alternate with *sampéyan* or *panjenengan sampéyan*, unambiguously and indexically referential of the addressee. This suggests that *panjenengan* became a pronominal alternant to *sampéyan* in much the same way that pronominal *abdidalem* (and, derivatively, *(a)dalem*) evolved from the phrase *abdidalem kula*.

One text (Sastrasubrata 1924) contains a dialogue in which a priyayi addresses a Dutchman (or at least someone identified with the title *Tuan*) with *panjenengan*, but then quotes speech to persons gathered in a formal ritual context (a *slametan*) using *sampéyan*. This usage might indicate that *sampéyan* was a more proper, formal, or conservative pronoun than *panjenengan*, or that this speaker was more concerned to honor his high-status, foreign speech partner than guests at a small gathering. It is evidence at least that the two forms were used in similar if not identical ways. A proposal (Sastrawirya 1931) that *panjenengan* replace *sampéyan* in basa address to those of comparable rank may have been a ratification of an already or almost completed change.

Panjenengan has long since been fully assimilated to the second-person pronoun paradigm and has entirely displaced *sampéyan*, which counts for priyayi in Surakarta now as outgroup madya usage. They use *panjenengan* in basa to their approximate equals, with or without honorifics. *Panjenengan* thus lost its morphosyntactic complexity and semantic content as an automatized simplex unit which has since been colloquialized (like *abdidalem, ijengandika,* and *sampéyan*) by fast-speech processes to *penjenengan* and *njenengan*. This latter alternant is used by modern but not conservative priyayi, who generally acknowledge its existence but fault it as "improper."[19]

Commoners obviously had a role in the process, emulating priyayi and appropriating this prestigious feature of priyayi usage as they appropriated *dalem*. A simple way of demonstrating this process is a prescription of proper personal pronoun usage made to me by an elderly, uneducated commoner in fairly frequent contact with members of the remaining courtly circles in Surakarta:

19. Bambang Kuswanti Purwo has noted (personal communication) that it is sometimes shortened still further to *penyan*, by elision of the second and third syllables and assimilation of the affricate to a palatalized nasal. In Surakarta I did not observe or hear reports of such a form.

Sampéyan is for young children. But sometimes even people here [Surakarta?] don't understand its meaning... it lacks, lacks politeness. It means [one] doesn't know etiquette.... Don't, if you can avoid it, don't use *sampéyan*... only if you're speaking to kids, say if you're speaking to one of your students, you can use *sampéyan*. If they're young.

Her statement bespeaks an ongoing change in criteria for appropriate personal pronoun use among non-priyayi from traditional status to relative age. She obviously invites the inference that she would not object should I, considerably her junior, address her as *panjenengan*. Priyayi on the other hand would find such usage entirely incompatible with her status, like use of *dalem* by commoner child to commoner parent. But one does hear *panjenengan* and its short forms in use by younger commoners (e.g., pedicab drivers) to older commoners (e.g., market sellers) in madya styles of address. Like the conservative priyayi observation on use of *dalem* quoted earlier, this prescription can be taken as a contemporary manifestation of long-standing commoner awarenesses of and attitudes toward proper usage that have led them to use and expect use of previously elite pronominal usage.

Priyayi second-person pronoun repertoires were further elaborated by the assimilation of the formerly figurative, indefinite expression *panjenengan dalem*, now used not just to refer to the king and royal offspring but in address to a wider group of noble elite including *wayah dalem*. *Panjenengan dalem*, now hardly used to refer to non-addressees—older, conservative priyayi accepted hypothetical examples of such use, but I never observed it—has lost formal and semantic transparency vis-a-vis the code, and so been subject to fast speech rules yielding the short alternant *nandalem*,[20] used more widely as a second-person pronoun and metalinguistic term (see Chapter 2) than the more formal, perhaps more deferential "full" form. But *panjenengandalem* and *nandalem*, unlike *panjenengan*, are used only in conservative priyayi circles; modern priyayi and educated non-priyayi recognized it but identified it with those speakers who are part of an outgroup they perceive as old-fashioned (*kolot*).[21]

20. Some priyayi who had grown up in courtly circles in Yogyakarta reported use there of another variant, *ndandalem*.
21. Sometimes called the 'palace group' (*kalangan kraton*) or 'ningrat group' (*kalangan ningrat*) as mentioned in Chapter 3 and discussed in Errington 1985b:84–88.

Terms for persons   131

PRAGMATIC SALIENCE AND PRONOMINAL CHANGE

As the pragmatic values of "high" deferential personal pronouns have been progressively diminished, priyayi have had repeated recourse to indefinite figurative expressions as a source of new personal pronouns that have been rapidly codified to replace devalued elements, and in turn been susceptible to strategic use. New personal pronouns have been introduced at the "top" of stylistic paradigms by those speakers at the "top" of the social hierarchy, but the social impetus for change has had broader social roots. Non-priyayi are no less sensitive to the values of personal pronouns as mediators of social relationships and markers of speech partners' relative status, and they have been quick to strategically use and so in effect appropriate "high," honorific personal pronouns into their repertoires of polite basa speech. Patterns of strategic use of these pragmatically salient elements that can be glimpsed in the speech of priyayi and non-priyayi now ("Everyone likes to be *dalem*ed") had analogues in usage a century ago.

There is no reason to expect that longstanding processes of appropriation and devaluation will not continue; the erosion and increasing permeability of traditional elite/nonelite distinctions may have lent these salient forms a new, perceived accessibility for non-priyayi. The recent patterns of strategic use are less innovations than an accelerated continuation of longstanding patterns of lagging emulation that led to the devaluation of *ndika* and its replacement by *sampéyan* more than a century ago. The progressive spread of *panjenengan* and *dalem* as polite but not necessarily deferential usage may represent the last phase in more than a century of appropriation and lagging emulation that will soon culminate in the loss of all conspicuous variation in pronominal usage across traditional priyayi/non-priyayi social boundaries.

The social motivations for strategic uses that have transformed conventional pragmatic value are hardly obscure to anyone, Javanese or otherwise, who recognizes that self-abasing, other-exalting behavior may be advantageous to oneself. It is not really surprising that pronominal usage should be interactionally strategic means to antecedent social goals. This historical sketch shows how the striking structural elaboration of personal pronouns, adduced as evidence of their pragmatic salience in Chapter 4, is an idealized (and in the lit-

132   Terms for persons

erature usually prescriptive) synchronic hypostasis of longstanding, recurring, and ongoing interactional strategies in speech.

Less obvious but just as interesting are the recurring assimilative processes through which terms originally expressive of deferentiality through their semantic content outside the speech style system were rapidly drawn into stylistic oppositions within it. New pronouns were not created out of whole cloth as fillers for empty slots in the paradigms, but evolved from indefinite figurative expressions which were in prior use, and came to replace the indexical referential terms for persons to which they were originally only quasi-obligatory prefatory additions. Their correlative semantic and social significances changed together, because the shift to indexically definite referentiality meant also a shift to conventionalized oppositive stylistic significance. The term pragmatic value has been particularly useful for describing this latter type of social significance of speech elements. Only when their indexical referentiality and system-internal pragmatic values were established could these new pronouns' sound shapes, newly opaque with respect to their original semantic meaning, be colloquialized through regular fast-speech processes that yielded subsidiary stylistic pronominal variation.

It is worth considering why these figurative terms were used in the first place and why, assuming textual evidence to be valid, they were used most often as prefatory expressions to personal pronouns, rather than kin terms, titles, or other referential material. An answer to both questions is suggested by the fact that, of all these terms for persons, only personal pronouns are indexically direct in referential meaning by virtue of the existential and interactively immediate connections they presuppose between the persons who are at once parties to and objects of pronominal reference: the speech partners engaged in face-to-face interaction. Occasions of pronominal use can be thought of as having a significative directness shared with all indexically significant speech elements, inside and outside the speech styles, and use of figurative expressions can be taken as a first example of how polite, refined, *alus* speech is muted in its indexical significances. Indefinite figurative expressions muted acts of pronominal reference by rendering them acts of pronominal reference to speech partners' statusful attributes, rather than to speech partners per se. A simple but necessary interpretive step to construe referent from act of reference to part endows them with a quality of indirectness or significative allusiveness that unadorned personal pronoun or proper name use does not have. Figurative expressions were more commonly used with personal pronouns than with nonindexical kin terms and titles because the latter are not necessarily indexically referential or existentially embedded within the same occasion of use.

Recurring transformations of figurative indefinite terms (e.g., *panjenengan dalem* 'honor of the royal house') into indexical terms referential just of a speech partner ('you') result from two distinct, complementary kinds of interactive pressure. First, personal pronouns have been subject to strategic self-abasing, other-exalting use by priyayi and non-priyayi, and as appropriate and normative use widened, their pragmatic values were "pulled down," creating a need for new, highly deferential personal pronouns for those at the "top" of the social hierarchy. Second, the significative directness of pronominal reference was recurringly muted in address of exalted others by appending figurative expressions that were consequently an extrinsically motivated source of candidates for new, highly deferential personal pronouns.

The remarkable rapidity of these recurring devaluations testifies to the fit between these two different aspects of politeness of demeanor, and to the interactive privilege of speaker and addressee as potential referents and mutually ratified partners in acts·of reference. The rapid narrowing of the referential range of figurative, indefinite terms and their concomitant refunctionalization as personal pronouns is attributable, by this argument, to the nature of speakership and addresseeship as social attributes of pragmatically salient objects of and participants in other-raising, self-lowering acts of reference. Speech partners are socially privileged as copresent candidates for objects of figurative reference, an availability that has helped "push" indefinite expressions into indexical modes of referentiality and so into the personal pronoun paradigms.

The complicated history of priyayi personal pronoun repertoires suggests a kind of tension between the interpenetrating social and referential significances of Javanese personal pronoun use, which turn on the double nature of indexical acts of reference. On the one hand, they are socially expressive, strategically usable mediators of interaction. On the other hand, personal pronouns are intrinsically immediate and significatively direct means of personal reference that have been repeatedly muted by use of figurative and semantically deferential expressions. Other aspects of this directness, and other ways it is muted, are dealt with in Chapters 6 and 7.

Kin Terms, Inside and Outside the Speech Styles

Kin term repertoires encode dyadic ngoko/krama inggil oppositions and appear to resemble other paradigmatic sets containing honorifics discussed in Chapter 6. But there are obvious restrictions on ranges of use of honorific kin terms, which suggest their distinctive roles in linguistic etiquette.[22] Although kin terms are not intrinsically restricted in referential range to speech partners, some honorific kin terms are (or were) unavailable for acts of address to speech partners. Use of honorific kin terms meaning 'father', 'elder male sibling', or 'younger sibling' for reference to a speech partner is virtually never appropriate, even if that person is otherwise spoken of with the full range of honorific vocabulary. At the same time, there are (or were) interactively crucial stylistic oppositions between kin term variants that are outside the speech styles, and come into play just for vocative and parenthetical usage. Vocative and parenthetical usage is not necessarily referential but is contextually dependent and significatively direct, like pronominal usage, in that it identifies some person who is presupposed as a prospective or established speech partner. So the distinction between referents who are and are not speech partners is as important for a study of kin terms as for personal pronouns.

Kin terms are ubiquitous, interactionally crucial means for referring to an addressee or perhaps to oneself,[23] and are endowed then with social expressiveness that, like that of titles, is relatable directly to their semantic content independent of any oppositional value they may have in the speech style system. For instance, switches in kin

---

22. More extensive treatments of kin terminology are Koentjaraningrat 1957 and 1985, and H. Geertz 1961. The system described by Geertz does not include a classificatory distinction between parent's sibling's children, called *nak-sanak* in south-central Java, and parent's parent's sibling's children, called *nak-misan* in south-central Java.

23. Acts of self-reference with kin terms are possible, but cannot be considered here in any detail.

term use (but not perhaps to use of name alone, *njangkar*) may be independent of and need not be accompanied by switches in address style or honorific usage. At the same time, social significance of kin term use in address as in sentence 3 is interactively relational insofar as it depends not just on semantic content but also, like personal pronouns and speech styles, on a pattern of exchange of which it is part. Two women of forty and fifty years of age might reciprocate the non-honorific kin term *ibu* 'mother' in address until, becoming relatively intimate, they switch to asymmetric, more intimate exchange of *mbak(yu)* 'elder female sibling' and *dhi* 'younger sibling'.[24] A man of twenty might address a new acquaintance of his father's generation with *bapak* and receive *((kang)mas)* 'elder male sibling', but if they become familiar switch to a kin term glossable as 'father's elder sibling' (*pak dhé*) and so, in the words of one of my informants whom I observed make such a shift, treat the addressee like "real family." The elder, conversely, might switch to *anak* 'child' or, to communicate real intimacy, *njangkar* with the addressee's name (probably a nickname) without a kin term.

Kin term use signifies or presupposes common, comparable characteristics of persons speaking, addressed, and spoken of, and whether or not it furnishes acquaintance with the referent's gender, it signifies or imputes to the referent seniority in relation to someone else. In predicative use (e.g., "She is a mother") kin terms signify an enduring relation of descent or consanguinity; in referential use as in sentence 3 above it minimally presupposes that referent is adult and male. What symmetric exchange of a kin term in address glossable as 'father' conveys socially between forty-year-old and twenty-year-old male speech partners (roughly speaking, respect or formality) depends on what other terms could conceivably be used: a kin term meaning 'elder male sibling', 'child', or no kin term at all by the elder speech partner; a term glossable as 'parent's elder male sibling' (*pak dhé*) or 'parent's younger male sibling' (*pak lik*) by the younger.

In this very basic sense, kin term usage is relational in a way title usage is not. Like titles, kin terms can be used predicatively to char-

---

24. I ignore here the now slightly quaint *jeng*, from the descent title element *ajeng*, sometimes used for intimate and younger women in conservative priyayi circles.

136   Terms for persons

acterize group membership or some relationship between individuals. But title use presupposes membership in a social hierarchy that is increasingly irrelevant in contemporary Surakarta, and so title use is increasingly restricted to ingroup use in shrinking conservative priyayi circles. It is being supplanted by kin term use which has become widespread for both priyayi ingroup and outgroup interaction. A single example must suffice to illustrate the difference in their social significances and concomitant appropriate uses. The following is an explanation of use by an older priyayi who still works in what remains of the palace administration:

> If *gusti* X calls me into his office [in the palace] and orders me to make a phone call to arrange for *gusti* X to talk with an employee in some office in Jakarta I answer "As you say, *gusti*." If after I leave his office and someone asks me where I'm going, I may answer "*gusti* X wants to talk to *pak* ['father'] so-and-so in Jakarta." But then, when I call Jakarta and talk to that employee, I will refer to *gusti* X as *pak* X.

Less direct and more polite than use of unadorned proper name, less overtly or traditionally hierarchical than use of a title, kin terms' semantic and social expressiveness interpenetrate inside and outside the speech styles alike. Here I consider briefly interactively significant stylistic variation in vocative and referential kin term use, the social logic that restricts the referential range of some honorific kin terms, and the patterns of change in kin term use outside the system resulting from strategic linguistic etiquette use.

ELABORATION OUTSIDE THE SYSTEM: VOCATIVE AND REFERENTIAL USE

Nonhonorific/honorific oppositions between kin terms are distinct from other nonhonorific/honorific oppositions in the speech style system because honorific kin terms are generally unavailable for reference to speech partners, even though they are commonly used to predicate kin relations of them. An example is the ngoko/krama inggil pair *bapak/rama*. *Rama* is not used to address a speaker's biological father or anyone else.[25] But as non-speech partner object of

---

25. *Rama* appears fairly commonly in letters and the older literature, in at least one case by low-ranking priyayi for reference to the king (Winter 1848:249). If Padmasusastra intended to portray usage after 1893 in the *Serat Urap Sari*, then Pakubuwana X, if not his father, was addressed by his own

reference a man addressed as *bapak* may and in some cases must be spoken of with *rama* to characterize his kin relation to someone else, as in "You are my friend's father". It is significant in this respect that the majority of honorific kin terms, not used to refer to addressee, have been quite stable in their pragmatic values as honorifics. These include krama inggil terms *putra* 'child' (ngoko *anak*), *rayi* 'younger sibling' (ngoko *adhi*), *raka* 'elder male sibling' (ngoko *kakang, kangmas*, on which more later), and *wayah* 'grandchild' (ngoko *putu*). There have been just two honorific kin terms in regular use to refer to addressee—*ibu* 'mother' (ngoko *mbok*) and *éyang* 'grandparent' (ngoko *mbah*)—and both have been mutable in pragmatic value. As such they are evidence of the ways that acts of address are foci of strategic, other-exalting interactional use.

Uses of nonhonorific kin terms to identify addressees are stylistically nuancable in several other ways. In polite acts of reference, address, and vocative/parenthetical use, kin terms were traditionally combined with titles of office (not descent) or proper names, usually in some shortened form (with *bapak*, for example, in expressions like *pak menggung, pak béhi*, etc.).[26] With the anachronization of title use, other longstanding stylistic alternations between "full" and "short" forms of kin terms became interactively conspicuous in just those acts that, like use of personal pronouns, always and only identify a speech partner—vocative and parenthetical use.

Bapak, the full form of the kin term glossable as 'father', has a short alternate *pak* with which it alternates in vocative and parenthetical use. Priyayi regularly use *pak* as simple vocative and parenthetical expression to lower-class, outgroup postadolescent males, and *bapak* in more formal circumstances and to honored persons to whom they do not use titles. In contemporary Surakarta a persistent social stratification informs the choice between full and short voca-

---

children as *bapak* (SUS:137–42) in otherwise extremely deferential language. Just two out of fifteen conservative priyayi, both *wayah dalem*, reported using *rama* in address of elder male kin (one to her father, the other to his father's elder brother), and I never observed an act of address with *rama* save to Catholic priests, to whom it is virtually titular.

26. *Menggung* and *béhi* are short forms of the official titles *tumenggung*, now used for cabinet ministers, and *ngabéhi*, their immediate inferiors.

tive forms, which can be sketched with a stereotypical example that priyayi often adduced to illustrate proper use to me—how to talk with *pak bécak* (*bécak* 'pedicab'), the ubiquitous pedicab driver with whom one engages in brief, transactional interaction.

Priyayi of all ages and ranks agree that vocative and referential use of *bapak* to a pedicab driver is much too refined (*kalusen*). Better, they said, to use just *pak*, as when hailing one on the street, a quintessential example of vocative usage. Interaction that I observed and examples I elicited yielded no cases of referential use of *bapak* to lower-class males. Priyayi avoid addressing pedicab drivers as *bapak* by avoiding constructions in which the short vocative form would be grammatically unacceptable, for instance, in subject and topic position of a sentence. Rather than ask a question translatable as "How much does *bapak* [idiomatically in English "do you"] want to go to the market?", for example, priyayi elide reference to addressee and append *pak* as short parenthetical form: "How much to the market, *pak*?" It is easy to avoid nonvocative, nonparenthetical use of kin terms, especially in service encounters that involve short, stereotyped utterances and specific, predefined ends. But even in longer encounters with lower-status commoners which I observed, priyayi consistently avoided use of *bapak*, choosing often instead a second-person pronoun (usually *sampéyan*, but once *njenengan*).

This structurally unobvious but interactionally important linguistic mark of status distinctions has become increasingly important since the 1930s because the kin term *(ka)kang* 'elder male sibling', discussed later, has fallen out of use among priyayi for virtually all postadolescent, lower-status males. Because of the disjunction between referential content of *bapak* and the socially appropriate vocative/parenthetical use of *pak*, the latter has highly attenuated semantic content, as is quite clear when a dignified sixty-year-old priyayi uses *pak* to hail a seventeen-year-old pedicab driver and haggle a fare.

Analogous social distinctions accrue to vocative and parenthetical uses of the "full" kin term *mbakyu* 'elder female sibling' and its two short variants *mbak* and *yu*. *Mbakyu* (derived historically from *mbok ayu* 'pretty mother') is commonly used as a referential expression that has no stylistic variant in the speech style system. But there is a marked contrast in the social significances of vocative/parenthetical use of *mbakyu, mbak,* and *yu* (combinable also with other referential material, usually names, in complex expressions). Such use is keyed to relative intimacy with addressee or to addressee's social status. *Mbak* counts as relatively polite use in comparison with *yu,* which, at least for contemporary priyayi, marks a younger addressee's stereotypically rural, uneducated, status. *Mbakyu* contrasts with *mbak* as relatively more formal and polite. Here too alternations between forms of kin terms usable always and only to speech partners turn out to be important mediators of social relations outside the speech style system.[27]

These and other cases of interactively significant stylistic elaboration outside the speech styles all demonstrate the privileged status of speech partners as potential referents and targets of vocative and parenthetical use. They also raise the issue of restricted referential ranges of honorific kin term use, which can be broached by considering the ways kin terms' semantic content bear on the social significances of their use. A convenient way to do this is to consider an extinct, essentially priyayi form of pronominal use from the turn of the century mentioned previously: the second-person pronoun *ijengandika.*

HONORIFIC KIN TERMS AND *IJENGANDIKA*

The common semantic attribute of honorifics and their alternants is that they signify possessions, attributes, states, and actions of persons. Insofar as kin to persons count as personal attributes, they fall into that category. But kin are obviously unique as personal attributes because they are social entities in their own rights, parties to multiple enduring biological and social relations who may be spoken of through their own intrinsic attributes. These two aspects of personal identity are clear in referential expressions like "mother of *X*"—where *X* is a personal pronoun, a name, or some other

27. This does not mean that some types of vocative kin term usage do not usually go together with a speech style. *Pak,* in use to a pedicab driver but not necessarily to an intimate of some status, typically goes together with some style of madya address. *Yu,* used almost exclusively to women perceived by priyayi to be uneducated and lower class, typically at the market, goes together with madya.

term—which refers to *X*'s mother as a kind of attribute or adjunct of *X*, a little like a body part or possession. Use of such an expression containing an honorific kin term in address of *X* could be construed, then, as marking the high status of the nonaddressee/referent of the kin term (the mother), the addressee in relation to whom that referent is identified (*X*), or both. Kin to persons of high status may be of high status in their own right, and the interplay between dyadic, enduring, statusful kin relations and dyadic, occasional, interactional speech partner relations makes for multiple possible interpretations of honorific kin term use in expressions like "Your mother."

In traditional priyayi society, uses of honorific kin terms in such phrases were construable as expressive of respect for either the nonspeech partner referent, addressee, or both, and this multiple interpretability had practical implications that were more than matters for idle conjecture. It often happened that nonaddressee referents of such expressions were of high status which warranted honorific reference, but that the addressee (for example, royal concubine) who was also kin to that referent (for example, a princess) was of markedly lower status than referent. Such acts were traditionally disambiguated by use of a special second-person pronominal form. If the addressee was inferior to referent/kin, the second-person pronoun *ijengandika* was prescriptively used in *basa* possessive constructions of the form *X ijengandika* 'your *X*'. This marginal use seems to have been the last stage in the history of *ijengandika*, which is now extinct.

This same ambiguity in acts of reference to kin of addressee informs strategic usage to foreground one of two kinship status relations that bear on interpretation of use. Although krama inggil lexemes are normatively unacceptable for self-reference in phrases like 'my *X*', in some contexts honorific kin term use for one's own relatives can be felicitous: a mother might refer to her newborn in addressing her mother-in-law with the honorific kin term *wayah* 'grandchild' (ngoko: *putu*) in the phrase *wayah dalem* (STC:83), thereby attributing high status to addressee/grandparent through reference to addressee's kin, simultaneously suspending the relevance of her own kin relation to the referent to foreground that between ancestor/addressee and descendant/referent. For this speaker to refer to her offspring in this context with the phrase *putra kula*, 'my child (honorific)', on the other hand, would be a breach of etiquette, because it signifies no kin relation other than that between referent and speaker.[28]

Such strategic honorific usage shows how construal of kin term use may require recourse to knowledge of social relations between speech partners, but also knowledge of constellations of enduring, interpenetrating kin and status relations. It also suggests a way of accounting for nonuse of honorific kin terms to refer to addressees: if acts of address with honorific kin terms implicitly recruit an addressee to some putative kin relation with speaker, they would also be construable not just as honorific of addressee but as self-raising by the same kind of interpretation that use of *ijengandika* once served to block in reference to kin of addressee. That social significances of honorific kin term usage need to be characterized vis-a-vis identities of speech participants and referents is symptomatic of their semantic complementarities with personal pronouns as linguistic mediators of social relations.

KIN TERMS IN STRATEGIC USE: *IBU* AND *ÉYANG*

Two traditionally honorific kin terms, *ibu* 'mother' and *éyang* 'grandparent', once used only in reference to very exalted addressees, have been subject to such widespread strategic use and appropriation that they have become marginal to the honorific kin term vocabulary. Like personal pronouns they came into use for reference to addressees, and then likewise became highly mutable in pragmatic value. Both are thus doubly exceptional and doubly significant examples of change in pragmatically salient terms for the speaker.

The krama inggil *éyang* was traditionally reserved for reference to and perhaps address of persons of the highest noble and official status but was sometimes not used even for those in the most exalted noble circles. Pakubuwana X, for instance, was addressed and referred to by

28. In other situations such usage could be felicitous. Padmasusastra (STC:159) has an older, lower-status intermediary in marriage negotiations address his younger, higher-status, prospective affinally related speech partner as *putra kula*. This apparent violation of the rule of nonuse of krama inggil for self-reference strikes the right note of intimacy with esteemed, prospective in-law, and can be construed not as self-elevation of speaker as fictive parent of addressee, but of addressee *tout court*.

142   Terms for persons

his grandchildren (*wayah dalem*) as *kakèk*, now an archaic term for grandfather (corresponding to *nini* or *nènèk*, 'grandmother').[29] In other high-ranking families use of *éyang* was keyed primarily to the referent's descent status, and so might be used to address and refer to just one high-ranking parent's parent(s) but not the other. Ngoko *mbah* was apparently used in almost all traditional priyayi households of middling to low rank for and to grandparents, often in complex expressions with honorific terms of gender: *mbah kakung* 'male grandparent' and *mbah putri* 'female grandparent'. The fact that ngoko kin terms were combinable with honorifics in this way is yet another symptom of the distinct social significances of use of kin terms as opposed to other honorific lexemes.

One conservative priyayi likened these two expressions, which he used as a child, to halfway points between plain ngoko and the krama inggil *éyang*, which he had been scared (*wedi*) to use in public as a boy because he would sound conceited (*gumedhé*). But he frankly acknowledged that he addressed and referred to his parents' parents as *éyang* at home, with other household members. *Mbah* was then felt not to be so much non-honorific as ordinary usage, respectful by virtue of the relative seniority and concomitant status it attributed to addressee. A popular folk etymology relates *mbah* as a short form to *si mbah* (*si* a personal article, mentioned previously) and this in turn to *sembah*, the word for the gesture of fealty prescriptively given to one's grandparents.[30]

Nowadays *éyang* is widely used by educated urban speakers, both priyayi and non-priyayi, in reference and address to their own grandparents. As one older conservative priyayi speaker sniffed, "everybody asks for *éyang* these days." Some conservative priyayi find

---

29. These are two of several kin terms that were in use at least as recently as the turn of the century but are now practically extinct in Surakarta. Others are *uwa* 'parent's elder male sibling', *paman*, 'parent's younger male sibling', and *biyung* 'mother'. A treatment of the history of these terms in city and village would further illustrate the pragmatic salience of kin terms, but would require more space than can be spared here.

30. Folk etymologies (*jarwa dhosok* 'forced renderings') are important to Javanese conceptions of language and symbolism but cannot be discussed at length here; in effect they involve treating the code itself as a text susceptible to explication; see Becker 1979:236.

themselves in the same bind with use of *mbah* and *éyang* as they do with *kula* and *dalem*: they prescribe usage that is at odds with what they themselves receive from their grandchildren, who have been trained by their own parents, my informant's offspring, to address and refer to their grandparents as *éyang*. Three older priyayi who called this 'accepted error' (*salah kaprah*) to my attention noted with some perplexity that they called their own grandparents, of much higher descent status than themselves, *mbah*, yet their own grandchildren address them as *éyang*.

They have little choice but to accept this new de facto norm, and prescriptions and complaints notwithstanding, some tacitly accept and expect it in address to themselves. During a visit with an older conservative priyayi who had cited use of *éyang* (among other things) to show how linguistic etiquette was deteriorating, I happened to be present for a son's arrival from Jakarta with his family. Coaxed by her parents, the elderly priyayi's four-year-old granddaughter shyly came into the visiting room carrying a package that she gave him saying *Kanggo bapak* (*kanggo* ngoko: 'for', krama: *kanggé*, krama inggil: *kagem*). Her grandfather's somewhat surprised but gentle admonishment was *Kok kanggo bapak!? Kagem éyang!* ("What d'you mean '*Kanggo bapak!*'? [you should say] *Kagem éyang*.") His spontaneous reaction betrays the degree to which priyayi expectations about usage have come into conformance with norms established outside the traditional priyayi community. Like the personal pronouns discussed previously, *éyang* has been appropriated outside traditional elite circles, the range of referents of whom and to whom it is used has grown, and its pragmatic value is transformed as it has been progressively deprived of honorific import. Its present availability for use for reference to one's own kin suggests that it may eventually be assimilated to the krama vocabulary of polite address.

Mbok and *ibu* ('mother') have undergone similar shifts although norms for their traditional use differed from those for *mbah* and *éyang*. The krama inggil *ibu* was used to refer to and address a first wife in priyayi households by her inferior household members, including concubines who were spoken to and of as *mbok*. *Ibu* was not a title, and was not necessarily used in address or reference to such a first wife by her superiors, who might call her *mbok* but could add the descent title *mas* to mark regard for their noble descent. Nowa-

144   Terms for persons

days *mbok* is hardly used by any educated speakers to their own mothers, or anyone else they count as an educated urbanite. *Ibu* has been appropriated and spread so rapidly among non-priyayi that mothers in some commoner families are addressed as *(i)bu*[31] by their own children, but refer to and address their own mothers as *mbok*. As *mbok* has been progressively displaced by *ibu*, it has become increasingly identified as 'village language' (basa *désa*) like the second-person pronoun *ndika*. Although some modern priyayi said that they sometimes use *mbok* to market sellers (typically villagers), that choice must be made carefully to avoid offending one's addressee.[32]

Parallels between personal pronoun and kin term change strongly suggest that the latter serve in address of speech partners as similarly crucial mediators of social relations, and are equally susceptible to strategic use just in case they are available for reference to an addressee. Another broadly parallel pattern of change in kin term usage deserves special consideration for two reasons. First, it has led to the incorporation of a former descent title to the kin term vocabulary through a process very much like that which led to the incorporation of figurative expressions into personal pronoun paradigms. Second, the patterns of use that brought about this relatively recent shift hinge on the difference between interactional statuses of referents who are speech partners and non-speech partners, the same social difference that underlies all other changes in linguistic etiquette discussed in this chapter.

STRUCTURAL SHIFT OUTSIDE THE SPEECH STYLES: *KANG* AND *KANGMAS*

Traditional vocative use of the ngoko kin term *kakang* 'elder male sibling' is keyed to a choice between the short form *kang* and full form *kakang*, presupposing of relative familiarity or social distance, respectively. Such usage was therefore broadly parallel to use of *bapak*. *Kakang*'s krama inggil alternant *raka*, like most other honorific kin terms, was never used vocatively or referentially for addressee,

   31. *Ibu* and *bu* are both available as vocative/parentheticals, but the choice is diacritic less of social status of (would-be) speech partner than of relative intimacy.
   32. According to Keeler (1984:11), the same change is occurring in rural south-central Java.

but only to speak of kin relations. *Adhi* 'younger sibling' was similarly used in address as a vocative in alternation with *dhi* or *dhik*. Its honorific equivalent *rayi* has likewise never served as vocative or independent means of reference to an addressee.

Convenient examples of differing ranges of nonhonorific and honorific usages of these kin terms can be drawn from complicated repertoires of terms for reference to and address of spouses. A husband may address his wife with *dhi(k)* or some teknonymous form, and receive in turn some expression glossable as 'elder male sibling' or teknonymous form. A speaker relatively familiar with two high status persons related as spouses may refer to one in address of the other with a construction including the honorific equivalent to the term that addressee uses to the referent: *keng raka* '(your) elder male sibling' (the one you address as elder male sibling, i.e., your husband) or *keng rayi* '(your) younger sibling (the one you address as younger sibling, i.e., your wife).[33] But that same speaker would never use either of those honorific kin terms, *raka* or *rayi*, in address of either spouse.

In traditional usage plain, unadorned *kakang* or *kang* in address presupposed lower and in all likelihood non-priyayi status of a speech partner. Far commoner in priyayi address of other priyayi were combinations of *kakang* or *kang* with the lowest descent title *mas* (discussed in Chapter 3) in *kakang mas* or, less formally and more commonly, *kang mas*. Similar expressions were constructed with *(a)dhi* (*(a)dhi mas*), *mbok* (*mbok mas*), and *anak* (*(a)nak mas*).[34] No dictionary or grammar from the nineteenth century describes *mas* as anything but a low title or word meaning 'gold',[35] and in older texts

33. *Keng* is a variant of *kang* (formal ngoko, krama: *ingkang*), a relative clause and topic marker that could be glossed in this construction as 'the one who is'. Koentjaraningrat 1957:86 and 1985 provides a sense of the complex calculations involved in use of terms for spouses when terms glossable as 'spouse' and elaborated in the speech style system are considered.

34. Short forms of *kakang* and *adhi* here fit the broader pattern of short kin term plus title as in *pak menggung, den béhi*, and so on. *Anak* is relatively rare nowadays because those so addressed are usually markedly inferior or younger intimates appropriately spoken to by name alone.

35. Some speakers appealed to this meaning to etymologize its sense of 'elder male sibling' as the one who, one informant said, 'we must treat like gold'.

146 Terms for persons

it usually appears as an independent element in vocative/parenthetical use to low-ranking priyayi. Only among persons of low descent status would such a title be relevant; others would be addressed as *radèn*.

Since the turn of the century *mas* has assimilated to kin term repertoires of urban and many rural Javanese. Older, conservative speakers recognize and use the constructions *(a)dhimas* and *(ka)kangmas* vocatively, to refer to addressees and nonaddressees, and they report (as do written sources) that *kangmas* is a reduced form of *kakang mas*. *(Ka)kang*, fifty or sixty years ago a common mode of address to male commoners like *bécak*s, is nowadays demeaning and may provoke angry reactions which I was told to avoid at all costs. This is one reason why the range of appropriate use of *pak* has extended to relatively young speech partners.

Mas is now commonly used vocatively and referentially by and to educated speakers.[36] Where conservative speakers say it is a short form for *kangmas*, modern priyayi and commoners alike use it as a term glossable as 'elder male sibling' not just as a vocative but as a kin term for reference to both speech partners and non-speech partners. So when asked to translate the Indonesian sentence "That's my friend's elder sibling" (*Itu kakak teman saya*) into Javanese, for example,[37] all younger, modern priyayi used the simple term *mas* in both ngoko (*Kuwi masé kancaku*) and krama (*Menika masipun kanca kula*.) Most older, conservative priyayi used *kangmas* in their translations, although they accepted the use of *mas* as a 'common error' (*salah kaprah*). Some younger priyayi characterized *kangmas* as a rather formal and, several suggested, "old-fashioned" variant on *mas*, and three added that *kangmas* is really redundant, because *kang* was 'village language' (*cara désa*) for *mas*. *Adhimas* is recognized and used (albeit rarely) by conservative speakers, but hardly known to

---

36. This change may not be recent, and this usage is hardly restricted to Surakarta. H. Geertz 1961 reports it in Paré, as does Keeler 1984:11 in villages in south-central Java. Unlike all other authors of word lists and dictionaries, Keeler and Nothoffer (1981:map 133) treat *kangmas* as a krama alternate for ngoko *kakang*. None of my informants identified or used them in any way which suggests they be classified as parts of that vocabulary.

37. Because *kakak* is not differentiated for sex, I specified that third-person referent was male in the hypothetical context of use.

younger speakers, particularly those who are not priyayi. Several non-priyayi between the ages of thirteen and seventeen answered my questions about it by saying, somewhat perplexedly, that the term does not make sense because it is a combination of words for younger sibling and older sibling. Their modern priyayi peers recognized *adhimas* as usage they hear among their elders, but do not use themselves.

To all appearances, then, a title once appended to a kin term has itself evolved into a kin term, displacing the term to which it was politely appended among priyayi and other urban speakers. It seems likely too that this rapid assimilation began shortly before or soon after changes in rights to titles (discussed in Chapter 3), which effectively detached *mas* from the descent title hierarchy.

The only evidence of the former semantic content and polite expressiveness of *mas* in usage by modern priyayi is the reluctance they share with their conservative elders to use *mas* to lower status persons. The idea of using *mas* to a pedicab driver they find ludicrous even if they are at a loss to explain why it is overrefined (*kalusen*) or politer than *bapak*, apparently going against the logic that age and esteem can be simultaneously signified by kin term use. But this broadly class-stratified pattern of use hardly prevents lower-class males from being addressed or referred to as *mas* by other lower-class speakers. However incorrect such usage seems to more educated speakers, they acknowledge that market sellers (*bakul*), for instance, address pedicab drivers as *mas* if they feel those addressee/referents are too young for *(ba)pak*. As a kin term, *mas* is undergoing much the same pragmatic devaluation as *ibu*, *éyang*, and formerly honorific personal pronouns.

Obvious differences between the transformation of title to kin term and figurative expressions to personal pronouns throw into sharp relief underlying parallels between both processes. The initial combinability of *mas* with kin terms to mark respect for the referent is structurally analogous to, if significatively different from, the ways figurative expressions combined with personal pronouns. *Kangmas* became automatized and idiomatic, its formerly titular component shifting in semantic motivation as it became a detachable equivalent of the formerly complex whole. So too formerly figurative expressions became semantically equivalent to and independent of the

148   Terms for persons

personal pronouns with which they had formerly combined. As independent expressions, *mas* and formerly figurative expressions have all displaced elements to which they had been appended in relatively polite use.

As important as the parallel between these developments inside and outside the speech style system are the obvious differences between the transformations and their results. The transformation of *mas* cannot be allied with the evolution of personal pronouns from figurative expressions because, as we have seen, the latter's novel construability in use was directly dependent on the special statuses of their referents as speech partners. But it is very likely, given stylistic alternations between kin terms like *bapak* and *pak*, and between *mbakyu*, *mbak*, and *yu*, that *mas* came to be detached from and used in place of *kang* in vocative and parenthetical use, just those occasions of use that always identify an addressee, and whose social expressiveness bears always and only on the speaker/addressee relation. *Mas* very likely came to be opposed to *kang* first in vocative and parenthetical expressions that identify the addressee in subjective, occasional ways as presupposed speech partner.

That these changes in pronominal and kin term repertoires share certain processual features should not obscure differences between the resulting social expressiveness of use of either sort of term. Choice of *mas* over *kang* (to the degree the latter is still in use) is not keyed to the kinds of interactional status relations marked and mediated by personal pronouns, but indicates evaluations of much broader kinds of class membership. Nor is the choice between *mas* and *kang* at all structurally integrated with the use of other elements of the speech style paradigms.

But patterns of kin term change outside the speech style system do broadly resemble personal pronoun change in the system, both through the social pressures that have been exerted on each, and the types of use through which those transformations have articulated. The broad semantic and social significative properties that thus inform use of linguistic etiquette in general and speech styles in particular lead back to the general issues broached at the beginning of this chapter and the end of the last: How is it that interactive and noninteractive statuses of participants and referents recurringly interpenetrate in use of speech?

Salience, Use, and Change

Javanese terms for persons are nuancable mediators of interaction because they are multiform, transient symbols of persons whose attributes—unique and shared, occasional and enduring, imputed and actual—they presuppose and signify. Patterns of change have served as clues to various ways encoded meanings of terms integrate with and have been strategically manipulated to mediate interaction. Social change has rendered titles anachronistic, like the hierarchies in which they are semantically based. The invariable semantic nature of personal names lends their use a constant, invariable quality of directness and familiarity. But an integrated description of complex changes in kin term and personal pronoun repertoires turns out to require analytic distinctions broad enough to subsume all four ways of speaking of people not just as parts of speech styles but as linguistic etiquette.

The practical need for an integrated approach stems from broadly similar change in social and semantic significances of terms for persons inside and outside the speech styles that results from broadly similar patterns of strategic uses among priyayi and non-priyayi alike. Taken together with evidence of changes in title use described in Chapter 3, this account of personal pronoun and kin term repertoires provides diachronic evidence of the pragmatic salience of all three classes of terms for persons. All have been susceptible to recurring strategic use, which is manifested by rapid structural change in and leveling of stylistic marks of traditional social distinctions.

This finding may not be terribly surprising. It is intuitively plausible that stylistic contrasts between terms for persons should be among the most interactively important among encoded means for reference and predication. But there are unobvious parallels between the significances of uses of kin terms and personal pronouns, and changes in both paradigms, which have hinged on acts identifying speech participants referentially and vocatively. Strategic patterns of use have affected all terms used for persons who are speech partners, including now devalued honorific kin terms.

It follows from this account that these special uses of terms are significatively direct, insofar as they presuppose direct acquaintance with participants in the *hic et nunc* of use. Terms used in indexically and significatively direct acts turn out to be foci of both elaboration and avoidance. Elaboration of and change in *basa* personal pronoun repertoires cannot be explained independently of figurative expressions that, regardless of their semantic content, conferred an intrinsic indefiniteness or allusiveness on acts of pronominal reference or response to vocative use. That priyayi have had recurring and ongoing recourse to such expressions, together with highly deferential personal pronouns, suggests an intuitive preference for an indirect means of deferential reference in refined linguistic conduct. The recurring assimilation of those expressions to personal pronoun paradigms seems to have been possible just because speech partners are privileged objects of reference. Just as obviously, personal pronouns have been especially salient, strategically usable terms for persons just because speech participants are salient objects of reference.

Because most honorific kin terms are normatively used just for reference to non-speech partners, and never vocatively, use of nonhonorific kin terms to refer to speech partners are subsistent for social expressiveness on their semantic content and perhaps referential indefiniteness of use. At the same time, nonreferential but significatively indexical vocative and parenthetical kin term use turns out to be elaborated in ways having nothing to do with the speech styles, and to have been a focus for change in kin terms for 'elder male sibling', which articulated through just such occasions of significatively direct, contextually dependent use.

Priyayi quite consciously emphasize the prescriptively allusive, indirect qualities of polite conduct, linguistic and otherwise, that they call *alus* in Javanese. This account of terms for persons resonates with such broad observations because it shows how communicative indirectness and referential allusiveness is implemented in acts of speaking of people with both figurative expressions and kin terms. It has drawn out semantic and pragmatic correlates of what priyayi "naturally" focus on in polite linguistic conduct, and explored the pragmatic salience of personal pronouns within the speech style system. Pragmatically salient acts are not just uses of relatively elaborate repertoires, but acts significatively anchored in the *hic et nunc* of subjective, occasional relations.

In the next two chapters a similar expository strategy is directed to similarly broad issues: significative connections between the stylistic expression of deference in acts of lexical reference, and relations between honorific lexemes and speech acts of which they are parts. Answers to these questions involve another kind of "indirectness" in honorific usage with other broad structural reflexes in an apparently homogeneous honorific vocabulary.

6

Deference, Reference, and the Encoding of Status

Most ngoko words for persons' actions, states, and possessions have at least one honorific alternant which serves to mark something about the social status of someone to whom it refers. Hair, servants, blankets, states of anger and sleep, and acts of sitting and speaking all are personal attributes, and onto acts of reference to such attributes can "naturally" be mapped judgements of social status. As a rule, honorifics share semantic significances and morphosyntactic valences with just one ngoko (and perhaps a krama) alternant for which they may substitute as isomorphous semantic equivalents in acts of honorific reference. These intrinsic, obvious links between semantic range and pragmatic function make it is easy to think of honorifics as a relatively small and homogeneous class: a basa vocabulary with a distinctively narrow semantic range, free from co-occurrence restrictions like those on other speech style elements, and distinctive in their pragmatic significances.

But in each of these respects honorifics exhibit interesting systematic class-internal contrasts that correlate directly with their semantic significances. There are obvious differences in paradigmatic structures of sets containing honorifics, most of which have just a krama inggil (KI) member, others just a krama andhap (KA) member,[1] and still others both a krama inggil and krama andhap member.

1. Members of the two vocabularies will sometimes be identified with these superscripted abbreviations for the reader's convenience.

Deference, reference, and the encoding of status 153

These structural differences in fact correlate not only with broad contrasts in honorifics' semantic significances, but also with the ranges of status relations involving speech partners and non-speech partners on which they serve to mark judgments. By pursuing these "natural" links between honorifics' referential and potential deferential significances, we can reapply distinctions between modes and objects of reference to paradigmatic structures of sets containing honorifics, and the pragmatic functions of honorifics in use.

This outline of class-internal differences suggests less obvious contrasts between subclasses of honorifics. One has to do with the relative deferential expressivenesses of honorific usage. These are usually described as being the same for all members of the honorific vocabulary, in that use of any honorific for a given person ostensibly entails use of all others when possible. But in fact the relative deferential expressiveness of honorific usage varies as a function of semantic subdomain, distribution of knowledge in the community, and the kinds of social intimacy that "little-known" krama inggil lexemes and their non-honorific equivalents presuppose in acts of reference (honorific or not) to certain attributes of persons.

There is another significant contrast in what can be provisionally called the relative semantic indeterminacy encoded in subclasses of honorific lexemes, which makes for contextual dependency and allusiveness in acts of honorific reference. A common assumption in word lists, pedagogical texts, and dictionaries is that honorifics and nonhonorific equivalents are mutually substitutable on the basis of morphosyntactic and semantic properties. This assumption is valid enough to make it convenient to characterize honorifics' semantic content through their ngoko alternants, that is, through elements of the "basic" language of which they are "synonyms." Every honorific word list is based on the assumption that honorifics share signifieds with some ngoko lexeme(s), that only their signifiers differ, and that "basic" ngoko lexemes are therefore a uniquely accurate and convenient metalanguage for describing honorifics' semantic content.

But the generalization is not entirely valid because, as every word list also indicates, some honorifics alternate with more than one ngoko "synonym," that is, honorific lexical resources in some semantic domains are relatively impoverished so that several ngoko terms share a single honorific alternant. To avoid terminologically prejudging the nature of sense relations between these single honorifics and their several ngoko alternants, we can provisionally call these honorifics semantically indeterminate.[2] It is worth considering the possibility of whether some cases of encoded indeterminacy involve honorifics which can be thought of as polysemous, and so ambiguous in use between one of the several specific related senses signified by one of its ngoko alternants, or whether they are vague and lack semantic specificity with respect to any and all ngoko alternants. Contextual dependencies of honorific usage lend qualities of semantic allusiveness to acts of reference to deferred-to persons like the indirect or allusive uses of figurative and indefinite expressions considered in Chapter 5, similarly construable through collateral knowledge of social and discursive context.

Semantically indeterminate honorifics are numerous and idiomatic enough to be describable completely only in a short dictionary, grammar, and ethnography of speaking that would complement and complete traditional word lists. But a specific concern with honorifics' places in linguistic etiquette suggests a more specific focus: the allusive qualities of speech stemming from referential avoidance encoded in alternations not just between distinct signifiers, but distinct (if related) lexical signs. That indeterminacy obtrudes in particular semantic domains, and suggests that in Javanese (or at least priyayi) society there are socioculturally important aspects of interaction that are subject to special linguistic treatment in quasi-euphemistic referential acts in which, as Benveniste puts it (1971:266), "[e]verything hinges on the nature of the idea that one wishes to bring to mind while avoiding naming it specifically."

To proceed from semantic and structural features of the speech style system to the expressive and interpretive aspects of interaction that speech mediates is to explore the connection between those "ideas," the terms that signify them, and acts of use. To extend the approach set out in Chapter 4 we can consider the structures of paradigmatic sets that contain honorifics, and differences in the range of

2. The meaning of the word "indeterminate" is hardly less indeterminate than the meaning of the word "vague" is vague, as Binnick (1970) points out in the source for the distinction between ambiguity and vagueness I draw too crudely here. For discussion of particular examples, though, I believe it provides a provisional distinction with polysemy.

social relations over which use of honorifics can mark evaluations of status relations. The concept of *exchange* turns out to be crucial in both respects: as a type of mediated social interaction that may be spoken of honorifically, but also a type of social conduct, including speech, which honorifics may be used to perform.

Semantics, Paradigmatic Structure, and Pragmatic Range

Because the honorific vocabulary includes the personal pronouns *dalem* (krama andhap) and *nandalem* (krama inggil), discussed in Chapter 5, those indexically referential signs can be classified with honorifics by slightly recasting the description of their referential significances: they are indexically referential signs that presuppose for their denotative meanings features of contexts of use, and particularly the identities of participants in acts of speech exchange which mediate social relations between speech partners. Personal pronoun use presupposes a referent's subjective, occasional status as an agent or recipient of act of speech exchange in which a pronominal token appears.

As a semantic domain, the notion of exchange serves to distinguish lexemes significative of mediated or more generally coordinated interaction from others, and is a useful classificatory rubric that correlates with broad differences in the structures of paradigmatic sets. Indexically referential pronouns presuppose exchange of messages of which they are part for their referential significances, while some other honorific lexemes and their alternants may be used to predicate and in some but not all cases simultaneously to perform acts of linguistic exchange. Figure 4 shows how these two classificatory distinctions, presupposing/nonpresupposing and predicative/nonpredicative of coordinate activity, can be used to subclassify paradigmatic sets in ways that correlate the structures of those sets and their members' shared semantic content.

Krama andhap and krama inggil forms are complementarily distributed in the first-person and second-person pronoun paradigms because of their modes and objects of reference, on one hand, and the most general ethics of interaction on the other. Because honorific personal pronouns denote speech partners *qua* speech partners while simultaneously marking respect for status of referent/speech partner,

Figure 4. Classification of paradigmatic sets containing honorifics

	Presuppose exchange?	Predicate of coordinate activity?	Set membership
Personal pronouns	yes	no	KI (2nd prsn. prn.) KA (1st prsn. prn.)
Coordinate activity	no	yes	KI and/or KA
Other honorifics	no	no	KI, no KA
Performatives	yes	yes	KA

there are none available for use in ways which would violate norms of humble (*andhap-asor*) conduct. Conventions for humble behavior likewise preclude the linguistic marking of one's superior status even if it is otherwise apparent and mutually acknowledged by both speech participants. To use krama inggil lexemes for reference to oneself or krama andhap lexemes to predicate actions of which one is either the patient or recipient would be neither ungrammatical or nonsensical—utterances like "my house^{KI}," and "Give^{KA} it to me" are neither—but would be socially unacceptable: they mark speaker's judgment that he/she is of higher status than speech partner/addressee (in the first case) or agent of action (in the second). As violations of broad, overriding norms of humility, such acts count in most situations as faux pas of the first order. Traditional high ranking priyayi did sometimes engage in such self-referential honorific usage, but it is now almost universally regarded as arrogant (*digsura*) except when teaching linguistic etiquette in ways touched on below. Acceptability or nonacceptability in use for self-reference is a convenient test of basa lexemes' pragmatic values for research on the changing membership of the krama inggil vocabulary.

This interpenetration of broad ethics of interaction and specifically linguistic/referential significances of use is manifested in the structure of paradigmatic sets in which krama inggil and krama andhap elements are necessarily complementary: personal pronouns. Self-

Deference, reference, and the encoding of status 157

elevation by speaker/agent of speech exchange over presupposed addressee/recipient is generally impossible, and so there is no occasion for use of a krama inggil form for self-reference (i.e., a first-person pronoun).[3] But often a krama inggil pronoun is appropriately chosen for an addressee, presupposed as a high-status recipient of speech. The krama andhap pronominal is available for reference just to speaker, marked as inferior to speech partner who is presupposed as a high-status person in relation to whom speaker is being compared.

Most paradigmatic sets of verbs significative of exchange and other coordinate activities (second row of Figure 4) contain both krama inggil and krama andhap members as pragmatically complementary honorifics for marking status asymmetries between agents and recipients/objects of such actions. The krama inggil honorific root *paring*, for instance, used to predicate acts of giving by superior agent to inferior recipient, is complemented by the krama andhap *caos* (krama andhap) used to predicate actions of giving by inferior to superior. Aside from such minimally three-place predicates, a few verbs significative of other sorts of mediated, coordinate social conduct (e.g., 'accompany', 'pay a visit to') also fall under this classificatory rubric. Relatively few sets contain krama andhap members (about twenty) but among them are honorifics that are most semantically indeterminate, most idiomatically used, and for which ngoko lexical distinctions collapse most strikingly.

Some of these paradigmatic sets contain a krama inggil member or a krama andhap member, but not both; these signify activities that presuppose social status asymmetries between participants, and so are appropriately engaged in only by inferior in relation to superior or vice versa. So sets of verbs used to predicate activities normatively engaged in only by inferiors in relation to superiors (e.g., paying a visit to, accompanying) contain krama andhap but not krama inggil honorifics, and sets of verbs for activities engaged in only by superiors in relation to inferiors (e.g., scolding) contain krama inggil but not krama andhap honorific alternants.

In this classification most paradigmatic sets containing honorifics fall into the large, negatively defined class of paradigmatic sets (third

3. I ignore here the first-person pronoun used by the king in palace language, discussed in Errington 1982 and 1984.

row of Figure 4) whose members are significative of noninteractional attributes and contain krama inggil but no krama andhap alternants: kin terms (discussed in Chapter 5), terms for body parts, possessions, physical states and attributes, and so on. Cases of semantic indeterminacy are relatively fewer and less striking among these roughly 120 sets of terms for bodily actions and functions, which collectively bear out the assumption that ngoko/honorific relations are isomorphic. But many are little known in the community at large, and are something of a specialty in the small and shrinking conservative priyayi speech subcommunity.

One small but crucial class of terms remains—performatively used verbs, represented in the last row of Figure 4, which are at once predicative and constitutive of the acts of linguistic exchange they denote. Performative uses of these verbs of speaking derive their distinctive, intrinsically indexical significances from existential relations between their tokens and interactional contexts.[4] Two krama andhap honorific verbs of speaking serve in highly idiomatic performative formulas to perform deferential directives, expressive of social acts through their deictically anchored semantic content. Krama inggil roots are not used in performative formulas for the same reason that no krama inggil first-person pronoun exists: both would presuppose speaker, who can never mark his or her own superior status to addressee, as agent or referent of action thus performed and named. Directive uses of these verbs provide striking, perhaps limiting examples of semantic indeterminacy in which mode and object of reference converge in a special focus for encoded indirectness.

This classification implicitly distinguishes between occasions of honorific usage for reference to persons who are and are not speech partners, and is naturally extended to differing ranges of possible status relations between speech partners and non-speech partners for which each subclass of honorifics distinguished previously is available to mark judgements. Differences in such availability, what can be called the pragmatic range of honorifics, may be relatively wide or narrow, as indicated schematically in Figure 5.

4. See on the indexical nature of performatives, which cannot be discussed at length here, Harris 1978, Spielmann 1980, Silverstein 1977b:143–45, and Welsh and Chametzky 1983.

Deference, reference, and the encoding of status 159

Figure 5. *Referential and pragmatic ranges of honorifics*

Mark judgement on status relation between:	Speech participants?	Speech participant & non-speech participant?	Non-speech participants?
Personal pronouns	yes	no	no
Exchange/ coordinate activity	yes	yes	yes
Others	yes	yes	no
Performatives	yes	( )	( )

Acts of exchange or coordinate activity may involve either, neither, or both speech partners (assuming singular addressee), and so a speaker's evaluations of status relations between persons can be mapped onto acts of honorific predication of such actions involving both, either, or neither speech partner (columns 1, 2, and 3, respectively). To speak of one person's act of visiting or giving something to another (row 2) is to speak of occasional coordinate conduct between them, use or nonuse of an honorific verb then marking an evaluation of an enduring status relation. So, to say the Javanese equivalent of "Mary gave Bill a book" one may use the krama andhap predicate glossable as 'give' (*nyaosi*, ngoko: *mènéhi*, krama:*nyukani*, krama inggil:*maringi*) to mark a judgment that Mary is of lower status than Bill. In principle if not practice[5] that judgment is made independently of the context in which, and the addressee to whom, honorific or nonhonorific alternants are used, unless Mary and Bill are also speech partners.

Performative uses of verbs of linguistic exchange (row 4) are intrinsically limited in their social and linguistic significances to the

5. Status relations between speech partners, and the interactional status of addressee as opposed to third person, may complicate honorific usage in ways too involved to be dealt with here. See Poedjosoedarmo et al. 1979:32–6.

speaker/addressee relation and, like personal pronouns in all uses (row 1), are in a crucially indexical relation to context of use. Null signs in columns 2 and 3 of Figure 5 are supposed to show that this limitation is a function of the indexical significativeness of performative acts, rather than the intensional meaning of their component verbs of speaking.

Honorifics in the largest, negatively defined class (row 3) serve to mark status of referent relative to a speech partner, presupposed as party to that status relation. Honorific use to speak of a non-speech partner ordinarily presupposes speaker as honorific user to be party to the status relation so judged. The krama inggil honorific glossable as 'examine', used in a Javanese equivalent of the sentence "Mary examines Bill's hand," for instance, may mark Mary's relatively high status in relation to speaker if Mary is addressee or non-speech partner, but in relation to Bill only if Bill is speaker. Use of a krama inggil honorific glossable as 'hand' for Bill will ordinarily be subject to the same range of possible interpretations, marking Bill's high status relative to speaker, who may or may not be Mary. To use both honorifics would similarly mark judgments on aspects of status relations between a speech partner and both referents, but would not necessarily directly mark anything about the status relation between Mary and Bill.

But there are nontrivial exceptions to the rule that honorific use marks something about status relation between referent and speaker, and the characterization of pragmatic range in the middle column of Figure 5 accurately reflects this fact. Most honorifics can be used to mark status relations between addressee and some object of honorific reference by strategically shifting the center of social deixis from speaker to addressee in an act Javanese call *mbasakaké*.

Speaking for Others: *Mbasakaké*

As a term for strategic use, *mbasakaké* can be glossed as something like 'to use language as another should or would', which presupposes the type of role relation implicit in Koentjaraningrat's translation of the phrase (1957:99) as 'to speak the speech of the children': parent/elder/superior to child/junior/inferior. To *mbasakaké* is to perform

Deference, reference, and the encoding of status 161

what Goffman (1974:535) calls a say-for, "projecting mimicked words into the mouths of figures that are present," and as such is broadly analogous to kin term use in English to refer to someone as addressee would refer to that person. That Javanese in fact most frequently explain *mbasakaké* with examples of kin term usage is further evidence of the pragmatic salience of kin terms in linguistic interaction.

The master of a house may *mbasakaké* a servant to whom he speaks of his wife by saying *Ndara putri wis tindak durung?* ("Has the female *ndara* gone out yet?"), where the terms glossed as 'female'(*putri*) and 'go out' (*tindak*) are krama inggil. Because his wife is not his superior, he would not ordinarily use that honorific to refer to her when speaking with (for example) friends or with her; his use of *tindak* therefore indirectly affirms the addressee's status relation to referent. In priyayi households this pattern of use commonly extends to parents' acts of reference to an elder sibling in address of a younger.

One may *mbasakaké* to instruct indirectly but also to affirm the status relations between speech partners that the strategy normatively presupposes, that speaker/agent of instruction is of higher status than addressee/recipient. For the speaker to appropriate an addressee's place in a status relation with some referent, "projecting an image of someone not oneself while preventing viewers from forgetting . . . that an alien animator is at work" (Goffman 1974:534) is to introduce a strategic ambiguity into the speech situation that must be mutually recognized. For this reason *mbasakaké* is doubly presupposing of the speaker's high status in relation to referent and to addressee. Were the speaker's status not higher than or at least comparable with referent's, no apparent anomaly in honorific usage would exist to signal the indirect prescriptive force of the usage. Were the speaker not of higher status than addressee, it would be inappropriate for him or her to take it upon him/herself to prescribe to or impose on addressee in speech style use.

To *mbasakaké* with a personal pronoun, limited in referential range just to a speech partner, is to prescribe something about the addressee's usage to just the person engaged in the act of *mbasakaké*: the speaker enacts the very mode of address behavior he or she

162   Deference, reference, and the encoding of status

wishes the addressee to adopt, and so reverses the apparently proper marking of status relations between partners. I learned of this strategy during my first visit with a middle-aged, low-ranking priyayi in Surakarta to whom I initially used the first-person pronoun *kula*. I soon learned that he felt this was not fitting, when he began to refer to himself as *dalem*, apparently placing himself in a lower-status position by creating a conspicuously asymmetric exchange of pronouns. He thus made me uncomfortable enough, given obvious differences in age, to switch to *dalem*. He then switched to *kula*, and having thus effected a reversal of usage and the status relations marked by usage, we maintained that pattern for the remainder of our acquaintance. In this type of *mbasakaké* (for other speakers identified it as such) my speech partner referred to himself qua speaker to me qua addressee as (he felt) I should speak of myself to him. Whereas use a nonindexical honorific to *mbasakaké* is effectively to prescribe "speak of this referent as have I," use of a personal pronoun to *mbasakaké* prescribes "when you adopt the relation in speech exchange to me that I am now in to you, refer to yourself as I am now referring to myself."

Indeterminacy and Semantic Domains

To focus on relations between semantic content, paradigmatic structure, and pragmatic range is to characterize negatively the vast majority of paradigmatic sets, which contain single krama inggil honorifics. They are neither indexically referential nor significative of acts of exchange and, in use, map judgments on status relations involving at least one speech partner. Another correlate of these distinctions can be drawn from very general contrasts between the proportions of ngoko lexemes in each of these semantic domains that share some honorific alternant. Table 5 shows how intraset and interset structure correlates with an extended (if still crude) distinction between a physical subdomain (terms significative of body parts, functions, states) and a psychosocial domain (voluntary conduct, psychological states and attributes, coordinate activities).

Obviously no clear-cut line can be drawn between voluntary noncoordinate actions and body functions; eating and drinking, for instance, are both. It is difficult to say whether terms glossable as 'to

Deference, reference, and the encoding of status 163

Table 5. Intraset and Interset Relations by Semantic Subdomain

	Total # ngoko lexemes	# with distinct krama alternants	# sharing honorific
Physical subdomain:			
body parts	39	7 (18%)	4 (10%)
possessions	44	14 (32%)	9 (20%)
body functions, states	52	18 (35%)	9 (18%)
TOTAL	135	39 (29%)	22 (16%)
Psychosocial subdomain:			
voluntary noncoordinate actions	25	21 (84%)	14 (56%)
psychological attributes, states	26	14 (54%)	15 (58%)
coordinate activities	29	19 (65%)	19 (65%)
TOTAL	80	54 (68%)	48 (60%)

kiss' and 'to have sexual intercourse' should be treated as members of the physical subdomain, like terms glossable as 'vomit', 'be sick', and 'have missing teeth', or whether they count as volitional activities like walking and riding. All are placed here under the first rubric, because they signify essentially physical attributes. The distinction is unproblematic in most cases, and suggests two significant generalizations.

As column 2 indicates, fewer than one-third of the ngoko lexemes that fall into the "physical" subdomain are described in the literature as having krama members, whereas more than two-thirds in the psychosocial domain have distinct krama equivalents. This is a structural clue to relative frequency of use of set members because, roughly speaking, krama alternants to ordinary non-basa words are concentrated among the most commonly used morphemes of the language, the "core" vocabulary, as noted in Chapter 4. Relative proportions of krama-containing paradigmatic sets in each extrinsically defined semantic domain thus provide a rough structural index of relative frequencies of use of members of these sets, even without a count of text frequencies, which would be difficult for practical and methodological reasons. Speakers more frequently choose between members of sets that contain krama elements than those that do not, and so choose between honorifics and nonhonorifics that alternate with krama forms more frequently than honorifics that alternate just with ngoko forms. By this line of reasoning lexemes in paradigmatic sets in the physical subdomain, and especially body parts, are little used. Certainly they are among the least widely recognized honorifics, and are considered in the next section.

The other general structural contrast within each semantic subdomain has to do with relative proportions of sets which share honorific members, an aspect of intraset relations shown in the rightmost column of Table 5. In the physical subdomain more than five in six honorifics (80%) alternate isomorphously with just one ngoko and perhaps krama equivalent, standing to them as semantically transparent honorific equivalents. Fewer than one in seven (14%) ngoko nouns referential of body parts and possessions, and one in five (20%) ngoko verbs referential of bodily functions and states share honorific equivalents.

But more than half of the ngoko verbs significative of volitional, non-coordinate activities (56%) and of psychological attributes and states (58%) share honorific equivalents, and almost two in three (65%) ngoko verbs of coordinate activity share krama inggil alternants, krama andhap alternants, or both. In this domain the assumption of isomorphous alternations between non-honorific and honorific lexemes is least valid, and semantic indeterminacy in honorifics is most conspicuous.

Table 5 does not show contrasting degrees of indeterminacy encoded in the subdomain of (linguistic) exchange and coordinate activity; distinctions between as many as five ngoko lexemes appear to collapse in the honorific vocabulary, making for the most strikingly obligatory types of indirect lexical reference. It is in this domain that performative and nonperformative honorific usage is most crucially dependent on contexts of use for construal, and in which honorific usage makes for the most referentially allusive indirect acts of speaking.

Little-known Krama Inggil

Most honorifics that alternate straightforwardly with ngoko terms signify body parts (about forty), body functions (about twenty), and possessions (about forty) ordinarily in close physical contact with persons' bodies (medicine, pillow, blanket, etc.). Many are rarely used, little known, and are falling out of use or now being refunctionalized into the vocabulary of krama address style markers. In one way it is intuitively plausible that this should happen. Why should there be honorific terms glossable as 'break wind', 'phlegm', or 'buttocks'? It seemed as peculiar to the Javanese I felt comfortable asking as it did to me that there should be honorific terms for genitalia, intercourse, defecation, and other topics one might expect to be avoided in speech about and perhaps with those of high status. It is hard not to sense that these should be taboo topics (in the sense of the word explored, for instance, by Leach 1964:28), and to wonder about the social implications of speaking of just these attributes, seemingly at odds with the qualities of social relations normatively presupposed by honorific usage.

The point is suggested also by two other special Javanese lexicons not often dealt with as speech style vocabularies, that share this semantic subdomain. One, ordinarily used for reference and address of children as a vocabulary for baby talk, is referential (like baby talk in many languages) of physical actions and states, and expressive of extreme intimacy. The other is a set of highly abusive 'crude' (*kasar*) words for reference to body parts and physical functions of persons who are objects of anger and scorn (see Poedjosoedarmo 1968b:190). Yet within this same semantic range, stylistically elaborated with forms expressive of intimacy on one hand and scorn on the other, are also vocabulary items expressive of respect and deference.

Today many priyayi find the semantic content of these honorifics presupposing of an intimacy at odds with the stylistic deference they convey as parts of the honorific vocabulary. But in traditional priyayi circles these were complementary rather than competing aspects of a social relationship: intimacy (physical or otherwise) did not necessarily mitigate status differences or the need for their linguistic diacritics. An older priyayi responded to my question about the krama inggil *cawik* (ngoko *cawok*) 'to clean the anus after defecating' by illustrating how a servant or concubine might use it to say of a royal child or grandchild "Oh, the young *gusti* has dirtied himself or herself, I'll clean him or her up right away (*dalem cawiki rumiyin*)."

These intimate honorifics, like the interactional mores they bespeak, are less relevant and less known in Surakarta now. Intergenerational variation in priyayi knowledge of such honorifics indicates that many are falling out of use among younger priyayi who have little opportunity or inclination to learn or use deferential terms whose meanings presuppose just the sort of intimacy that, for them, contraindicates the use of linguistic marks of deference.[6] I chose twenty-five ngoko terms reported in the literature to have krama inggil alternants, and asked informants if they had *alus* 'polished' alternants, avoiding more specific classificatory terms that might condition the answer. Speakers who supplied a form I then asked "Can it be said, my _____," using the elicited form in the blank with the krama first person pronoun. In this way I tried to exploit the general restriction on use of krama inggil for self-reference to determine without using problematic metalinguistic labels whether the form in question counted as honorific or nonhonorific basa for the speaker. If they accepted this construction, I asked about the same construction in ngoko to see if (as turned out to be the case) the form co-occurred only with and so was classifiable as krama vocabulary.

I deleted three of these twenty-five words from my list after I found out that none of the first ten informants knew them, and two because all informants knew them. I asked about no more than four or five (and often just one) during any one conversation to avoid quizzing speakers, especially younger ones, who might feel they were expected to know about things they did not. There is no guarantee that a person who can produce a certain form in an elicitation session will use that word in just the ways they report, but in a study of such manifestly little-used terms among an intergenerational sample of the

6. Some of these terms are so extremely limited in their range of reference and marginal in honorific usage that they can only be called krama inggil if one ignores real differences between them and more commonly used honorifics. Some Surakartans, both priyayi and non-priyayi, characterize such terms as *basa kedhaton* 'palace language', which is accurate insofar as they are (and probably were) used predominantly in and by those closely associated with the palace. See Errington 1982.

community I could only test a necessary and not a sufficient condition for their use.

The fairly coherent distribution of responses displayed in Figure 6 suggests that age is a primary but not the sole correlate of knowledge of honorifics. Informants 1 through 4, who knew the greatest number, are all more than fifty years old and still have fairly close familial and occupational connections with the court.[7] Informants 9 and 15, on the other hand, nobility of that same generation, know fewer forms than informants 7 and 8, both some thirty years their junior. The relevant social information is a little less obvious: 9 and 15 were both active for fifty years in national politics and the federal government in Jakarta. (Informant 9 had retired to Surakarta but still made frequent trips to the capital.) Informants 7 and 8 are both daughters of informant 1, as shown in Table 6, are of high nobility, and have never been out of close contact with their extended family around the palace.

They are agemates of informants 19, 20, and 21, offspring of informant 15, and of informants 17 and 18, offspring of informant 9. But these latter two sets of siblings knew far fewer honorific equivalents. Those who knew the fewest, informants 22 and 23, are commoners of no traditional status but, in contemporary Surakarta, are coequal classmates of other young informants. Figure 6 also shows that several honorifics are apparently used by some younger speakers as part of the krama vocabulary of polite address, not the krama inggil vocabulary of polite reference. This usage may be a recent development, insofar as only one speaker who reported at least one term to be basa usable for self-reference is older than twenty-five (informant 6, is in his mid-thirties).

In a curious way little-known honorifics are endowed with greater deferential expressiveness than others, just because they are known and used in restricted circles and presuppose relative intimacy with a referent. Commonly known honorifics are used by even the most conservative priyayi to some commoners, if only in formulaic salutations,[8] but use of other honorifics, whose meaning presupposes

---

7. For convenience of comparison, numbers used here identify the same informants as in Errington 1985:80–98.

8. For example, compare use of the honorific (*tindak*) 'go' in the madya

Figure 6. Distribution of knowledge of little-known krama inggil

(Ng, KI: gloss)	1	2	3	4	5	6	7	8	9	10	11	12	13	14	15	16	17	18	19	20	21	22	23	Percent known:
nangis/muwun: 'cry'	X	X	X	X	X	X	X	X	X¹	X	X	X	X¹	X¹	X	X	X	X¹	X	X	X	X¹	X¹	100
untu/waja: 'tooth'	X	X	X	X	X	X	X	X	X	X	X	X	X	X	X	X	X	X	X	X	X¹	X¹	X¹	100
umur/yuswa: 'age'	X	X	X	X	X	X	X	X	X	X	X	X	X	X¹	X	X	X¹	X	X	X	X	X¹	X¹	100
mata/paningal: 'eye'	X	X	X	X	X	X	X	X	X	X	X	X	X¹	X¹	X¹	X	X	X¹	X¹	X	X	X	X	100
irung/grana: 'nose'	X	X	X	X	X	X	X	X	X	X	X	X	X	X	X	X	X	X	X¹	X	X	X	X	100
tangi/wungu: 'wake up'	X	X	X	X	X	X	X	X	X	X	X	X	X	X	X	X	X¹	X	X	X	X	X	X	100
cangkem/thuthuk: 'mouth'	X	X	X	X	X	X	X	X¹	X	X	X	0	X	X	X	X	X	X	X	X¹	X	0	X¹	96
rambut/rikma: 'hair'	X	X	X	X	X	X	X	X	X	X	X	X	X	X	X	X	X¹	X¹	X¹	X¹	X	X¹	0	96
cukur/paras: 'haircut'	X	X	X	X	X	X	X	X	X	0	X	X	X¹	X¹	X	X	X¹	X¹	0	0	X¹	X¹	0	87
rai/(pa)suryan: 'face'	X	X	X	X	X	X	X	X	X	X	X	0	X	X	X	X	X	X	X	X	0	0	0	83
dada/jaja: 'chest'	X	X	X	X	X	0	X	X	X	X	0	X	X	X	X	X	0	0	0	0	0	0	0	61
kringet/riwé: 'sweat'	X	X	X	X	X	X	X	X¹	X	X	X	0	0	0	X	X	0	0	0	0	0	0	0	61
gulu/jangga 'neck'	X	X	X	X	X	X	X	X¹	X	X	X	X	X	X	X	0	0	X¹	X¹	0	0	X¹	0	61
alis/imba: 'eyebrow'	X	X	X	X	0	X	X	X	0	0	0	0	X¹	X¹	0	0	X¹	X¹	0	0	0	X¹	0	48
gelang/binggel: 'bracelet'	X	X	X	X	X¹	X	X	0	0	X	X	0	0	X¹	0	0	X	X	X	X	0	0	0	39
pipi/pengarasan: 'cheek'	X	X	X	0	X	0	0	0	X	X	X	0	0	0	0	0	0	0	0	0	0	0	0	35
brengos/rawis: 'moustache'¹	X	X	X	X	X	0	0	0	X	X	X	0	0	0	0	0	0	0	0	0	0	0	0	35
dengkul/jengku: 'knee'	X	X	X	X	0	0	X	X	0	0	0	X	0	0	0	0	0	0	0	0	0	0	0	30
geger/pengkeran: 'back'	X	X	X	X	0	X	0	0	0	0	0	0	0	0	0	0	0	0	0	0	0	0	0	26
sikut/siku: 'foot'	X	0	0	0	0	0	0	0	0	X	0	0	0	0	0	0	0	0	0	0	0	0	0	7
Percent known:	100	95	95	95	85	80	80	75	75	75	75	70	65	65	60	50	50	45	45	45	45	40	35	

"X" = Known by informant; reported to be unusable for speaker
"X¹" = Known by informant, reported to be usable for speaker
"0" = Unknown to informant

¹ Some sources list an alternate KI form, *gumbala*; no informant provided this as a KI form.
Percentages are calculated on the basis of knowledge of term only, and not reported mode of use of term.

Deference, reference, and the encoding of status 169

Table 6. Cross-Generation Variation in Knowledge of Krama Inggil

PARENT (% known as deferential)	OFFSPRING (% known as deferential)
1 (100%)	7,8 (75%)
4 (95%)	12,13 (65%)
9 (80%)	17 (50%)
	18 (45%)
15 (65%)	19–21 (45%)

social intimacy, serve as more than pro forma marks of respect and are inappropriate for reference to commoners who, older priyayi consistently suggested to me (focusing on reference to addressee), would not know them anyway.

This pattern helps to justify claims about relative deferential expressiveness of honorifics made on "nothing more than an impressionistic basis" by Wolff and Poedjosoedarmo:

> We may divide the honorifics into four groups: (1) honorifics which are used when an honorific is appropriate at all; (2) honorifics which are frequently used but which are occasionally omitted where an honorific is appropriate (they imply a higher status than (1)); (3) honorifics which are confined to careful speech and imply a very high status; (4) rarely-used honorifics.... [Group 4 is m]ost of the rest of the honorific vocabulary ... not common in ordinary conversations ... and ... normally used only to address or refer to persons to whom particularly high status is assigned (1982:40).

In effect they classify the bulk of the honorific vocabulary in an implicational hierarchy that correlates distribution of knowledge, frequencies of use, degrees of deferential import, and semantic domain. Honorifics glossable as 'going' and 'giving' are widely known and used, and fall into Wolff and Poedjosoedarmo's group 1. At the other extreme are honorific terms for body parts and functions, neither widely known nor commonly used, more markedly deferential, and falling into their group 4. In both respects little-known and little-used krama inggil count as a priyayi specialty, and the progressive

---

version of a common greeting *Ajeng tindak pundi?* ("Where are you going?"). On conservative priyayi use of honorifics in madya speech styles, see Errington 1985:155–56.

170 Deference, reference, and the encoding of status

loss of these honorifics reflects the progressive simplification of priyayi linguistic etiquette and lack of felt need to mark deference for intimates.

Indeterminacy, Ambiguity, and Vagueness

In word lists and dictionaries some honorifics are listed as alternants to several ngoko (and more often than not krama) roots, suggesting that their use introduces ambiguity, systematic or unsystematic, in Binnick's (1970) sense, into speech by encoding several distinct significations of several distinct if related ngoko terms. It is assumed that a given honorific serves in a given context of use as a semantic equivalent for just one such ngoko alternant, can therefore be assigned a reading just like that alternant, and so counts as polysemous. But the meanings of some ngoko roots that share a single honorific alternant are related clearly enough to suggest that their honorific "equivalent" may have a single signification that subsumes but is more abstract and general than all or some of them, or shares semantic content with just one ngoko lexeme and together with it subsumes the more specific significative content of its other ngoko alternants. Alternatively, honorifics may have meanings that are broader or more general than any single ngoko alternant, or may simply be indeterminate with respect to its ngoko equivalents and as such construable in communication as having content not exactly like that of any one ngoko term.

Whatever their system-internal nature, these nontransparent sense relations make for relatively indirect acts of reference in honorific as opposed to nonhonorific usage and require crucial recourse to syntactic, discursive, and social-contextual information for construal. They have possible analogues in ceremonial speech styles in aboriginal Australian languages like Dyirbal (Dixon 1971) and Guugu Yimiddhir (Haviland 1978). The Dyirbal at one time spoke a special "mother-in-law language," *Dyalnguy*, rather than "everyday" or "ordinary" language, *Guwal*, when in earshot of persons to whom they stood in certain proscribed kin relations. Verbs in Dyalnguy's comparatively limited lexicon stand in one-to-many relations at least superficially similar to those between honorifics and nonhonorifics in Javanese.

Deference, reference, and the encoding of status 171

Like Javanese speech styles, Dyalnguy and Guwal share phonological and grammatical systems but unlike ngoko, madya, and krama address styles share no vocabulary items at all. An obvious social functional difference is that Javanese honorifics are not parts of an address style per se, but a vocabulary for marking aspects of a social relation involving a referent. Use of Dyalnguy is keyed to the presence of an honored, avoided bystander who is neither addressee nor referent. Still, the relative parsimony of the two "special" vocabularies in relation to their respective "ordinary" vocabularies is suggestive, especially in light of Dixon's sophisticated analysis of the Dyirbal case. He has shown that one of several Guwal alternants counts as the "basic" or what he calls "nuclear" equivalent to a Dyalnguy verb, and is structurally superordinate to the rest in descriptions of underlying sense relations. Where the intensional content of nuclear verbs can be represented componentially with semantic primes, those of nonnuclear morphemes are treated as configurational complexes of nuclear and non-nuclear semantic material. The mother-in-law language is parsimonious yet semantically adequate because its verbs realize structurally basic elements of a single underlying system, supplementable and specifiable in discourse with added lexical material.

This patterned semantic relation suggests that the parsimonious Javanese honorific lexicon, concentrated in a relatively narrow semantic domain, could be treated as a similarly impoverished set of lexical resources. Consider in this respect the widely known krama inggil root *asta* (ngoko *tangan*) 'hand' and its derived verb forms *ngasta*, active transitive or intransitive, and *diasta*, passive and transitive.[9] Speakers who were asked to supply ngoko words that had *ngasta* for a polished (*alus*) equivalent all provided the forms listed in Table 7.[10] Later I presented these same speakers with the ngoko

---

9. In what follows I use for convenience sake the impersonal passive forms (ngoko: *di-*, krama: *dipun-*). Other transitive forms of *asta* inflected with the affixes *-i* and *-aké*, rarely used and only marginally acceptable, will not be considered here.

10. Older written sources (Walbeehm 1897, Gericke and Roorda 1901) do not mention *ngasta* as a possible alternant of *nggawé* or *nggawa*, and Walbeehm lists *ngasta* (transitive) as an honorific substitute for *nggebug* 'beat with a stick', which none of my informants accepted. More recent sources

172   Deference, reference, and the encoding of status

Table 7. Ngoko Alternants of *Ngasta*

nyekel	'grasp, grip, hold'
nggawé	'make'
nggawa	'carry'
nyambut-gawé	'have a job'

words in Table 7 and asked which was the 'basic' (*baku* or *pokok*) alternant to *ngasta*. Faced with this forced choice, four chose *nyambut-gawé*, five chose *nyekel*, and three chose *nggawa*.

They made their choices with difficulty and reluctance, all but one requesting a context of use. Any example would minimally eliminate the systematic transitive/intransitive ambiguity because the latter usage always involves lexical material referring to the object of whatever action is being carried out. *Ngasta* in sentences 1 and 2 can only share senses with some transitive nonhonorific equivalent, but in sentence 3 can only count as intransitive and so as an intransitive alternant to *nyambut-gawé* or *nyambut-damel*.

1. Mas Har mréné, ngasta[KI] layangan.
   Mas Har came here, carrying/holding/and made a kite.
2. Mas Har ngasta[KI] menapa?
   What is Mas Har carrying/holding/making?
3. Mas Har ngasta[KI] wonten kantor.
   Mas Har works in an office.

On other occasions I presented these speakers with a choice between the impersonal passive transitive ngoko equivalents of the verb *diasta*, and again asked for a "basic" ngoko equivalent, a task they found no easier outside of a context of use. Five speakers indicated that *dicekel* was somehow more basic, while four chose *digawa*.

The lack of consensus contrasts strongly enough with Dixon's results to suggest that sense relations between special and ordinary vocabularies in the two languages are basically different. Other evidence of differences between the two cases can be drawn from sense relations between some ngoko hyponyms of *gawa* presented in passive transitive form in Table 8.

(Poedjosoedarmo 1968b, Horne 1974) do treat *nggawé* and *nggawa* (and their krama equivalents) as alternants of *ngasta*.

Table 8. Some Hyponyms of *Digawa*

	... on the head'	*disunggi*
	... under the arm'	*dimpit*
digawa 'carried ...		
	... in the fingers'	*dicangking*
	... with a shoulderpole	*dipikul*

All speakers chose *digawa* as the basic member of this group, recognizing the same hyponymous relation exploited by one Javanese lexicographer (Poerwadarminta 1939) to characterize verbs in the semantic domain. They all further agreed, but no word list indicates, that *diasta* would be used rather than any of these hyponyms of *digawa* to speak of an honored person, although there are contingent reasons why the honorific would be rarely so used: persons of high status do not ordinarily carry objects on their head or on a shoulder pole, and so occasions on which speakers (or at any rate priyayi speakers) would consider speaking honorifically of someone engaging in either action would be rare.[11]

More important here is the fact that in use as honorific equivalent to these hyponyms of *gawa*, transitive *asta* can be used to speak of actions that do not involve the hand at all. Speakers found the notion of using some form of *mpit* 'to carry something under the arm' to refer to an honored person ludicrous, appropriate only by way of a joke. They preferred transitive *asta* even though the action thus predicated differs fundamentally from others of which *asta* may be predicated involving use of the hand, most obviously holding (predicated with forms of *cekel*). There is thus no obvious way to treat transitive *asta* as "equivalent" to both *gawa* and *cekel* save by assigning it some still broader, vaguer, or indeterminate meaning compatible with but distinct from both.

Different though the Dyalnguy and Javanese cases seem to be, the comparison between them is instructive as a demonstration of the vagueness that may accrue to some deferential usage, even if honor-

---

11. An idiom reported to but never observed by me allows an intimate male superior to be spoken of as bringing his wife with some form of the verb *cangking*.

ific lexemes are implicitly treated as polysemous when listed as equivalents to several distinct but related ngoko alternants. This underlying connection between the marking of deference and allusiveness of acts of reference is even more striking in honorific predicates of exchange.

Predicates of Exchange

The semantic domain of exchange includes krama inggil and krama andhap honorifics with relatively wide pragmatic ranges, and still more striking asymmetries between honorific and non-honorific linguistic resources. The collapse of semantic distinctions between honorifics quite effectively effaces differences between acts that do and do not involve exchange—that is, interaction that does and does not necessarily involve two social entities and is or is not mediated by an object of exchange. This is obvious, for instance, in correspondences between the honorific root *pundhut* and its ngoko "equivalents" (shown in Table 9) which are glossable as 'request' (*jaluk*), 'take' (*jupuk*), and 'buy' (*tuku*) and have a collective semantic range too broad to be easily glossed in Javanese or English. Like 'acquire' in English, *mundhut* may be used in some contexts to predicate acts of acquisition that do and do not involve exchange (like 'buying' and 'taking', respectively) but unlike any English or Javanese root can also be used like the ngoko lexeme *jaluk* to predicate acts of requesting, that is, utterances that serve to make known the speaker's desire to acquire something.

As Peirce (CP 2.86)[12] so clearly showed, actions of exchange—such as buying, giving, borrowing, lending, accepting, or speaking—are essentially triadic, involving at least two parties and a mediating object of exchange. Acts of requesting made by someone to someone for something, and acts of buying something by someone from someone, presuppose that the patient of the action has the right and capability to participate or not in the action; where there is no reciprocal orientation, there is no exchange. Actions of taking, on the other hand,

---

12. I use here and elsewhere the de facto standard form of citation—volume number (here 2) and paragraph number (here 86) from Peirce's *Collected Papers*, edited by C. Hartshorne, P. Weiss, and A. Burks.

Deference, reference, and the encoding of status 175

Table 9. Honorific Verbs of Acquisition

Ngoko	Krama inggil	Krama andhap	Gloss		
tuku	mundhut	—	buy	X buys Y from Z	(Z necessarily a person)
njaluk	mundhut	nyuwun	request	X requests Y from Z	(Z necessarily a person)
njupuk	mundhut	—	take	X takes Y (from Z)	(Z not necessarily a person)

do not intrinsically involve two persons in mediated conduct and reciprocally defined roles, nor are they in and of themselves acts of exchange. A structural correlate of this semantic contrast is that *pundhut* has a krama andhap equivalent (*suwun*, discussed later) as an alternant of the ngoko root glossable as 'request' (*jaluk*)[13] but not 'take' (*jupuk*).

The indeterminacy of *pundhut* thus effaces the semantic distinction between mediated social actions involving interactively coequal parties and simple physical actions that lead to acquisition by the agent of the action. This dichotomy is reflected in speakers' responses to requests for a "basic" ngoko equivalent for *mundhut* (the active form of *pundhut*). Ten of twelve speakers chose *njupuk*, even though *jupuk* can't be treated as somehow nuclear or "basic" with respect to *jaluk* 'request' and *tuku* 'buy'; no configuration of lexical material including *jupuk* (or 'take' or 'acquire') adequately represents the meaning of *jaluk* (or 'request'). A request counts as an attempt to acquire, but not all attempts to acquire count as requests.

Pundhut is semantically indeterminate with respect to *tuku* and *njupuk* in something of the way that "acquire" is indeterminate with respect to "buy" and "steal," so significatively broad as to be really

---

13. That there is no krama andhap verb equivalent to *tuku* can be attributed to the fact that high status persons do not normatively sell things (on which more later) and so are not normatively bought from. In fact, it is not uncommon in everyday use for persons to have recourse to nonhonorific euphemisms when speaking of buying in such situations glossable as 'exchange' or 'change for'.

vague, and in use highly dependent on context for construal. This collapse in lexical distinctions between actions of acquisition that do and do not involve exchange involves an obvious, obligatory lack of semantic explicitness in speech, and so too for a correspondingly crucial context dependence for proper construal of use.

'Request' (transitive verb) is used here as a gloss for *njaluk* and *nyuwun* not because of its stylistic feel compared with 'ask' or 'ask for', but because its syntactic behavior more closely resembles that of the Javanese verbs. Like *njaluk* and *nyuwun*, 'request' is ordinarily followed by syntactic material referring to the thing requested/asked for (sentence 4) rather than to the person who is requested of/asked (sentence 5), and can be used in grammatically well-formed sentences with a complement (in Javanese usually marked with a complementizer *supaya* 'in order that') that refers to a state of affairs that the asker wishes or hopes will be brought about (sentence 6).

4. Aku njaluk/nyuwun[KA] buku (karo Pak Har).
    I requested a book[KA] (from Pak Har).
*5. Aku njaluk/nyuwun[KA] Pak Har buku.
    I requested Pak Har[KA] a book.
6. Dhik Har njaluk/nyuwun supaya Ibu kondur.
    Dhik Har requested that mother go home.

The pragmatic significance of *suwun* is in flux, apparently being assimilated to the krama vocabulary of polite address, and so displacing its former krama alternant *tedha*, which at one time was the krama alternant to ngoko roots meaning *pangan* 'eat' and *jaluk* 'request', but now has only the former meaning. The change is recent, and not entirely complete. Were *suwun* still functioning solely as a krama andhap honorific, sentence 7 would be pragmatically unacceptable, and would not have been provided by speakers as the *alus* equivalent to sentence 8 to predicate an act of deferential request to speaker.

7. Dhik Har arep njaluk dhuwit karo aku.
8. Dhik Har badhe nyuwun[KA] artha kaliyan kula.
    Dhik Har will request money from me.

Some older priyayi used the active form of *tedha* to translate sentence 7, and I observed its use by an older, conservative speaker once in spontaneous interaction, but all agreed that such usage was unusual nowadays. Use of *nedha* in place of *nyuwun* made sentence 8

Deference, reference, and the encoding of status

Table 10. Honorific Predicates of Disposal

Ngoko	Krama inggil	Krama andhap	Gloss
wènèh	paring	caos, atur, unjuk	give
saji	paring	caos	make an offering
dokok	paring	—	place, put
sèlèh	paring	—	lay down, place

nonsensical for younger speakers, meaning 'Dhik Har will eat money with me.' Another reflex of the ongoing change in pragmatic value of *suwun* is the fact that it can still be used by all priyayi speakers in ngoko speech as in sentences 4 and 6 (i.e., the style called ngoko *alus* in Chapter 4) like honorific but not krama lexemes.

What can awkwardly be called honorific predicates of disposal, listed in Table 10, are also vague and also stand in opaque sense relations to their four ngoko verb roots. They share the single krama inggil "equivalent" *paring,* and the two ngoko roots significative of actions of exchange (*wènèh* and *saji*) have, as one would expect, krama andhap equivalents. Here too honorific referential resources efface distinctions between terms significative of the actions of high-status persons through which they do or do not dispose of or relinquish something through actions of exchange.

Unjuk is the least widely known of the three krama andhap terms, used only by priyayi in and around the palace, and at one time had the general sense 'to raise up'. Now it is used in the sense of 'give' only by conservative priyayi for such actions directed to those of very high status.[14] It is the much more widely known as a transitive, unsuffixed krama inggil verb meaning 'drink' (ngoko, krama: *ombé*), once used figuratively and allusively in the sense of 'to raise up', of a vessel.

Caos (or *saos*) is the krama andhap alternant to ngoko *wènèh* and *saji,* used to predicate actions of giving of things to persons as well

---

14. In these cases, it is used with the petrified active verb marker *-(u)m-* in *munjuk,* or in a transitive forms marked by *-i* and *-aké*. In some treatises it is classified as "palace language;" see Errington 1982 and sources discussed there.

as offerings to supernatural beings (*sajèn*). (Both were probably derived from *saji* by the sorts of semiregular sound changes discussed in Chapter 7.) Their semantic ranges are relatively narrower than *atur*, which may be used to predicate actions of exchange of physical things, but also actions of speaking in constructions discussed in the next section. *Paring* does not count as an alternant of *saji* because an act of making an offering is always carried out by an inferior to superior, perhaps supernaturally powerful entity. But forms of *paring* do count as krama inggil equivalents of forms of the ngoko verb roots *wènèh* 'give' and *sèlèh* or *dokok* 'place, put', effacing the lexical distinction between honored persons' actions that do and do not involve actions of exchange. Most speakers asked to provide a basic ngoko equivalent of *maringi*—active transitive form of *paring* suffixed with *-i* to mark indirect object of the action of giving—chose *mènéhi* with little hesitation. But *wènèh* cannot be treated as underlyingly equivalent to *paring* any more than *jupuk* can be treated as equivalent to *pundhut*, because acts of exchange predicable with forms of *wènèh* are not reducible to actions of placing, relinquishing, or giving up. There is an analogous set of sense relations between honorific forms based on the two roots: where someone other than honored person is benefactee/recipient of an action of exchange, the lexical distinction between the two sorts of disposal is suppressed.

These most striking cases of nonisomorphic correspondences between nonhonorifics and honorifics show that the semantic domain of exchange is the focus of encoded, obligatory indeterminacy which obliges one to speak of persons honorifically not as purchasers but takers, not as givers but relinquishers. In effect, the identity of other, inferior parties to such mediated exchange are downplayed in favor of a pregiven lexical focus on the enduringly superior party to the occasion of exchange. Outside of the performative utterances considered in the next section, however, krama andhap verbs of exchange have relatively restricted meanings in the domain of exchange and alternate transparently with their nonhonorific equivalents. Honorific roots serving to refer to and perform acts of speaking, special types of speech exchange indexically bound to face-to-face interaction, are a different case that must be considered in some detail to make sense of the system as a whole.

Acts of Linguistic Exchange

Honorific verbs of speaking are the most irregular and idiomatic basa lexemes, and least satisfactorily fit the generalization that ngoko/basa alternations are isomorphic and transparent. So it is difficult to describe them concisely, and here striking semantic discrepancies between performative and nonperformative uses of krama andhap roots are sketched with an eye to performative directives, in which honorific usage is maximally indirect. As Table 11 shows, krama andhap verbs of speaking are few in comparison with ngoko and krama inggil lexicons.

Of immediate interest are the two ngoko verb roots *kandha* and *crita*,[15] glossable as 'speak' and 'tell about' and inflectable for object focus in the ways cataloged in Table 12. Both can be used intransitively, as can their krama inggil and krama andhap alternants *ngendika* and *matur*. *Ngendika*, used transitively and intransitively, is a petrified active verb form.[16] *Matur* is a petrified, active intransitive verb form marked with the archaic infix *-(u)m-*, realized with vowel-initial stems like *atur* as *m-*. Both roots can be used in active and passive transitive constructions suffixed with *-i* to focus on indirect object/addressee, or with *-aké* to focus on direct object/content of speech. Forms in the first column of Table 12 would thus be used in response to a question like "What is she doing?" the second to a question like "Who is she talking to?" and the third to a question like "What is she talking about?"

Matur's syntactic idiomaticity may be an indirect result of its pragmatic function as marker of low status of speaker/agent of exchange in relation to someone else presupposed and/or referred to as addressee/recipient of exchange. It may be used with a following object not headed by a preposition (as in sentence 9), where *kandha* (10 vs. 11) and *ngendika* (12 vs. 13) may not. *Ngendika* marks high status of referent in relation to one or both speech partners, but is not keyed to the status relation between parties to speech exchange.

15. I ignore here the many roots, some onomatopoeic, that are used to describe acts of speaking in terms of its affect and sound quality; lists and descriptions of some of these can be found in Padmasusastra 1912.

16. It can, for instance, be passivized as in *dingendikani* 'be spoken to', which is, however, rare for reasons discussed later.

180   Deference, reference, and the encoding of status

Table 11. Some Verbs of Speaking

Krama inggil	Ngoko	Krama andhap	Gloss
ngendika	kandha	(m)atur	speak
paringi priksa	crita	aturi/caosi priksa	tell about
pundhut priksa	takon	suwun priksa	ask
timbal	undang	atur	summon
dhawuh	kon	atur	order
—	celuk	atur	use a vocative to
—	ulem	atur	invite

Table 12. Inflected Verbs of Speaking

0 (act)	-i (addressee)	-aké (content)
kandha 'speak'	kandhani 'tell to'	kandhakaké 'speak about'
crita 'relate (a circumstance)'	critani 'relate (a circumstance) to someone'	critakaké 'relate a circumstance'
ngendika	ngendikani	ngendikaké
matur	aturi	aturaké

```
 9. Har arep    matur^KA       Bapak.
10. Har arep    kandha  karo   Bapak.
*11. Har arep   kandha         Bapak.
        WILL    SAY     WITH
    Har will speak to/tell Bapak.
*12. Bapak arep ngendika^KI            Har.
13. Bapak arep  ngendika^KI   kaliyan  Har.
        WILL    SAY           WITH
    Bapak will tell Har.
```

More obvious and striking are idioms commonly used to predicate honorifically acts of speaking that are focused on the recipient of the action. As Table 12 indicates, *aturi* and *ngendikani* can be so used in active or passive constructions, although the former is much more common than the latter, which I heard only once, and was character-

Deference, reference, and the encoding of status 181

ized by several informants as giving the feeling that a superior was advising or admonishing an inferior.[17]

Other very common expressions contain an honorific root glossable as 'give'—*aturi* or *caosi* in krama andhap, *paringi* in krama inggil—in combination with the verb root *priksa* (alternatively *pirsa*), itself a polysemous root glossable as 'know', 'understand', 'see', or 'examine'.[18] These are not syntactically regular configurations of verb and object noun phrase, but idiomatically frozen phrases that explicitly (i. e., lexically) represent the nature of such actions as exchange of which inferior is agent and superior is recipient. *Priksa* cannot be treated syntactically as either as topicalized direct object (sentence 14) (compare *buku* 'book' in 16) or indirect object (sentence 15) (compare *Bapak* in 17).

* 14. Sing dicaosaké^{KA}/diaturaké^{KA}/diparingaké^{KI}, priksa.
* 15. Sing dicaosi^{KA}/diaturi^{KA}/diparingi^{KI}, priksa.
     What was given was knowing.
  16. Sing dicaosaké^{KA}/diaturaké^{KA}/diparingaké^{KI}, buku.
     What was given was a book.
  17. Sing dicaosi^{KA}/diaturi^{KA}/diparingi^{KI}, Bapak.
     The one who was given to was Bapak.

Passive forms of these constructions are acceptable when the focus is on addressee/recipient of the action, as shown by sentence 19 (equivalent semantically to 18), sentence 21 (equivalent to 20) and sentence 23 (equivalent to 22).

  18. Sapa sing dikandhani?
  19. Sapa sing diaturi^{KA}/dicaosi^{KA}/diparingi^{KI} priksa?
     Who was told?
  20. Sing dikandhani Mas Har.
  21. Sing diaturi^{KA}/dicaosi^{KA}/diparingi^{KI} priksa Mas Har.
     Mas Har was told.

17. *Ngendikakaké*, on the other hand, carried no such overtones though, according to Walbeehm (1897), at one time it was used to signify speech acts that are orders.

18. *Priksa* and *pirsa*, historically distinct roots with similar meanings, have now effectively merged in many priyayi and non-priyayi dialects. *Priksa* is an example of an honorific that has a distinct sense as a "plain" ngoko verb (meaning 'examine'), but when used in a wider sense is endowed with honorific import.

22. Bapak arep takkandhani.
23. Bapak arep takcaosi[KA] priksa.
    I will tell Bapak.

These constructions are pragmatically idiomatic in the sense that the krama inggil *priksa* is neutral with respect to status of person of whom it is predicated, combining with both krama andhap and krama inggil predicates of exchange to speak of lower-status or higher-status agent, respectively.[19] In these constructions *priksa* is not significative of a state of 'knowing' which is predicated either of an agent or a recipient of an act of telling, but is merely diacritic of the expression as referential of exchange of speech to inform rather than summon or order, on which more below.

Constructions in which the verb of exchange is inflected to focus on the content or act of speech itself, like sentences 24 and 25, are unacceptable to almost all speakers. Topics or content of acts of speaking predicated with these constructions are more commonly introduced with an optional prepositional phrase, as in sentence 26.

?24. Sing diaturi[KA]/diaturaké[KA] priksa apa?
?25. Sing diparingi[KI]/paringaké[KI] priksa apa?
     What was told about?
26. Bapak wis takaturi[KA] priksa bab soal kuwi.
    I've already told/spoken to Bapak about that problem.

More interesting examples of *priksa*'s diacritic function are krama responses (28 and 29) to directive 27, hypothetically used by a mother to her child to instruct him or her to inform his or her father that the speaker has gone to the market. It contains a morphological ngoko imperative form (see later discussion) of the root *atur*, marked for focus on the recipient of the act of speaking that the child is being directed to make. Thus the mother uses the strategy of *mbasakaké* with respect to the child's act of speaking to the father, as well as to her own act of going out (with the krama inggil verb *tindak*).

27. Bapak-   -mu   atur-[KA] -ana   yèn   aku   tindak[KI] pasar.
    FATHER   YOUR   SAY   IMP. IO THAT   I   GO   MARKET
                                 FOCUS
    Tell[KA] your father that I've gone to the market.

19. Prescriptively inclined conservative priyayi told me that in use for acts of telling by high-status to low-status speech partner, krama and ngoko alternants to *priksa*, krama *sumerep* or ngoko *sumurup*, should be used. I never observed these or any other speakers using such constructions.

28. Inggih, (Bapak)   mangké kula atur-ᴷᴬ -i   priksa.
    YES   FATHER   LATER   I   SAY   IO MRKR   KNOW
    Yes, later I'll tellᴷᴬ father.

?29. Inggih, (Bapak) mangké kula atur-ᴷᴬ -i.
     YES   FATHER   LATER   I   SAY   IO MRKR
     Yes, later I'll speakᴷᴬ to father.

Sentence 28 is typical of the responses speakers provided as responses to 27. Sentence 29 they accepted as grammatical but "lacking appropriateness" (*kurang cocok*) in the context provided. Several amended sentence 29 by adding a complement phrase referring to the content of the message to be relayed.

Honorific verbs for asking a question—alternants of the ngoko verb glossable as 'ask a question' *takon* (krama: *takèn*)—combine *priksa* with the krama inggil verb *pundhut* 'acquire' (sentence 30) or the krama andhap verb *suwun* 'request' (sentence 31). The ungrammaticality of sentences 32 and 33 shows that here too *priksa* functions neither syntactically as direct object nor pragmatically to confer high status on the agent or recipient of acts of asking.

30. Bapak mundhutᴷᴵ priksa kaliyan kula.
    Bapak askedᴷᴵ me (a question).
31. Kula nyuwunᴷᴬ priksa kaliyan Bapak.
    I askedᴷᴬ Bapak (a question).
*32. Sing kula suwunᴷᴬ (kaliyan Bapak), priksa.
    What I requestedᴷᴬ (from Bapak), is knowing.
*33. Sing Bapak mundhutᴷᴵ (kaliyan kula), priksa.
    What Bapak acquiredᴷᴵ (from me), is knowing.

The important point here is that all of these constructions explicitly (i.e., lexically) encode reference to acts of speech as species of exchange, yet do so with honorific verbs (*aturi, priksa*) that are themselves ambiguous or indeterminate.

Affixed with -*i*, *atur*'s strikingly broad semantic range extends beyond those of *wèneh* 'give' and *kandha* 'speak' to other verbs of speaking in Table 11 glossable as 'invite' (*ulem*), 'summon' (*undang*) and 'use a vocative to' (*celuk*). Attempts to elicit a "basic" ngoko equivalent of either the active or passive form of *aturi* were almost entirely unsuccessful because, even in as neutral a syntactic context as that of sentence 34, speakers' forced choices varied almost equally between forms of *wèneh*, *kandha* or *crita*, and *undang*. All accepted as possible alternants *celuk* and *undang*.

184 Deference, reference, and the encoding of status

34. Bapak wis di- -atur-^KA -i.
    ALREADY IMPRSNL ? IO
       PASS   MRKR

Informants regularly used *aturi* as honorific alternant to *undang* ('invite, summon') in hypothetical responses to sentence 35,[20] of which sentence 36 is typical; they added lexical material, in seven of ten cases the krama *mriki* (krama, ngoko *mréné*) 'to come here', thereby explicating the nature of the future action predicated of a lower-status speaker to some higher-status speech partner. All found responses like sentence 37 (compare 31), without additional material, to be inappropriate (*kurang cocok*). They disambiguated *aturi* here much as they did in the sense of 'tell' (*kandha*), by adding lexical material.

35. Eyang-^KI -mu mengko undang- -en mréné, nak.
  GRAND- YOUR LATER INVITE IMP. COME CHILD
  PARENT   IO   HERE (PAREN-
             FOCUS   THETICAL)
  Later, invite your grandfather over here, child.

36. Inggih, éyang mangké kula aturi^KA mriki.
?37. Inggih, éyang mangké kula aturi.^KA
  Yes, I will invite(?)^KA grandfather (to come here).

In the sense of *celuk* 'call to, use a vocative to' as in sentences 40 and 41, hypothetical basa responses to 38, active and passive forms of *aturi* both apparently serve in predicates of acts of address. But speakers all rejected the passive construction [first person pronoun + *aturi*] in sentence 40, syntactically equivalent to that in 39 with *celuk*, and offered instead (if I had not already proffered) the active verb form as in 41.

38. Kowé N- celuk wong kuwi piyé?
  YOU ACT. CALL PERSON THAT HOW
     VRB. TO   INTERR.
     MRKR
  How do you address/call to that person?

20. Ordinarily priyayi would *mbasakaké* to the child by using a form of *aturi* rather than *undang*, but speakers accepted sentence 35 as hypothetically possible usage.

39.	Wong	kuwi	tak-	-celuk	Bapak.
?40.	Tiyang	menika	kula	aturi[KA]	Bapak.
	PERSON	THAT	I	CALL	
				PASS	

That person I address as/call Bapak.

41.	Kula	N-	-aturi[KA]	tiyang	menika Bapak.
	I	ACT.	CALL(?)	PERSON	THAT
		VRB.	(KA)		
		MRKR			

I call[KA] that person Bapak.

Here too speakers avoided passive *aturi* in utterances referential of speaker as agent and addressee as recipient of speech. In doing so they also avoid an idiomatic deferential performative formula endowed with directive force.

Deferential Directives

The ways Javanese communicate their wishes concerning others' behavior and the states of affairs others might bring about—ranging from blunt, straightforward orders to manipulations of prosody, context, lexicon, and conversational inference—all deserve a chapter of their own. In all speech styles speakers use various devices—invitational or optative particles, hedges, question markers, impersonal passive constructions, and others—to soften and dissemble the force of directive utterances that count as "attempts ... by the speaker to get the hearer to do something" (Searle 1972:13). Crucial for present purposes are deferential directives performed with krama andhap verbs of speaking, and especially use of *aturi* to perform directives that are in a sense not directives at all, and limiting cases of honorific lexical indirectness.

A convenient way to sketch polite imperatives is to contrast the felt deference of forms of the verb roots *atur* 'to say, give' and *suwun* 'to request' in directive uses. These contrast strikingly with their apparent semantic content. Speakers consistently evinced feelings that directives performed with *suwun*, like sentence 42, are somehow less honorific (*urmat*) and refined (*alus*) than those performed with *aturi*, like sentence 43. Both have the 'feeling of an order' (Indonesian *rasa perintah*), as one

42. Mas Har kula suwun[KA]   (supaya)   mundhut buku   menika.
43. Mas Har kula aturi[KA]   mundhut buku   menika.
    I   ASK(?)[KA]   IN ORDER TAKE   BOOK   THIS
         SAY TO(?)[KA]   TO
Mas Har(= addressee) I ask(?)/order(?)[KA] to take this book.

speaker put it, but sentence 42 generally felt, to quote the same speaker, more "pushy," (Indonesian: *mendorong*), more (said another) as if one was trying to "force" (Javanese: *meksa*) the addressee who "had" (*kudu*) to do something. The speaker who provided sentences 42 and 43, in fact, contrasted their felt effect by saying: "With *suwun* it feels as if I want you to buy it because I need the money. With *aturi* it feels as if I'm telling you to do something that's for your own good, that you'll do well by doing what I'm asking." A reflex of this general feeling that *suwun* is less refined (*alus*) in these performative constructions is the relative awkwardness of combining it with the first-person pronoun *dalem* with which it is not "equal," (*seimbang*) as one person said, because *dalem* is addressed only to those of markedly higher status, but *suwun* is not. *Dalem* with *aturi*, on the other hand, is fine.

Suwun is commonly glossed as and alternates quite transparently with *jaluk* 'to request' in syntactic constructions structurally similar to many in which 'request' appears in closest English translations. *Aturi*, on the other hand, appears to alternate with *kon*, 'to order', and no other ngoko verbs of speaking in performative constructions like those in sentences 44 to 50. In simple constructions with predicates of states and no complementizer, as in sentences 44 to 47 the only ngoko verb acceptable is *kon* (44) and the only acceptable honorific verb is *aturi*(45).[21] Both ngoko *jaluk* (49 vs. 47) and krama andhap *suwun* (48 vs. 46) require a complementizer glossable as 'in order to be' (ngoko *supaya*, krama *supados*). Use of *kandhani* 'say to' (50) is unacceptable with or without a complementizer. Crucial here is the contrast in interpretations speakers gave for sentences 44 (with *kon*) and 49 (with *jaluk*). Use of *kon* was consistently construed as descriptive, rather than performative, of an act of ordering.

21. More common are directives of states or qualities with the relativizer/topicalizer *sing* (ngoko, madya) or *ingkang* (krama), to which can be optionally added elements that clearly mark or soften imperative force.

44.	(Kowé)	tak- -kon	sabar.
45.	(Panjenengan)	tak- -aturi[KA]	sabar.
*46.	(Panjenengan)	tak- -suwun[KA]	sabar.
*47.	(Kowé)	tak- -jaluk	sabar.
48.	(Panjenengan)	tak- -suwun[KA]	supaya	sabar.
49.	(Kowé)	tak- -jaluk	supaya	sabar.
*50.	(Kowé)	tak- -kandhani	(supaya)	sabar.
	YOU	I		PATIENT

(You) be patient.

Ngoko imperatives are commonly marked with an elaborate morphological modal paradigm, which cannot be discussed at length here,[22] and *kon* is practically always used and construed as nonperformative in force. Speakers all placed sentence 44 in a context of use to speak of some past, habitual, or potential act of ordering, rather than an act of issuing an order in the present. Some speakers spontaneously repeated the example I offered them, adding some particle or time adverbial that clearly presupposed its referential nonperformative use. It is remarkable for more reasons than can be discussed here that performative use of *kon* is at best marginal and, to the degree it is in use, is relatively polite just because it is not necessarily or even normally construed as a directive.[23]

Sentences 48 and 49, which can be translated more closely as "(You) I request in order to be patient," have active equivalents with obligatory complementizers as in sentences 51 vs. 52.[24]

22. Partial descriptions of imperatives and other directives may be found in Keeler 1984:227–31, of imperatives and related voluntatives and modal forms in Ras 1982:133–41, of imperatives and propositives (see Chapter 7) in Robson 1976:75–78. Examples are sentences 27 and 35.

23. It suggests, for instance, that McCawley's remarks (1981:208) on the availability of verbs of speaking in all languages for performative use need to be qualified. In some thirty-five hours of spontaneous conversation recorded in my absence, I have just one performative use of *kon*, that by an adult, educated daughter to her uneducated mother. Another possible example combining performative *kon* with a morphological marker is in Padmasusastra 1907:87.

24. Some speakers accepted active *jaluk* and *suwun* without complementizers if pronounced with a clear, almost stylized rising intonation on the verb, and followed by a brief pause to mark prosodically the beginning of the complement.

51a. Aku nyuwun[KA] supaya (panjenengan) sabar.
51b. Aku njaluk supaya (kowé) sabar.
   I request that (you) be patient.

*52a. Aku nyuwun[KA] sabar.
*52b. Aku njaluk sabar.
   I request be patient.

Complements of both *suwun* and *jaluk* obligatorily contain material referential of an agent of requested action (so, 53a and 53b are ungrammatical) who may be specified as addressee (as in 54, 55, 57, and 59) or not (56, 58). The object of a transitive verb in the complement phrase may be fronted to the beginning (55, 56, 59) or out of that complement (57, 58).

??53a. Aku nyuwun[KA] (supaya) mundhut[KI] buku iki.
??53b. Aku njaluk (supaya) njupuk buku iki.
   I ask take this book.

54a. Aku nyuwun[KA] (supaya) panjenengan mundhut[KI] buku iki.
54b. Aku njaluk (supaya) kowé njupuk buku iki.
   I ask that you take this book.

55a. Aku nyuwun[KA] (supaya) buku iki panjenengan pundhut[KI].
55b. Aku njaluk (supaya) buku iki kok- -jupuk.
   I ask that this book be taken by you.

56a. Aku nyuwun[KA] (supaya) buku iki dipundhut[KI].
56b. Aku njaluk (supaya) buku iki dipundhut[KI].
   I ask that this book be taken.

57a. Buku iki taksuwun[KA] supaya panjenengan pundhut[KI].
57b. Buku iki takjaluk supaya kok- -jupuk.
   This book I ask that you take.

58a. Buku iki taksuwun[KA] supaya dipundhut[KI].
58b. Buku iki takjaluk supaya dijupuk.
   This book I ask to be taken.

59a. Taksuwun[KA] supaya buku iki panjenengan pundhut[KI].
59b. Takjaluk supaya buku iki panjenengan pundhut[KI].
   I ask that this book you take.

On the other hand, no lexical material may occur between directly used *aturi* or its lexical equivalent *kon* and any following verb, but both allow an object noun phrase to be fronted out of a complement phrase (as in 60a and 60b). This may be the only construction in Javanese in which an active verb is allowably preceded by its object noun phrase. *Jaluk* and *suwun* do not (61).

```
60a. Buku iki  (panjenengan) tak- aturiᴷᴬ           mundhutᴷᴵ.
60b. Buku iki  (kowé)         tak- -kon              njupuk.
*61a. Buku iki (panjenengan) tak- suwunᴷᴬ (supaya)  mundhutᴷᴵ.
*61b. Buku iki (kowé)         tak- jaluk   (supaya)  njupuk.
     BOOK THIS YOU            I    PASS    IN        TAKE
                                           ORDER
                                           THAT
```
This book (you) I ask(?)/(order?) to take.

This clear syntactic parallel between *atur* and *kon* may make it seem peculiar that constructions with *aturi* should somehow be felt as more "refined" than those with *suwun*, which corresponds so closely to *jaluk*. Performative use of *aturi* has imperative force, presupposing speaker's right to compliance from an addressee, whereas *suwun* has the force of a request that under some circumstances an addressee may reasonably decline to fulfill. Two reasons why this should be the case suggest themselves.

The first reason is that this distinctive syntactic parallel between *aturi* and *kon* is found between an obligatorily performative formula in the former case, but a nonperformative, descriptive use in the latter. Sentences like 60a are indubitably imperative in their illocutionary force, yet to all structural appearances resemble sentences with ngoko verbs like 60b that are not performatively used and so are nonindexical in their significances. Constructions with ngoko *jaluk* as in sentence 61b, on the other hand, are performative just like those with their basa equivalent *suwun* in 61a. Despite the politeness attributable to use of *suwun* by virtue of its overt lexical content, the indexicality it shares in performative use with its ngoko alternant seems to endow its use with a quality of immediacy and makes it, recalling one speaker's term, 'pushy' (*mendorong*).

The second reason for the relative politeness of *aturi* is its encoded indeterminacy, that is, its availability as an alternant for a large number of ngoko terms. *Suwun* alternates only and quite transparently with *jaluk*, but *atur* alternates with four distinct ngoko verbs of speaking, and a verb glossable as 'give'(*wénèh*) as well. Performative directive use of *atur* is construable as such not just semantically, that is, by assigning it the intensional meaning of the ngoko *kon* 'order', but configurationally because the highly idiomatic formula [first person passive + *aturi*] is used just to perform a directive, and avoided in nonperformative utterances. There is no semantic reason why the active form *ngaturi* should never be used to perform an imperative (40 vs. 41) or that nonperformative uses of the construction [first person pronoun + *aturi*] should be consistently avoided or signaled by additional lexical material (28 vs. 29, 36 vs. 37). The reason is rather that directive force of *aturi* is signaled configurationally by the frozen construction in which it is so used, rather than the semantic content it shares with some basic ngoko verb of speaking.

If one simply assumes that such honorifics' meanings are the sum or shared content of the meanings of their several ngoko "equivalents," it is difficult to avoid the peculiar conclusion that when speaking basa it is more polite to order (i.e., perform directives with the honorific "equivalent" of *kon*) than to request (i.e., perform directives with the honorific "equivalent" of *jaluk*). That very peculiarity is symptomatic of the fact that honorifics used in just these indexically significant directives do not really count as semantic equivalents to nonhonorifics. Rather than consider *aturi* an honorific verb for speaking that is stylistically opposed to a range of ngoko verbs, it may be better to consider it as the honorific verb negatively opposed to the only other krama andhap verb of speaking, *suwun*. Because of its highly impoverished semantic content, it lends allusiveness to performative usage. That *aturi* alternates in directive constructions with no ngoko verb of speaking suggests that in performative directive acts—presupposing socially of relative statuses, rights, and duties of speech participants, and referentially of the face-to-face relation between agent and recipient of directive use—we find the limiting case of encoded avoidance in the deferential lexicon. *Aturi*'s mode of reference is then indexical, and its referential content is then conveyed configuratively in a construction that mitigates both the indexical mode of significance and semantic specificity of the performative verb it contains.

Honorific Reference and Avoidance

As a set of terms with pragmatic significance keying to identity of referent, honorifics resemble so-called taboo vocabularies found in other languages in Indonesia, Southeast Asia, the Pacific, and elsewhere in the world.[25] Under the assumption that ngoko is the "underlying" language, and therefore the best metalanguage for all basa vocabularies, each honorific can be said to diverge from the "normal" way of speaking of persons and to be less "direct" insofar as honorific use requires a further significative step from signifier of the "special" word to signified of the "ordinary" word. Unlike basa address vocabularies, most honorifics in this respect can be seen as a means for avoiding "ordinary" words proscribed for honored persons. Given the general tenor of deferential behavior traditionally adopted to superiors, and the semantic overlap between socially contrasting vocabularies of deference, intimacy, and abuse, it is not difficult to see honorifics as vehicles of recurring, interactionally important proscriptive linguistic rituals that, as Goffman (1967:62) puts it, allow one to "keep at a distance from the recipient" (where "recipient" is referent who may or may not be speech partner.)

Whether or not this is an appropriate way to deal with most honorifics that stand in one-to-one correspondences with ngoko alternants, it is very suggestive for honorifics that stand in one-to-many relations with their ngoko alternants and therefore encode lexical indeterminacy in the speech style system. We have seen how these lend a very real communicative indirectness to honorific reference, especially when speaking of acts of exchange, and above all when predicating and performing acts of linguistic exchange. Although it is generally correct to assume that each honorific signifier shares a signified with a single ngoko alternant, conspicuous exceptions in just these semantic domains suggest that they are interactively crucial and socially salient objects of indexical or nonindexical reference.

25. For speculation on historical relations between Javanese basa vocabularies and *saali* words in Galela, spoken in the Malukus, and other Indonesian ethnic languages, see Kern (1917). Other related phenomena in the area are *andung* words used of the dead among the Batak, and so-called camphor vocabularies and tin mining words on the Malay peninsula (Shaw 1971, Skeat and Blagden 1906).

192 Deference, reference, and the encoding of status

Performative acts are structurally and semantically treated so as to have real lexical indeterminacy. Because it conflates lexical distinctions between acts that do and do not involve exchange, the krama inggil lexicon semantically effaces inferior's partnership in acts of exchange as partner to a superior. Because it conflates lexical distinctions between all acts of speaking that are not acts of requesting, krama andhap verbs of exchange semantically foreground speaking as an act of exchange while effacing the difference between directive and nondirective speech acts.

The special social sensitivity of acts of exchange can be traced to underlying tensions between the enduring differences in social status that honorific use presupposes, and the complementary, reciprocal equality of parties to exchange, which intrinsically involves agents and recipients of acts of (linguistic) exchange. It seems to be this aspect of exchange to which the the semantic indirectness of honorifics "naturally" keys. To speak honorifically of exchange is to forgo some ngoko term that would name it specifically, and simultaneously to rely on shared knowledge of context to construe use of some semantically broader honorific. This is another face of the allusiveness, indirectness, or what Javanese call the *alus*ness of polite speech. Idiomaticities of honorific use, nowhere clearer than in deferential directive formulas, provide configurational clues to the intended sense of a honorific usage at the same time that they lend an indirect feel to the communicative process, and mark status of some referent.

The semantic indirectness encoded in the honorific vocabulary, characterizable in fairly precise ways by using ngoko terms metalinguistically, is generally ignored in the literature in favor of their functions in what Goffman calls prescriptive presentational rituals: "acts through which the individual makes specific attestations to recipients [here, referents] concerning how he regards them"(1967:71) and "depicts his appreciation of [them]"(1967:73). This after all is the basic social function of any basa vocabulary—to convey appreciation of others in interaction by ritually treating them as special objects of address, reference, or both. Honorifics and honorific usage can be viewed from two different perspectives and perceived to serve simultaneously two significative functions, which interpenetrate as do honorifics' semantic significances and social import. It is as if speaking honorifically of people in certain socially special respects is to speak indirectly of them, avoiding their person as object of overly direct reference while simultaneously marking their person as object of felt deference.

7

Address Styles and the Muting of Gesture

The phrase "address style" can be used in a narrow sense to designate ngoko and basa morphemes of the speech style system, and the combinations in which they are diacritic of structurally and pragmatically distinct ngoko, madya, and krama styles of speaking. But in a broader sense, "address style" counts as a rubric for all aspects and qualities of acts of linguistic conduct, part of an interactive, presentational gestalt that involves much more than use of the speech style system. From any save the narrowest system-internal viewpoint it is artificial to deal with speech style vocabularies and the styles they distinguish independently of their fit with other, broader aspects of linguistic conduct.

As stylistically contrasting mediators of social relationships, ngoko, krama, and madya address styles can be located and opposed on a cline of polish from relatively "low," crude (*kasar*) ngoko to "high," polished (*alus*) krama. At the same time their use can be gauged as relatively appropriate or inappropriate in a given interactional context and as part of a speaker's general demeanor, which ordinarily fits or, to use a Javanese word, is *keplok* with the sensible impact of other perceptible qualities of one's conduct. Priyayi's prescriptive criticisms and negative examples of basa use make clear how the choice of address style is of a piece with other sensible features of speech—intonation, voice pitch, rate of speech, and so on—but also with other aspects of physical comportment: the way one composes one's face, one's posture, the way one points and sits, and other aspects of conduct alluded to in Chapter 2.

Address styles and the muting of gesture

There are more or less refined ways for performing virtually any action and for "polishing" (in Javanese *mbesut*) one's demeanor, linguistic and otherwise. Full or elided realizations of segmentable speech elements in slower or faster, precise or slurred speech can shade sensible qualities and overall impact of speech. Slow, measured tones and literary words that are not necessarily parts of the speech style system can add weight to advice bestowed on a child in ngoko; the allegro patter of colloquial krama, hardly different from madya, can mute the sense of formality conveyed in krama usage. These aspects of linguistic etiquette are related to but analytically independent of address style use in the narrow sense, and are hardly touched on in accounts of the speech styles. They make for expressive shading in speech that allows priyayi to make their presentations of self less a matter of following rules, as one insightful priyayi said to me, and more like painting a portrait: skillfully done, it is difficult to locate the precise line between two shadings.

Not all aspects of refined behavior are consciously adopted or strategically informed like the kinds of usage discussed in Chapter 5. This chapter deals with the relation between lexical address styles and broader aspects of refinedness in conduct by extending the descriptive assumptions and expository strategies of previous chapters to other stylistically significant speech segments. The obvious starting point is the structure of the address style vocabularies, the ways they have changed, and the social pressures that have made for such change. These changes broadly complement those among relatively pragmatically salient terms described in Chapter 5. Basa address style vocabularies, especially those distinguishing madya and krama styles, have been relatively stable, and changes in the membership of the krama vocabulary have been subject to social pressures that have more to do with what can be broadly called, with Halliday et al. (1972), dialectal significances of usage, rather than interactionally strategic use like that discussed in Chapters 3 and 5. The krama vocabulary has long been growing through what can be called a drift to pattern symmetry (Sapir 1921:149–52) if one recognizes the social motivations through which semiregular sound patterns have been recurringly extended. Because knowledge of basa varieties is unevenly distributed across elite and nonelite communities, standard basa usage has long been perceived not just as polite but genteel speech, emblematic of priyayihood. Change in the krama vocabulary reflects the social dialectal significances of address style use, and can be presented by adapting Labov's so-called mechanism of linguistic change (1972) to a situation very different from that which it was developed to describe.

Basa address style vocabularies have been more stable than kin term and personal pronoun repertoires, and overall are far less semantically impoverished than the deferential vocabulary discussed in Chapter 6. But most of the few encoded collapses of ngoko semantic distinctions in krama and sometimes madya share a referential mode of indexicality: deictic use, on the one hand, and proscriptive, invitative, and propositive locutions, on the other, all count as indexically significant, and in krama if not madya all are performed with relatively impoverished resources. Much of the relative refinedness of krama use resides in the avoidance or muting of such gestural aspects of speech.

I use the word "gestural" for the common significative nature of use of these speech style elements to suggest the semiotic attribute that they share with other aspects of more or less refined conduct, linguistic and otherwise. In its common sense, something like "communicatively expressive movement of the body, head, or face," the word gesture most obviously applies to nonlinguistic indexically significant acts like pointing, which are forbidden or at least affectively muted in paradigmatically polite kinds of behavior discussed in Chapter 2. But the term is naturally extended to English speech acts, for instance, which can be called gestures of thanking, offering, inviting, and so on—otherwise diverse acts whose functional Javanese analogues turn out to receive special structural and interactional treatment in basa vocabularies and basa usage.[1] The term also covers indexically significant aspects of speech external to the speech styles but also muted in polite conduct. There are linguistic gestures performed with nonreferential, segmentable elements of speech used as interjections and exclamations, psycho-ostensive elements of speech that index subjective and occasional attitudes of a speaker. The term

---

1. Although the term gestural was first suggested to me by Ortega y Gasset 1959, I use it in a more specific way for more specific descriptive purposes. I further ignore the general issue of intentional and nonintentional gestures, a problem to which Husserl (1970:276–78) speaks usefully with his notion of intimation.

Address styles and the muting of gesture

"psycho-ostensive" is ugly but accurately and usefully captures the intrinsically indexical, contextually dependent nature of utterances of such signals of momentary emotional or attitudinal states. Unelaborated in the speech style vocabularies, and available for use in any address style (in the narrow sense of the term), psycho-ostensive particles are unobvious but ubiquitous modulators of the affective politeness or refinedness of linguistic etiquette and styles of address in the broadest sense of the term.

This wide range of linguistic variation and change, complementary to that discussed in Chapters 5 and 6, will be surveyed by again moving from the speech style system to linguistic etiquette, albeit in a different direction. To show how diverse speech elements inside and outside the system of speech styles modulate the refinedness of linguistic conduct is to explicate another facet of the integral relation between linguistic and nonlinguistic conduct, the communicative content and affect of *tata-krama* 'the ordering of conduct'.

Innovation and Standardization of Krama and Madya

Krama words contrast in phonaesthetically striking ways with their basic ngoko alternants and can lend speech a certain ceremony, as Gonda (1948) puts it, by refining the aesthetic impact of speech sounds. Because the vast majority of krama forms alternate isomorphically with exact ngoko semantic equivalents, this largest basa vocabulary best bears out the assumption that each basa form alternates with a single ngoko morpheme. Of the more than six hundred ngoko/krama oppositions listed in most sources, fewer than forty share krama members.

Because there are no intrinsic semantic or grammatical limitations on the range of krama vocabulary, criteria for determining krama vocabulary membership are extrinsic to the code and basically dialectal: krama words are those that educated (i.e., priyayi) speakers use when they speak basa. Because knowledge of this standard vocabulary has never been shared by all Surakartans, much less all Javanese, priyayi are (or traditionally were) right to say that the only way to learn really proper krama usage, "good basa," is by interacting with those who use it properly. Subcommunity variation in basa usage has long been recognized by Javanese, albeit sociocentrically and covertly, as a key linguistic diacritic of social status.

198   Address styles and the muting of gesture

Walbeehm (1896:4) distinguished between krama *words*, whose sound shapes are unrelated to those of their ngoko alternants, and krama *forms*, whose sound shapes are related to those of their ngoko equivalents through patterned analogy. His distinction is important enough here to warrant a more descriptive terminological distinction between nonderivative and derivative krama morphemes, respectively. Derivative krama morphemes fit semiregular patterns of analogous sound-shape alternations. Insofar as they are quasi-systematic they are formally allied with the grammar of language "from the formal point of view, inasmuch as a specific difference in meaning is coupled with a certain—though still imperfect—regularly recurring difference in form" (Uhlenbeck 1978:292). Derivative krama morphemes do not stand to their base ngoko forms just as derived (or inflected) words stand to root forms, but the terms "derivative" and "nonderivative" highlight the partial, noteworthy resemblance between Javanese address styles and the patterns of affixation used to "derive" polite forms of address in languages like Japanese and Korean.

Sound shapes of many derivative krama words contrast with their ngoko alternants as having closed rather than open root-final syllables, dissimilated vowels in adjacent root syllables, consonant clusters in place of single intervocalic consonants, and other obvious phonotactic changes. As Uhlenbeck has pointed out (1978:290), these alternations tend to apply to complementary types of ngoko root sound shapes. The social dialectal significances of use of derivative krama forms vary in several ways. Walbeehm (1896:4–5) for instance distinguished between krama words "according to use" as being either "usual" (*gewoon*) and obligatory among "cultured Javanese of Surakarta" or "optional" (*facultatief*) and nonobligatory among members of that community. Still other krama words he distinguished as *krama désa* 'village krama', which "from the point of view of cultured (*ontwikkelde*) Surakartans are not good [i.e., standard] krama" (1896:6). Walbeehm appeals to the elite "cultured Surakartan" standard-speaking subcommunity as a social reference point for this distinction, and so implicitly broaches the issue of dialectal variation in krama usage.

The term *krama désa* he probably borrowed from his informants; certainly it is commonly used by priyayi today to characterize what they count as nonstandard krama derivative forms.[2] It presupposes a geosocial distinction through which improper usage is stereotypically attributed to speakers at the rural periphery, and proper usage by implication to city dwellers. But as older conservative priyayi are quick to note, fewer people living in Surakarta speak good basa these days; people from villages are migrating to the city, and young educated people are not learning to speak krama as they should. These priyayi are still fairly sensitive to "substandard" krama usage and, as members of a traditional standardizing speech subcommunity, "oppose any increase in the number of *ngoko:krama* pairs. In the [substandard] dialects, on the other hand, where the pressure of the standard language is less strong, the productivity of the [ngoko/krama] opposition manifests itself very clearly" (Uhlenbeck 1978: 291). Like Walbeehm and Gonda before him, Uhlenbeck alludes here to patterns of innovation among communities of speakers of different basa dialects. Evidence suggests that the situation is more complicated because longstanding processes of innovation in both non-priyayi and priyayi speech subcommunities alike have contributed to the growth of the krama vocabulary.

These changes can be broadly sketched with Labov's well-known "mechanism of linguistic change," based on phonological variation and change in English. Peculiar though it may seem to invoke a model developed for and most successfully applied to a very different community and type of variation, Labov's distinction between complementary, interacting social forces operating on speech from above and below the level of social awareness does help make sense of the growth of the krama vocabulary. "Social awareness" refers here, as in Labov's work, to awareness of features of standard and nonstandard dialects, rather than alternations between relatively salient mediators of social interaction. These terms' low pragmatic saliences as strategically manipulable speech elements are complemented by their covert dialectal significances, which are apparent in patterned change in the krama vocabulary of address.

---

2. That conservative priyayi sometimes apply this same term and its urban analogue *krama kampung* to madya as well as krama vocabularies does not detract from the validity of that distinction; see Errington 1985:125–32.

CHANGE FROM ABOVE

Even the least prescriptively inclined priyayi pointed out to me that not all krama is "good" krama, and most provided an example or two of what they called *krama désa* for my instruction or amusement. After illustrating a sound shape analogy between ngoko and derivative krama words—for example, *tuduh/tedah* 'to point', *tunggu/tengga* 'to wait on', *cukup/cekap* 'enough'—they would give an example of how village people (ngoko *wong désa*, krama *tiyang dhusun*) who "don't know any better" coin and use what they think are "good krama" words, e.g., *welah* (ngoko *wuluh* 'a kind of bamboo'). This priyayi perception of *krama désa* as the result of uneducated speakers' incorrect attempts to speak standard basa is valid: in trying to approximate a target dialect of basa, uneducated Javanese extend analogical correspondences past limits of application defined by speakers of the standard dialect and so inadvertently coin new, hypercorrect terms.

Priyayi may be privy to such usage in just those contexts in which uneducated speakers feel most obliged to speak standard krama and are most aware of their limited ability to do so—formal situations and in address of priyayi themselves. Experiences of several priyayi with peasants on their best linguistic behavior, related to me as amusing or embarrassing, show the dilemma of uneducated speakers when obliged to address speakers of a target dialect they do not control. Certainly these uneducated speech partners were then doubly on the spot, because their substandard (or subordinate) dialect was then in direct contact with a standard (or superordinate) dialect in the sorts of contexts in which "linguistic forms produced by a speaker of the subordinate dialect in a formal context will shift in an unsystematic manner towards the superordinate" (Labov 1971a:450). Speakers' awarenesses of and attempts to approximate a standard target dialect make for what Labov (1972:179) calls "hypercorrection from above the level of awareness . . . a sporadic and irregular correction of the changed [here, krama] forms towards the model of the highest status group. . . ."

Some hypercorrect *krama désa* forms have been subject to extreme stigmatization, become "the overt topic of social comment," and fallen out of use with the exception of what Labov calls "stereo-

Address styles and the muting of gesture   201

types." Notable stereotyped examples for priyayi are place names and morphologically complex words based on folk etymologies. Villagers (as one priyayi said to me) will speak of Semarang, the capital of the province on the north coast, as Semawis, segmenting and changing the last two syllables by analogy with *arang/awis* (ngoko/krama 'scarce') and *larang/awis* (ngoko/krama 'expensive'). The nominal *kebupatèn* 'place of the *bupati* (a high level official)' is kramanized (*dikramakaké*) by segmenting the word as *kabu* and *patèn* according to a folk etymology tracing *kabu* to *kebo* (ngoko 'water buffalo') and *patèn* to *pati* (ngoko: 'dead') affixed with the nominalizer *-an*. Because the krama of *kebo* is *maésa*, and of *patèn* is *pejahan* (from *pejah*) the *krama désa* form is *maésapejahan*, highly stigmatized and probably little used in contemporary village speech communities.

But older conservative priyayi who complain that their own children and grandchildren cannot always tell "good" krama from "bad" do not realize how complex the situation is. They recognize that some derivative krama words have entered the standard priyayi repertoire, but are unaware that the processes of pattern extension that they attribute to villagers are operative within the priyayi class as well. Although priyayi may be linguistically conservative, they have themselves coined new basa words through a process that can be called, with Labov "hypercorrection from below."

CHANGE FROM BELOW

Walbeehm probably posited the category of "optional krama" to account for the transitional stage in the evolution of nonstandard into standard basa usage, but it is significant that the term has no widely used native counterpart and that priyayi recognize no distinct class of optional basa words. Certainly optional forms are interactively marginal in that variation in optional krama versus ngoko use from context to context and from speaker to speaker goes largely unnoticed and rarely commented on by even the most prescriptively minded speakers. Priyayi sometimes classify forms that they and their closest relatives sometimes use as *krama désa*. A good example is *bènten*, categorized by Walbeehm as optional krama for ngoko *béda* 'different'. Several older speakers told me that use of *bènten* is a common mistake (*salah kaprah*) because *béda* is both ngoko and krama. But at other times and in more spontaneous speech I observed several of these same speakers themselves use *bènten* as a de facto part of the standard vocabulary. *Teras*, used by some speakers as a basa alternant for ngoko *terus* 'right away', was characterized by two older speakers not just as a common error (*salah kaprah*) but 'real krama désa' (*krama désa tenan*). But *teras* is nonetheless in very common use among younger priyayi; on one occasion I observed its use by a girl in the presence of her father, who himself had classified it as *krama désa* in conversation with me some weeks before. He evinced no reaction to his daughter's ostensibly substandard use, I suspect, simply because he did not notice it.[3]

Such variation in and discrepancies between norms and actualities of krama usage are not always apparent to priyayi speakers, even in the speech of members of their own households. Their awareness of relative standardness of basa correlates with the degree of attention they happen to be devoting to the "properness" of speech, an aspect of what Labov oversimply calls the "formality" of the situation. In spontaneous, informal situations like that noted previously, priyayi make use of forms they will on other occasions label *krama désa*, and avoid using in more formal and linguistically self-conscious contexts. This is nothing new. "The same priyayi who would call *bènten* [from *béda* 'different'], *cobi* [from *coba* 'try'] ... *krama désa* and are careful in correspondence and conversation with their highest chiefs to avoid using them, have them repeatedly in their speech when outside of their civil posts ... (Walbeehm 1896:12). *Cobi* is now almost universally recognized to be standard krama and is, like *bènten*, a regular part of younger priyayi speakers' krama repertoires. Change from below the level of social awareness is bringing these formerly substandard forms into the standard dialect in a process complementary to that hypercorrection from above found among non-priyayi. It is a process that may be accelerating among younger modern priyayi in more intimate contact with commoners and are less self-conscious about their special traditional elite status.[4]

3. It seems unlikely that he wished to save her a lecture on usage in my presence, because during another of my visits he had given her one on her use of madya forms to address me.
4. For a plausible account of a microevolutionary process through which such change may articulate, see Householder 1983.

Address styles and the muting of gesture 203

The standard krama repertoire has to all appearances expanded through hypercorrective processes operative within the priyayi subcommunity itself, which answers Labov's description of "hypercorrection from below." Evidence that priyayi have themselves extended ngoko/krama sound correspondences are what Soepomo Poedjosoedarmo (1968:66a) has called hyper-krama forms. An example is *nami* 'name', hyper-krama from the original and, according to older priyayi, only standard krama, *nama* (ngoko: *jeneng* and *aran*). This derivation is based on analogical alternations between ngoko/krama pairs like *upama/upami* 'such as', *rada/radi* 'rather'.[5] *Nami* is not a new krama word filling a gap in the krama vocabulary of address, but the product of a mechanistic extension of a preexisting sound pattern to a standard krama form, one obviously known to just those who coined the hypercorrect form. *Nami* is regarded by older prescriptively minded priyayi speakers as an error—"It's like painting a crow black," as one said to me—but is de facto standard. A striking example of hypercorrect krama, apparently extant just among priyayi, is the form *krami*, which appears standardly as an alternant to *krama* in the phrase *tatakrama*, but in some priyayi usage is also used to the exclusion of *krama* as a metalinguistic term. Another example of hypercorrection from below is the hyper-krama *sedanten* (ngoko: *kabèh* 'all'), derived from the standard *sedaya*. Older speakers dislike *sedanten*, although it is, whether they know it or not, now in regular use by their own children and grandchildren. This form too results from the unconscious, mechanistic extension of sound patterns.

At the turn of the century the Dutch philologist J. L. Brandes published a vitriolic attack on Javanese linguistic etiquette in which he called the growth of the krama vocabulary a "superficial, sickly, phenomenon" which was the responsibility "at least in part of pedantic schoolmasters" (1889:134). More influential than pedantic pedagogues, in all likelihood, were native speakers of all classes who extended preexisting patterned alternations to ngoko forms with appropriate sound shapes.

From a narrowly structural viewpoint, oppositions between speech style vocabularies are merely diacritic of structurally distinct speech

---

5. My impression is that *radi* is hardly ever used by men and may convey a sense of effeminacy.

styles and make for a great deal of redundancy in the system. The very small class of three-member ngoko/madya/krama paradigmatic sets bear the main weight of distinguishing address styles, and the hundreds of two-way ngoko/krama oppositions serve structurally crucial functions only in the madya substyles *madyangoko* and *madyakrama*. In the standard dialect, at least, their presence elsewhere is totally predictable on the basis of knowledge of use of deictics and grammatico-syntactic elements, discussed later.

This structural peripherality of most krama lexemes suggests, as do patterns of change and variation in this largest basa vocabulary, that krama usage is as important as a covert diacritic of social status as it is of polite demeanor, an ubiquitous badge of speakers' backgrounds in a traditionally stratified society. That Labov's model of change in dialects turns out to be relevant to change in styles suggests that if any uses of krama address elements count as strategic, they are attempts to emulate statusful speakers, a very different kind of strategic use from those of deferential terms and personal pronouns discussed in Chapter 5. The former is significant as much as a marker of (claim to) knowledge of educated speech as it is a token of deference or formality in a relation with a speech partner.

Ngoko/madya/krama Alternations

Madya styles are usually treated as "middle" speech, occupying an intermediate position between "high" or formal (krama) and "low" or informal (ngoko) speech (see, for example, Wolff 1976:221, and Wolff and Poedjosoedarmo 1982:17). Because styles of krama may themselves be relatively formal or informal, however, drawing a firm line between madya and krama basa styles is difficult, as Uhlenbeck has pointed out. Paradigmatic alternations between style variants are complemented by variation between more or less full realizations of speech style variants to which colloquializing fast-speech processes apply. (The relation of interlevel and intralevel variation in address styles is discussed at length in Errington 1985b:135–55).

More notable here is another characteristic of the madya vocabulary—its stability. The class of ngoko/madya/krama sets has changed very little over the period for which written records exist (discussed in Errington 1985b:121–35). Outside of the personal pronoun paradigms there has been very little change in the membership of the class of distinctively madya forms. Symptoms of some change in priyayi madya usage exist, however, in differing attitudes to madya usage among conservative and modern priyayi that correlate with the degrees to which those speakers will "mix" informal krama and distinctively madya elements. This intergenerational variation appears to be resulting in shifting patterns of standard and substandard basa usage, change that is largely unobvious to speakers whose observations on madya usage (like substandard krama) are often notably inaccurate. Such change also fits broadly with Labov's postulated "change from below," and corresponds well with Kroch's Labovian theory of the evolution of social dialects (1978). Although Kroch alludes to ngoko/krama variation as an example of social dialect variation that bears out his general approach, his remarks fit much better the ongoing shift in use of madya and krama variants in priyayi repertoires, discussed in Errington (1985b:155–60).

Most madya elements alternate transparently with just one ngoko morpheme and one krama morpheme, but there are significant clusters of nonisomorphic ngoko/madya/krama alternations among just those address style markers that as a group serve what can be called gesturally communicative functions in speech. Encoded distinctions in the indexically referential demonstrative pronoun apparatus of ngoko collapse in single krama terms. These are the most obvious examples of the broad gestural muting of refined basa speech, distinguished from both ngoko and less polished madya styles. So they provide a good introduction to the nature of refinedness of speech, and to a basic, previously unnoted point of resemblance between madya and ngoko speech styles: madya preserves encoded gestural distinctions that collapse in polite refined (*alus*) krama acts of address.

Demonstrative Pronouns and Indexing Acts

Demonstrative pronouns are such conspicuous and ubiquitous markers of address styles that priyayi sometimes degradingly refer to madya as *basa niki-niku* 'this-that' [madya] language, alluding to two typical madya demonstrative pronouns. Table 13 shows how five series of ngoko and madya demonstrative pronouns encode a propor-

Address styles and the muting of gesture

Table 13. Overview of *Ngoko/madya/krama* Demonstrative Pronouns

	Ngoko	Madya	Krama
Correlational			
BASIC			
proximal	iki/ki[a]	niki	
medial	kuwi/ki	niku	menika
			(formal: punika)
distal	kaé/ké	nika	
MODAL			
proximal	mengkéné/ngéné	ngèten	
medial	mengkono/ngono	ngoten	mekaten
			(informal: ngaten)
distal	mengkana/ngana	ngaten	
QUANTITATIVE			
proximal	(se)méné	(se)mènten	
medial	(se)mono	(se)monten	semanten
distal	(se)mana	(se)manten	
Noncorrelational			
LOCAL			
proximal	kéné	ngriki	ngriki
medial	kono	ngriku	ngriku
distal	kana	ngrika	ngrika
DIRECTIONAL			
proximal	mréné	mriki	mriki
medial	mrono	mriku	mriku
distal	mrana	mrika	mrika
TEMPORAL			
up to now	sepréné	sepriki	sepriki
up to then	seprana	sepriku	sepriku

[a] Stylistic ngoko alternants are listed either full/short, or with elidable syllables in parentheses; see Uhlenbeck 1978:210–77.

tional three-way distinction involving three opposed types of contextual features presupposed for their tokens to convey information about or identify denotata, their locations, directions of movement, qualities, and quantities. There is also a two-member temporal series.

Like other languages Javanese encodes this analogical distinction

Address styles and the muting of gesture 207

in demonstrative sets with corresponding sounds and senses: proximal demonstratives have relatively high front vowels, medial members have relatively high back vowels, distal members have low back vowels. It is significant for present purposes that in each of what are called the basic, modal, and quantitative series in Table 13 there is just a single krama member that corresponds in sound shape with its respective distal ngoko/madya alternants, but counts as the krama alternant of all three members of the set. An obvious question follows: why do encoded semantic distinctions collapse in the krama members of some of these deictic series, but not others?

The notional labels used for each deictic series are borrowed from Uhlenbeck's careful study except that "basic" replaces "neutral" to avoid an unfortunate ambiguity that arises when he uses it in another crucially different sense, discussed later. Uhlenbeck's description of Javanese deixis (1978:210-277) corresponds closely enough with Fillmore's etic account (1982) that terminological distinctions from the latter can be matched with and in some cases conveniently substituted for those in the former. For present purposes we can overlook various nondenotative uses of deictics—anaphorically as coreferential with portions of discourse, syntactically to mark grammatical boundaries, and what Fillmore (1976:40) calls symbolically to refer to previously established topic—and consider these demonstratives just as means for referring in ways grounded in spatiotemporal and social context of use.

Proximal members of each demonstrative series serve to refer to that "in direct relation to the speaker of the sentence in which they occur," the medial to denotata "in relation to hearer, or at least to what is present or considered present in the speech situation," the distal to "what [is] outside the speech-event" (Fillmore 1982:222). Uhlenbeck calls the distal members of demonstrative series "neutral" deictics that function negatively in that they presuppose neither speech partner as deictic anchor for reference. So, he writes (1978: 224), it is appropriate for krama alternants to correspond to the distal members of these three-member sets:

> It is not surprising that krama should have only one demonstrative in contrast with the three ngoko forms: it is in the nature of krama to avoid excessive explicitness, to make use of periphrases, and to prefer neutral [sic] and impersonal modes of expression. In a situation which calls for

krama it will be inappropriate to use words such as *iki* and *iku*[6] which allude directly to speaker and hearer.

He thus identifies another kind of encoded avoidance in basa speech, one that is keyed to modes rather than domains of reference, but does not completely explain why deictic recourses should be impoverished in just three sets of demonstrative pronouns (basic, modal, quantitative) and not the others. Brakel addresses this question with a useful if cryptic suggestion based on Uhlenbeck's study:

> I would venture that the neutral [here, basic], modal, and quantitative series might be termed correlational, i.e., directly connected with the speaker, while the local, directional, and temporal series, being neutral [sic] in this regard, might be styled noncorrelational.... In the correlational sphere the personal involvement is too strong to be allowed to express itself fully in the vague, polite, krama idiom (1969:264).

It is intuitively plausible that there should be a difference in speakers' "connection" or "involvement" with what Brakel calls correlational and noncorrelational demonstrative usage, but his (and Uhlenbeck's) crucial uses of "neutral" in two different senses does not help to make his point clear. Speech partners are "involved" enough with use of proximal and medial ngoko local demonstratives (*kéné* and *kono*), for instance, that the deictics can be used to refer to speaker and addressee (respectively). But this connection, however direct, cannot be what Brakel is alluding to because the local series is, to use his term, noncorrelational.

What Brakel and Uhlenbeck only indirectly allude to as the difference between use of correlational and noncorrelational demonstratives has to do with their ostensiveness. There is for some but not all of these deictics an obligatory "connection" or "involvement" with an accompanying nonlinguistic gesture, what Fillmore calls an indexing act: "a stance, gesture, or non-incidental bodily orientation that can direct the Hearer's gaze."(1982:46) This difference between types of deictic reference most strongly suggests the notion of ges-

---

6. Here as elsewhere in his work, Uhlenbeck focuses on formal/literary variants of the morphosyntactic and deictic apparatus of the language. In the body of this text I cite the common, everyday form of the demonstrative, *kaé*, although this variation is secondary for present concerns. The krama element of the basic series corresponds quite transparently with the old-fashioned, literary distal ngoko element *ika*.

Address styles and the muting of gesture 209

tural muting. The encoded collapse of just those deictic distinctions that in use presuppose indexing acts can be demonstrated by first contrasting just the local and basic series.

Local demonstratives convey information about spatial locations, presupposing speaker's and/or hearer's bodily locations as deictic anchors (or Grounds, as Fillmore calls them). Uttering a token of "here" or *kéné* may in at least some circumstances identify the place of utterance independently of any accompanying nonlinguistic gesture because such use may presuppose knowledge just of the precise location of the utterer over and against addressee, or of the vicinity of speech partners together over and against some other nondemonstrable locus. In either case, usage may inform about the location by presupposing knowledge that is potentially available independently of any indexing act, whether or not an indexing act may be copresent and even in some circumstances necessary. *Kéné*, like "here," might be called with Kaplan (as described by Miller 1982:62) a "pure" indexical, tokens of which need not (but may) be accompanied by a nonlinguistic gesture or demonstration. Tokens of both demonstratives serve to identify a point copresent with the physical locus of user in a spatial manifold, not necessarily presupposing anything other than (co)presence of speech partners during an occasion of use of a token of the indexical.

With respect to this potential nonobligatoriness of indexing acts members of the basic demonstrative series contrast with locatives, because tokens of the former can only pick out and identify demonstrata together with some presupposed, copresent gesture on the part of the speaker to which the addressee is expected to attend. *Iki* and 'this', though proximals, are not "pure" indexicals in Kaplan's sense, because use of either must always be accompanied by some ostensive nonlinguistic gesture, a physical indexing act that helps furnish acquaintance with a demonstratum.

A similar contrast can be drawn between medial members of the local and basic series. *Kono* 'there' may serve to identify (things at) points in space that are either near the addressee, the speech partner who serves as secondary ground, or some distance from the speaker. The first type of usage can potentially be implemented without an accompanying indexical act, as on occasions when demonstratum is addressee. Use of the medial basic demonstrative *kuwi* on the other hand always presupposes some indexing act directed to the person or environs of the addressee. Distal demonstratives have an essentially negative (as Uhlenbeck puts it, neutral) significance, like impersonal pronouns, because they identify demonstrata negatively as being outside or on the periphery of speech partners' shared field. For this reason it is noncoincidental that the single krama element of the basic series, *menika*, should correspond in sound shape with the distal ngoko and madya elements, ending in a low back unrounded vowel.

Indexing acts accompanying use of proximal and medial demonstratives are typically directed to or associated with a speaker, addressee, or both, but an indexing act accompanying use of distal demonstratives has addressee for audience, not ostensible target or ground. One way of characterizing the differential "involvement" of speech partners in basic and local demonstrative usage is to say that uses of *iki*, *kuwi*, and *kaé* correlate or are necessarily copresent with and thus "involve" the speaker in an indexing act of which one or both speech partners may be target. And because distal members are negatively defined as a residual sort of demonstrative category, we may say with Uhlenbeck that their usage "points" to neither speech partner and so is neutral or impersonal.

The gestural muteness of refined behavior explicitly prescribed in texts on court etiquette like those discussed in Chapter 2 has here an obvious structural correlate in krama usage in less exalted situations. In fact, a complementary muting of demonstrative gesture is (or was) obligatory in complementary speech settings. Those engaged in conversation in traditional royal audiences, to which king was bystander obligatorily made use of a pair of ceremonial basic demonstratives, proximal *puniki* and medial *puniku*, but never any distal alternant (see Errington 1982).[7] The same logic of avoidance applied to socially complementary situations led to complementary suppression of correlative demonstrative usage.

This underlying difference between intrinsically gestural basic and nongestural local demonstratives extends naturally to other demonstrative series, which incorporate the same underlying semantic and

---

7. This entire vocabulary, like the ceremonial speech styles in Dyirbal and Guugu Yimidhir discussed in Chapter 5, counts as a set of what Comrie (1976) calls bystander honorifics.

Address styles and the muting of gesture 211

deictic distinctions. Aligned with the basic series (as their English glosses in Table 13 show) are the quantitative demonstratives ('as much as this . . . ') and modal demonstratives ('in the manner of/like this . . . '), which also presuppose copresent indexing acts.[8] The directional series, on the other hand, incorporates the significative content of the local series, whereas the two temporal deictics presuppose knowledge of a point in time (in spoken language) necessarily shared by speech partners independently of any gesture.

This link between polite and gesturally muted conduct at the interface between linguistically and nonlinguistically significant conduct, acts of linguistic reference and ostensive gesture, was noted more intuitively by Roorda (1855:336):

> In krama these varied forms [i.e., demonstratives embodying the proximal/medial/distal distinction] are ordinarily used only with the deictic pronouns for place [i.e., local and directional] but otherwise uniformly end in [a low back vowel]. The reason for this is none other than that the Javanese when speaking krama, the language of respect, may not let his eyes be seen, nor may he point with the hand; rather the eyes must respectfully be directed down, and the hands must be held against the body, without any sign which may be used to indicate but the thumb. So he can indicate no definite object, and all which is in his thoughts or which he would indicate with his thumb is rather removed. Therefore usage demands that in krama one must at all times, except only for indicating place, use the form as that with which one speaks of things at a distance.

Roorda's prescriptive account is based on limiting cases of polite, restrained self-presentation, and whether or not it is valid as an explanation of the asymmetry in the krama demonstrative paradigm, it fails to explain patterns of everyday contemporary usage in which it is hardly obligatory to direct one's eyes downward or hold the hands against the body when addressing someone in krama. Certainly it is permissible and sometimes necessary, as Roorda says, to point in properly muted fashion with a thumb. But the intrinsically gestural nature of linguistic and nonlinguistic indexing acts, semiotically related types of significant behavior, emerges clearly from the correspondence between different gesturally muted modes of self-presentation.

With this broad parallel between refined linguistic and nonlinguis-

8. The same is clear in their Javanese glosses given by Poerwardminto (1939), for the quantitative series—for example *ukurané padha karo iki*, roughly, 'the measurement of it the same with this'.

tic conduct in mind, and a first instance of gestural significances of speech, we can consider other cases of nonisomorphic ngoko/krama and ngoko/madya/krama alternations. A relatively small group of ngoko speech elements with an underlying gestural significativeness have either impoverished krama variants or none at all, and all serve in some indexically direct manner to refer to and intimate the utterer's attitudes, desires, and states, whether or not they are accompanied by an indexing act.

Formulaic Locutions

The rubric "formulaic locution" serves here for a diverse set of linguistic forms which are indexical and locutionary in the sense that their significances are keyed to speaker/addressee relations and are intrinsically subjective and occasional. They are subjective in the sense that in use they furnish direct acquaintance with a speaker's desires, wishes or attitudes, and occasional in that they do not refer to but indexically intimate something within the coexperienced context of use. This very general rubric covers performative imperatives discussed in Chapter 6, nonperformative locutions endowed with negative imperative force, and a special propositive construction. Negative imperatives are performed in a necessarily muted manner in krama, whereas the propositive form in ngoko and madya is simply not available in krama address. One respect in which madya speech is intrinsically less refined than krama is that lexical and grammatical distinctions in ngoko are preserved in madya but not krama. As in deictic usage, madya is a gesturally unrefined style of basa.

Other ngoko formulaic locutions that must also be characterized vis-a-vis contexts of use are significative of persons' states, attitudes to, and desires concerning something presupposed in context. All the ngoko locutionary formulas for inviting, forbidding, rejecting, indicating lack of knowledge, and so on are encoded in the speech style system so as to share krama stylistic alternants, or are simply unused in krama. Although they cannot all be dealt with exhaustively here, the impoverishment of distinctions between formulas in krama is worth sketching as another aspect of the muting of indexical significances of speech.

NEGATIVE DIRECTIVES

The range and relative politenesses of negative directives, construable as proscriptions of actions engaged in or states of affairs brought about by an addressee, are as complex as those of the directives incompletely discussed in Chapter 6. They can be considered in a similarly cursory manner to show just how these indexically significant acts are encoded in muted basa locutionary formulas.

One may deferentially communicate a desire that an addressee either desists from or does not begin an activity by using the performative formulas discussed in Chapter 6 with a negative particle attached to a verb in the complement, as in the krama sentences 1 and 2.

1. (Panjenengan) kula aturi mboten tindak (kemawon).
2. (Panjenengan) kula suwun supaya mboten tindak (kemawon).
   YOU   I   ORDER/ IN ORDER NOT   GO   ONLY,
                   REQUEST THAT   OUT   JUST
   I order/ask you not go.

Inferentially based, indirect, and more refined are statements regarding the unnecessariness of an action or its result, with or without explicit reference to addressee.

But there are also nonperformative locutionary formulas endowed with negative directive force. In ngoko, *wis* and *aja* can be uttered with directive force such that addressee desists from some activity already being engaged in at the time of the utterance. *Aja* but not *wis* can also be used to proscribe some projected, not yet initiated action. *Wis*, an auxiliary verb marking completive aspect, is expressive of directive force only when uttered in isolation as a single locution (unless followed by one of the kinds of interjections considered later). In a question like sentence 3 and a response like sentence 4, then, *wis* marks completedness of the action.

3. Dhik Har   wis   mangkat durung?
   YNGR   ALREADY   LEAVE   NOT YET
   SBLNG
   Has Har left yet or not?
4. Wis   (mangkat).
   ALREADY   LEAVE
   He has (left).

214 Address styles and the muting of gesture

In other contexts—uttered, say, upon seeing a child running through the yard—a simple utterance *wis* with falling intonation will signal to an addressee (here, child) the speaker's desire that he or she desist. The use of some verb descriptive of the proscribed action, (e.g., *mlayu* 'run' in *Wis mlayu!*) would mark the sentence as a (typically) elliptical statement meaning something like 'He already ran.' *Wis* is ambiguous, then, between a referential aspectual and a locutionary directive function, and in both senses has a madya equivalent *mpun* and a krama equivalent *sampun*.

Aja serves only to issue negative imperatives in ngoko speech, used either alone or in combination with verb phrases referential of the proscribed action, as in sentence 5. *Waé* 'only, just' or *dhisik* 'right away' are frequently appended to verb phrases with *aja* as in sentences 6 and 7, and its imperative force can be softened with a prefatory interjective particle *mbok* or *mbok ya*, which gives it a kind of an optative feel, like 'may it be/I hope that'.

5. (Kowé) aja mlayu.
 YOU NEG. RUN
 IMP.
 Don't run.

6. (Mbok (ya)) aja mangkat waé.
 NEG. LEAVE ONLY, JUST
 IMP.
 Don't leave.

7. (Mbok (ya)) aja mangkat dhisik.
 NEG. LEAVE RIGHT AWAY
 IMP.
 Don't leave now.

In krama *sampun* is the single krama alternant to both *aja* and *wis*, and so use may be ambiguous between meanings like 'already' and 'don't!', as the two English glosses for sentence 8 show. Its use with directive force is commonly marked with an appended modifier *(ké)mawon*, equivalent to ngoko *waé* (as in 9) or *rumiyin*, alternating with ngoko *dhisik* (as in 10).

8. Sampun tindak.
 ALREADY/ GO OUT
 NEG.IMP.
 He/she has already gone out. OR
 Don't go out.

Address styles and the muting of gesture   215

9. Sampun   tindak   (ké)mawon.
   NEG.   GO OUT   ONLY, JUST
   IMP.
   Don't go.

10. Sampun   tindak   rumiyin.
    NEG.   GO OUT   RIGHT AWAY
    IMP.
    Don't go.

11. Sampun   menika.
    ALREADY   THIS
    DON'T   THIS
    This is done/finished.
    Don't take/buy/eat . . . this.

Outside of context, the only disambiguating feature of highly elliptical utterances like sentence 11 may be intonation. A rising intonation peaking on the penultimate syllable of *menika* signals that the referent of that word—the object of some elliptically understood action—is the primary focus of the utterance, and *sampun* then marks a proscription vis-a-vis that action or state of affairs. If stress and high pitch fall on the second syllable of *sampun,* the primary information is signaled as involving the completion of the elliptically understood action and *sampun* as indicating completedness.

In madya speech the distinction between *wis* and *aja* is preserved by two forms that may be historically related to their single krama equivalent but are functionally distinct. These are *mpun*, equivalent to *wis*, and *ampun*, equivalent to *aja*. Here, as in the case of the correlational demonstrative pronouns, a distinction between ngoko forms collapses into a single form in krama but is preserved in madya. Elliptical utterances consisting of *mpun* and a madya modal demonstrative (sentence 12) can be glossed as 'It's already like that', whereas that demonstrative with *ampun* (sentence 13) means 'Don't be/do it like that'. Their shared krama variant, sentence 14, is ambiguous between both.

12. Mpun   ngoten.
    It's already like that.

13. Ampun   ngoten.
    Don't do it like that.

14. Sampun   mekaten.
    Don't do it like that.
    It's already like that.

Address styles and the muting of gesture

Sampun can be used in the complement clause to *suwun* or *aturi* in a deferential negative directive like sentence 15, conveying the feeling (according to several speakers) that the contemplated action is on the verge of being initiated, whereas with *mboten* (as in sentences 1 and 2) there is no such felt immediacy.

   15. (Panjenengan) kula aturi sampun tindak (kémawon).
       I ask(?) you not to go.

This is another example of the structural impoverishment of a basa vocabulary which contributes to the gestural and indexical muting of speech.

THE PROPOSITIVE

The ngoko first-person pronoun *aku* and passive clitic *tak-* are ordinarily replaced in madya and krama speech with the free morpheme *kula*, discussed in Chapter 5, but in ngoko there is an idiomatic construction in which *aku* and *tak* are combined with intransitive or active transitive verb forms and are uttered with propositive force, as in sentences 16 and 17.

   16. Aku tak-   -N-   -pangan (dhi)sik (ya).
        1ST 1ST PRSN ACT.   EAT   RIGHT   YES
        PRSN PASS   VRB.   AWAY
                          MRKR
       I'm going to eat now (OK?)

   17. Aku tak-   -turu   (dhi)sik (ya).
        1ST 1ST PRSN SLEEP   RIGHT   YES
        PRSN PASS   AWAY
       I'm going to sleep now (OK?)

These idiomatic constructions presuppose the speaker's intention to carry out the proposed activity and convey the presumption that it is acceptable to the addressee. But the construction has no analogue in krama because there is no distinct alternant in krama for *tak-*, and sentences like 18 are unacceptable. On the other hand, the propositive construction is available in madya sentences like 19, because in just this construction the passive clitic *tak-* can appear in basa speech.

  *18. Kula kula nedha rumiyin (inggih?)
    19. Kula tak- -nedha riyin   (nggih?)
        I'm going to eat now, OK?

Address styles and the muting of gesture 217

Taken together, these otherwise disparate structural differences between ngoko and basa speech produce qualitative differences in speech in ngoko, the relatively unrefined madya styles of basa, and more refined (*alus*) krama speech styles. Although this interlevel variation hinges on far fewer, less obvious nonisomorphic ngoko/basa alternations than among demonstratives, each involves indexically significant speech elements tied to the immediate context of interaction for referential and social meaning. Some of this structural muting of gesture is encoded quite clearly in repertoires of address style vocabularies, but elsewhere involve a categorical unavailability of indexically direct locutionary forms.

"I DON'T KNOW"

Uttered in isolation, ngoko *mbuh* is best glossed into English as "I don't know." Like that English sentence, it indicates a speaker's ignorance about some state of affairs presupposed as a topic of conversation. One symptom of the essentially locutionary, indexical significance of *mbuh* is the existence of a derived verb of the type Benveniste calls delocutive, "deriving from a locution of discourse and not from another sign of language" (1971:242). Just as *tutoyer* and *vousvoyer* mean respectively 'to say *tu* to' and 'to say *vous* to'—that is, to engage in an act of uttering a token of either—and the English 'to thank' means 'to say "thank you" to', the transitive form of *mbuh*, suffixed with the indirect object marker *-i*, counts as a metalinguistic item that signifies an occasion of speech.[9] So the sentence *Aku dimbuhi* means 'I was said *mbuh* to'—that is, 'Someone indicated to me they did not know about something by saying "*mbuh*"'. *Mbuh* can be used to refer to someone's state of ignorance by virtue of its semantic content describable with the gloss "Don't know," but in isolated use it is subsistent on context-dependent, formulaic acts and an indexical link between identity of token user and state of knowledge referred to.

Mbuh is not used in madya or krama speech, nor does it have a correspondingly simple basa formulaic locutionary equivalent. In

9. Although this form now seems to be marginal in Solo, it is reported in Poerwadarminta (1939) and was accepted by three older priyayi speakers.

218   Address styles and the muting of gesture

polite address speakers often have recourse either to nonindexical declarative sentences, usually basa equivalents of the ngoko gloss provided above, or the more honorific, idiomatic utterance *duka*, which is the krama inggil word for 'angry' (ngoko: *nesu*). To utter *duka* in this way counts as an elliptical performance of the act of 'asking for anger'—*nyuwun duka*, '(I) ask for (your) anger'—because a speaker does not know and cannot inform an addressee concerning what he/she wishes to know. The form *didukani* does not have the meaning 'to be said *duka* to' but 'to be the object of (honored) person's anger (*duka*)', that is, 'to be scolded'. Use of *duka* then, serves to communicate a speaker's lack of knowledge by referring to and so idiomatically presupposing a stereotyped consequence.

"HERE, TAKE IT," AND "LET'S GO"

Two ngoko formulas for inviting, *nya* and *ayo*, share madya and krama alternants which are therefore not exactly equivalent to either. To utter *nya* is to signal an offer of something to an addressee or to direct an addressee to receive something; to utter *ayo* is to signal an invitation to or a desire that the addressee do something. The contextual dependence of the first use of *nya* is quite clear from the copresent indexing act that ordinarily serves to point to or otherwise bring into the addressee's immediate proximity the thing offered. In this respect the best idiomatic English gloss of *nya* is something like 'Here, take it', which closely resembles Poerwardarminta's (1939: 123) ngoko gloss *iki lho, tampanana!*, literally something like 'this here [proximal basic demonstrative], y'see, receive [passive imperative] it!'. Children use *nya* much like the melodramatic English "Take that!" to celebrate as they watch the hero of a story give a villain his just deserts.

Ayo, as broad in its range of appropriate uses as *nya* is narrow, serves to issue invitations, to urge, and to indicate a speaker's expectation that an addressee engage in some action, and so may serve to soften directives. It can be glossed very crudely as 'Go ahead' or 'Let's go.' Now *ayo* and *nya* share a single krama equivalent, *mangga*, which is used in so many ways, and is appropriate in so many contexts, that it is perhaps the first word of Javanese a nonnative speaker learns. No delocutive verbs are derived from either *ayo* or *nya*, but a

Address styles and the muting of gesture   219

delocutive verb is derived from *mangga* with the causative/benefactive verbal affix (ngoko: -*aké*, krama: -*aken*). The impersonal passive form *dimanggakaké* can be glossed literally as something like 'to be addressed with the word *mangga*', 'to have "*mangga*" said to one' or, more fluently and with an eye to context and illocutionary force, 'to be invited'. *Mangga* is usually described as having a madya alternant *ngga* but both are heard in madya speech. By the same token the alternant *sumangga* is often classified as krama inggil, but *mangga* is commonly used to persons otherwise addressed and referred to in deferential ways.[10] These basa locutionary forms encode avoidance, as do the honorific vocabularies, through the substitution of one locution for several.

Interjections

Incidental though they are to an account of the speech style system, interjections are pervasive elements of speech and have indexical significances that are suppressed in relatively polite, gesturally muted speech. Every language offers conventional means for intimating feelings and attitudes on what Jakobson (1960:354) has called the "purely emotive stratum of language." Interjections like "gee" "hey" or "the hell" (as in "What/who/when . . . ") signal subjective psychological and emotional states of an utterer at the time of the utterance and, as indexes of a speakers' feelings and attitudes, share a mode of significativeness with personal pronouns discussed in Chapter 5, demonstrative pronouns, and locutionary formulas. Some interjections signal a speaker's attitudes about or feelings concerning the way an addressee should regard the force or content of what the speaker says, roughly as does "Y'know" in English. They serve what Jakobson (1960:255) calls a conative function, intimating speakers' feelings and attitudes, and have an indexical significativeness that heightens

---

10. From *sumangga* are derived with -*aké*/-*aken* verbs best translated as 'to leave in someone else's hands, to do/leave to be done as someone wishes', but which mean literally (in active form) 'cause to be uttered *sumangga* to', (i.e., 'to say *sumangga* to'). *Sumangga* is historically an active verb derived from the root *sangga* 'to hold up' with the infix -*um*-. *Mangga* has apparently come into use as an elided form resulting from the same fast-speech colloquializing processes that have affected personal pronouns.

the experiential immediacy and vividness of speech in face-to-face interaction.

Like other Malayo-Polynesian languages, Javanese has a fairly developed set of such forms, and these[11] can be called psycho-ostensive insofar as they furnish acquaintance with subjective, occasional states of a user, in ostensive, nonreferential, gestural ways. They are entirely unelaborated in the speech style system, subject to no obvious co-occurrence restrictions with address styles, and go largely unnoticed by speakers when they describe or criticize linguistic etiquette usage. Nonetheless, interjections serve to modulate the relative refinedness of use of each speech level, and this intralevel variation does in fact correlate with relative politeness of context in ways speakers often ignore in metapragmatic descriptions.

But speakers whom I asked neutral questions about differences between examples in which these particles do and do not appear said that examples without them are more refined *(alus)*, using the same term they apply to "lower" and "higher," less and more refined speech styles. I asked about such use in the first place because I had noted that priyayi at their most refined consistently avoided or used such particles only sparingly, and likewise were giving me positively prescriptive examples of proper basa in which they hardly appeared at all. Conversely, these particles were quite prominent in their negative examples of basa that were not sufficiently 'polished' *(besut)*, these occasionally being lampoons of country bumpkins or foreigners who fail miserably to achieve true refinedness.

In krama especially, abstinence from use of some of these particles unobviously but ubiquitously contributes to the relative flatness of affect in conduct. Others are tacitly but entirely excluded from polite usage. Like variation in pitch, intonation, and prosody, psycho-ostensive particles can be important modulators of the gravity of one's demeanor in any act of address with a speech style, and it sometimes happens that a shift in topic, or the arrival or departure of some bystander makes for a change in interactional tone and correlative use or nonuse of particles. But unlike pitch, prosodic, and intonational variation, psycho-ostensive particles are segmentable elements of the

11. See for instance Ikranegara 1975 on the Jakartanese dialect of Indonesian and references there. A complete catalog of psycho-ostensive particles in Javanese would cover *kok* and *lho* but also (at least) *(a)thik, dhing, ara, rak, ta* and *lha*. *(A)thik, dhing* and *ara* are never used in polite, krama address.

Address styles and the muting of gesture 221

code that are or are not present, and so more easily characterized. Just two, *kok* and *lho*, will be sketched here to show how and why their presence detracts from the refinedness of speech, and so how they function to modulate refinedness, formality, and perhaps deference. These particles serve emotively or conatively, depending on their placement in an utterance: immediately preceding syntatic material referring to some state of affairs, they index something about a speaker's reaction to that state of affairs; following such material they index a speaker's expectations regarding an addressee's awareness of that state of affairs.

Kok in the first of these uses expresses surprise. Learning that a servant has returned from the kiosk with two batteries rather than the three she was instructed to buy, the mistress of the house may remark to the servant in ngoko *Kok loro!?* (*loro* 'two'), which might be translated as 'How/why is it (that you/he/she only got) two?!' or, relying overheavily on tacit conventions for punctuation in English, 'What!? (only) two??'. If such use of *kok* is construed as a signal that an explanation is desired, and the servant says that the money provided for the purchase was insufficient because the price of batteries has risen, the mistress might respond, as much to herself as anyone else, *Kok larang!* (*larang* ngoko: 'expensive') signaling surprise but not disbelief as might the English 'Wow/well, that's expensive!'.

To express surprise in this way to a higher status person (unlikely, but convenient for contrastive purposes) one could make a simple declarative statement to the effect that two batteries might not be enough or inquire about some possible reason why only two were procured. Better is to say nothing at all. Appending a word meaning roughly 'yes' in the krama equivalent of the above example *(Kok kalih inggih?)* would be relatively polite because the final word explicitly indicates speaker's acknowledgment of and so mere surprise, not doubt, about the state of affairs reported. I observed that fairly formal interaction included speech in which *kok* and other psycho-ostensive particles were generally avoided, particularly in address of persons of markedly higher status. One insightful priyayi to whom I posed the observation as a question said this was because *kok* "displayed the feeling of surprise directly" *(ngétokaké rasa gumun langsung)*, as if one was overtly expressing doubt about something a speech partner had said.

Following material referential of some thing or state of affairs, *kok* conatively conveys to an addressee a speaker's conviction of the truth of that state of affairs described and that he or she would do well to believe and act on that knowledge or conviction. As an appended ostensive strengthener of assertive power, *kok* marks the evaluation a speaker expects on the part of an addressee about the validity of the utterance. In this use *kok* is likewise avoided in politer forms of address.

Lho,[12] uttered with falling intonation either in isolation or as a preface to an utterance, indexes feelings of surprise at some unexpected state of affairs, and its significative similarity with *kok* in nonfinal positions is indirectly evidenced by the frequency with which they are used together (*Lho, kok* . . . 'Why, how is it that . . . '). When pronounced with rising intonation either after a topic phrase or at the end of an utterance, *lho* signals the importance of what has been conveyed, and the speaker's concern that the addressee take heed. As such it may be used in utterances intended to warn or advise, to draw attention to some piece of information in the utterance, or to help draw the speaker's attention to some ostensively identified object in the context of utterance. It is noncoincidentally often used together with the negative imperative element (*Aja lho*) and demonstrative pronouns (for example *Iki lho*; see the previous discussion of *nya*) to emphasize indexically the affective force of the utterance and emphasize the focus of communicative attention.

All the psycho-ostensive particles that priyayi "naturally" avoid in their most refined conduct can be thought of, as one older priyayi said to me, "of a kind with ngoko" (*Tunggilipun ngoko*) insofar as ngoko is the most relaxed, least inhibited speech style. These indexical nonreferential speech components constitute a kind of stylistic overlay superimposed on lexically distinguished address styles, and these gesture-like linguistic resources subtly condition the presentational whole of which speech style use and speech are one part. They help, to recall the image offered by one priyayi, to make speaking less

12. This particle is spelled here (as in other texts) with *h* to mark the breathy phonation quality of initial *l* peculiar to this and one other psychoostensive particle, *lha*, which (roughly put) marks anticipation of or agreement with something forgoing in conversation. I do not accept James Siegel's suggestion (1986:27) that Javanese "exclaim *lho*, indicating that they are surprised, in order to avoid feeling it."

Address styles and the muting of gesture

like following a set of rules, and more like painting a picture. Because their most basic significative, nonreferential properties are skewed with those of speech style system elements, but their indexical representativeness nonetheless allies them with personal pronouns, demonstrative pronouns, and locutionary formulas, they are semiotically complementary linguistic parts of social interaction with their own affective impact on self-presentation.

Indexicality and Modes of Self-Presentation

One reason for carefully distinguishing between speech styles and linguistic etiquette is the existence of variation in use of segmentable speech features that are clearly part of the latter but not subsumed by the former. The cross-cutting classificatory distinctions between objects and modes of reference that organize the description of the speech style system are not readily extendable to psycho-ostensive particles, whose presence or absence does not affect the semantic content of an utterance. A broad notion of indexicality allows for a treatment of this aspect of linguistic etiquette as integrally related to speech style distinctions.

Speech style use is subsumed under broader norms of linguistic etiquette as a major part of but not equivalent to the "ordering of behavior," and the descriptive strategy adopted here to account for more conspicuous aspects of linguistic politeness has been naturally extended to other unobviously related aspects of self-presentation. Patterns of use and change in use, moreover, suggest that social significances of speech style use are more complex than has previously been noted.

Generically refined forms of behavior, linguistic or otherwise, share a common significative basis—the avoidance or muting of indexically communicative behavior. This avoidance is encoded quite clearly in the speech style system's referentially indexical correlative demonstrative pronouns, which stand at the interface between speech and the nonlinguistic acts of pointing that necessarily accompany their use in acts of reference. Such allusiveness in speech depends not on the context dependence of use of impoverished lexical resources like those described in Chapter 6, but the collapse of encoded distinctions between overtly gestural, indexical modes of lexical reference. Interjections and formulaic locutions may have no place in the structurally elaborated speech style vocabularies, and may not be differentiated in the speech style system, but they too are intrinsically gestural and in polite speech are performed less directly or simply avoided.

These various aspects of politeness inside and outside the address styles, in the narrow sense of the term, share underlyingly similar significative modes that bear in different ways on the perceived refinedness and politeness of speech. By framing discussion with distinctions that extend beyond the speech levels to etiquette more generally, the substance of priyayi remarks on the felt unity of etiquette, the ways these different "guided doings" are of a piece, can be rephrased: indexically significant elements—linguistic and kinesic, referential and nonreferential—obtrude if they are not normatively muted in relatively "refined" behavior. Underlying the structure of a system of lexical stylistic distinctions and the experienced qualities of conduct is a common significative dimension that priyayi intuitively recognize in all 'ordering of behavior' *(tata-krama)*. This review of patterned interaction between ways of representing states of affairs and intentions referentially, while presenting oneself interactively, helps articulate the interpenetration of Javanese language and etiquette in broadly semiotic terms.

8

Signs of Politeness

> *I have a strong conviction that one cannot expect to understand a principle with assurance, even when it is a universal, unless one first sees it in a language where it is highly developed.* (Pike 1975:16, italics in the original)

Javanese linguistic etiquette may interest sociolinguists because they have tacitly assumed what Pike suggests: its unusual structural elaborateness may be especially illustrative of general, perhaps universal principles of linguistic politeness. Semantic and semiotic contrasts within the speech style system do in fact suggest general correlations between speech style elements' linguistic significances, the aspects of contexts that they normatively presuppose, and qualities they lend to the social interaction that they serve to mediate. This account may make "the speech levels" seem a little less exotic, and may suggest some ways to follow Joseph Greenberg's advice (quoted by Frake 1980:62) "Whenever you are not surprised, stop and ask yourself: 'Why am I not surprised?'"

Some of the conclusions presented here are unsurprising, and could be drawn from any of several quasi-prescriptive accounts by applying the cross-cutting distinction introduced in Chapter 4 between significances of speech in acts of address and of reference. Treatments already analytically removed from use furnish evidence of the principles of stylistic elaboration discussed here which may be universal but are less developed in other languages. The speech styles' structure (in Peircean terms) might display iconically (and diagrammatically) some general, possibly universal features of linguistic etiquette. The structure of the system clearly suggests that there are two unsurprising properties of or tendencies in relatively polite speech: toward stylistic elaboration of address styles focused on the nonlexical, grammatico-syntactic apparatus, and toward expressions of deference focused on lexemes in the domain of person.

The classification of speech style elements by their objects of reference (personal, nonpersonal, or none) fits with the contrasting structural elaboration and social significances of segmentable speech elements in the system as a whole. Relative to the system as a whole, it is not surprising that diacritics of relatively formal (polite) address styles should be most elaborate among the frequently used morphsyntactic and deictic elements of the language. In this respect categorical krama/madya distinctions are unusually clear but not unique instances of stylistic contrast within repertoires of "nonordinary," non-ngoko *basa* address styles. It is also not surprising that krama/madya style alternations are characteristically between "full" and elided "fast-speech" sound shapes which have analogues in grammatico-syntactic apparatus of many languages (and even within ngoko itself; see Errington 1985b:137–40).

Because deference and esteem have persons for their objects, stylistic oppositions that mark or presuppose deference are unsurprisingly articulated among terms potentially or necessarily referential of persons. Although the Javanese honorific vocabulary is strikingly large and differentiated—in its class-internal structural contrasts between paradigmatic sets that have a krama inggil member, krama andhap member, or both, and that share honorific elements with no, one, or several other sets—its overall structure fits the general logic that objects of deference are socially marked in acts of linguistic reference. Stylistic elaborateness and referential indeterminacy both obtrude in just the semantic domain of mediated acts, first and foremost acts of exchange of which speech is a special subtype. Conversely, the ongoing extinction of what were called little-known honorifics for certain body parts and functions suggests a similarly unsurprising negative correlation between the social intimacy presupposed by acts of reference to certain personal attributes, and the deference presupposed stylistically by use of all honorifics.

Because speech partners are co-occupants of intersubjective, interactive speech partner roles, the structurally central place of pronominal means for referring to speech partners in the speech style system, terms indexically presupposing object of reference as party to act of reference, is likewise not surprising. Nor is it surprising that they are interactionally crucial in speakers' metalinguistic comments on and strategic uses of the style system as a whole. In many languages second-person pronouns are conspicuously elaborated as stylistic mediators of social relations between speech partners (see Head 1978), are highly susceptible to strategic use (see, for example, Friedrich 1972), and have shifted in patterned normative use in ways that reflect broader changes in social status and norms for interaction (see most famously Brown and Gilman 1960). Titles and kin terms, not indexically limited in referential range, also serve as socially significant terms for persons because of their semantic content and the types of enduring social attributes of their referents who may or may not be speech partners. It is unsurprising too that nonpronominal and titular terms in Javanese, as in Spanish, Japanese,[1] Balinese, Malay, and other languages, have been incorporated into personal pronoun paradigms.

Put strongly, these obvious structural contrasts suggest universal implicational relations between the semantic domains, grammatical functions, and social significances of stylistically elaborated segmentable speech element variants. More flexibly, they could be taken as evidence of core/periphery relations between foci of different kinds of socially significant stylistic elaboration. Structural diacritics of formal address style contrasts, whether or not they are available for asymmetric as well as symmetric exchange, will be more generally elaborate in the grammatico-syntactic apparatus of a language than among lexical classes. Stylistic markers of deference for individuals will be elaborated in the semantic domain of person and more differentiated, with or without an encoded semantic indeterminacy, among predicates of exchange and psychosocial states. Finally and perhaps least surprisingly, the most elaborate class of speech elements is most likely to be personal pronouns, elements referential of speech partners qua speech partners.

This analysis would be an overlong explication of the common substance of the literature, which also suggests these conclusions, were it not also concerned with patterns of change and variation in

1. I cannot deal at length here with the putative nonexistence of personal pronouns in Japanese, an issue debated in the literature.

228   Signs of politeness

speech style use, the relation of speakers' interactive strategies to normative pragmatic value and code structure, and the complementary applicability of different sociolinguistic models. To portray the speech styles as mutable, strategically usable mediators of social relations and parts of a larger system of etiquette, I have broached methodological issues of two general types. First, I have suggested that there are general correlations between the stylistic elaboration, referential objects, and significative modes of speech elements, and that indexical significances accrue to aspects of all sorts of etiquette: the speech styles, specifically linguistic etiquette, and more generally conduct in the broadest sense. Second, I have claimed that the effect of interactively oriented use on encoded system structure needs to be described with recourse to something like a "native speaker's point of view," allowing for the effects of recurring patterns of strategic use that assimilate speech variation as means to social ends extrinsic to norms of etiquette.

The concept of indexicality has been obvious and ubiquitous in both respects. The distinction between indexical and nonindexical modes of reference was first introduced in Chapter 4 to distinguish classes of speech style elements. In Chapter 5 I argued that the assimilation of indefinite nonindexical descriptive phrases to pronominal paradigms (*abdidalem, panjenengandalem,* etc.) occurred just because of their prior use as substitutes for or prefaces to pronominal, indexically direct terms for persons. I suggested there that indexically significant vocative use played a crucial role in the evolution of the title *mas* into a kin term. We saw in Chapter 6 that the limiting case of lexically indeterminate honorific use can be characterized by a semantic domain (exchange), but also by the indexical nature of the directive utterances that indeterminate *aturi* serves to perform. In Chapter 7 the muting of indexical significances of speech was traced beyond the gestural correlates of some demonstrative pronouns to a variety of less obviously indexically significant referential and nonreferential linguistic forms: negative imperatives, various locutions, interjections, and even nonlinguistic gestures.

The various indexical significances of conduct and speech are subject to various treatments in relatively polite conduct and deserve to be considered in light of the underlying significative base they share, to be considered semiotically, as Jakobson (1980:35) puts it, as "particular features of language in comparison with the specifics of other sign systems ... to define the common features that characterize signs in general." Possibly general if not universal properties of indexically significant conduct are suggested by Peirce's semiotic, the "quasi-necessary or formal doctrine of signs" (2.227), which can be considered with an eye to the forms and qualities of social interaction. Because speech style variants can be described in specifically linguistic and broadly semiotic terms, topics in sign theory and sociolinguistics converge in ways that are not too surprising if speech is viewed as conduct significant by virtue of shared knowledge of linguistic codes, but also of particular social contexts, persons, and relations between them.

I have considered these two sorts of knowledge as parts of a "native speaker's point of view," to which I have had recourse in descriptions of two distinct patterns of change in speech style structure. To deal with rapid changes in the structures and uses of personal pronouns, titles, and kin terms, and to justify my use of "naive" native speakers' descriptions of use of all three kinds of terms, I claimed that all are relatively pragmatically salient, interactively crucial linguistic mediators of relations between speech partners. For devaluations of all three types of terms, especially personal pronouns, which passed "out" from the center and "down" from the apex of society, I assumed that speakers pay special attention to them as interactively strategic linguistic means to extrinsic social ends which they bring to interaction. The stability of ngoko/madya/krama vocabulary sets in the deictic and grammatico-syntactic apparatus of the language I took to be a reflex of their low pragmatic salience and susceptiblity to quasi-mechanistic, hypercorrective pressures largely outside speakers' awarenesses. Correlative with these variants' lesser pragmatic saliences as linguistic mediators of speaker/addressee relations are their covert dialectal significances as linguistic badges of community membership.

The notion of pragmatic salience was defined abstractly and categorically in Chapter 4 to permit its transposition to other languages and cultures, and needs to be considered in light of the sociolinguistic and semiotic paradigms with which it was used. At issue in this treatment of style in the Javanese case is the heterogeneity not just of the social significances of and changes in the speech styles, but sociolinguistic models introduced to deal with them: Labov's inductive approach to phonological and grammatico-syntactic variation, and Brown and Gilman's account of second-person pronouns. To juxtapose these paradigms in descriptions of variation in a single linguistic subsystem is to invoke metatheoretical issues that still need to be addressed.

Style and Dialect Variation

If sociolinguistics as a discipline comprehends the study of all the diverse significances of human speech, there may be a healthy pluralism in the radically different assumptions, goals, and procedures associated with the paradigms developed by Labov and by Brown and Gilman. But in the face of the manifestly unitary nature of human communication, those disparities may, by the same token, be symptomatic of a debilitating fragmentation. Programmatic criticisms and sweeping slogans aside, points of fit or conflict between these partial, useful approaches to human communication have, with a few notable exceptions, been tacitly accepted or ignored. Differences between them may occasion little discussion because the models have never been used to develop competing descriptions for the same or closely related variational phenomena. But by opportunistically introducing both models I oblige myself to address this question, however briefly, by considering Javanese as a somewhat privileged case in point.

I have assumed that analyses like those by Labov and by Brown and Gilman can each be usefully applied to variation and change among different basa vocabularies, and further that native speakers are differentially aware of stylistic alternations that are more or less pragmatically salient as mediators of face-to-face interaction. Pragmatic salience can be reconsidered here in three general respects. First, it has implications for the congeniality of Labov's approach for nonsalient vocabularies (krama and madya elements), and of Brown and Gilman's approach for relatively salient vocabularies (basa personal pronouns and other terms for persons). Closely related is the issue of "strategic" use invoked to describe pronominal change, which can likewise be articulated in terms of relatively low and high pragmatic salience. The issue of communicative strategy furthermore raises points of difference between Brown and Levinson's (1978) "Model Person"-based approach to universals of linguistic politeness, and what I have called a native speaker's point of view.

From this perspective it is no coincidence that Labov's inductive variable rule approach to linguistic variation was first developed and has been most successfully applied to phonological and morphophonemic variation, which is minimally salient and only marginally obtrusive on native speakers' other-oriented awarenesses of interaction. Insofar as Labov claims that all markers of relative formality of speech situation (what he calls markers) evolve from linguistic symptoms of group membership (what he calls indicators), he assigns genetic and explanatory priority to dialectal variation and change, described mechanistically in terms of "internal, structural pressures and sociolinguistic pressures [that] act in systematic alternation" (1972:181).

Insofar as such variation im-mediately marks speaker group membership, it is susceptible to highly operationalized research techniques and quantitative analysis. Phonological variation offers Labov crucial advantages, most notable here that it "give[s] us a large body of quantitative data from relatively small samples of speech . . . " and is "to a large extent . . . independent of conscious control of the subject" (1972:111). Labov has gone to great lengths to demonstrate that native speakers' characterizations of speech variation reflect empirically groundless stereotypes too often to be dependable, and that an unbiased study of variation "in its natural setting" (Labov 1984) is therefore possible only with research methods that ostensibly bypass the speaker's sociocentric point of view. An abiding concern with generalizations about linguistic variation that emerge from data of talk, and are correlated statistically with speakers' socioeconomic and ethnic backgrounds, makes it plausible to residualize contextual influences on use placed under the oversimple rubrics of "formality" and "degree of attention to language." Labovian studies of unconscious allegiances to linguistic (sub)communities presume that contextually conditioned variation is secondary to and genetically derivative of dialect variation, and susceptible to unilateral manipulation by the investigator in the context of research.

If speakers in a real sense do not know what they are doing when they "choose" phonological variants in ways that are not possibly informed by or grounded in conscious communicative projects, Labov's variable rules account for im-mediate relations between noncontextual features of community status and linguistic behavior. In this analytic sphere the conceptual gap between inductively motivated rules drawn from *data* of talk and the interactively realized *process* of talk, to borrow a distinction from Fishman 1972, is relatively unobtrusive. Still, much sociolinguistic writing critical of the variable rule approach speaks directly or indirectly to the theoretical significance of this gap. The now dead controversy over the theoretical status of variable rules vis-a-vis generative models of linguistic competence (see, for example, Cedergren and Sankoff 1974) was also a controversy about the theoretical status of variable rules as descriptions of language as act (*parole*) or knowledge (*langue* or competence).[2] By the same token, several authors have criticized such oversimplistic equations of "formality" with "attention to language," and sought to explore the ways that "group membership and its reflection in speech [is] ... to a large extent ... mediated by the intervening variable of social relations" (Brown and Levinson 1979:291) even if they are "not necessarily explicitly statable by participants" (1979:294).

In retrospect it seems impractical and theoretically implausible to argue that the quantitative paradigm needs to be extended beyond phonological variation "if [the approach] is to make a significant contribution to the problems [of variation]" (Labov 1972:247). Theoretical and operational problems that have attended Labov's forays into syntactic description (see Lavandera 1976, Romaine 1982) and semantic description (see Fillmore 1975b:128) are symptomatic of intrinsic significative differences between phonological and nonphonological variation, differences that bear directly on the ways each can be described as "rule-governed behavior." Nonetheless, by convincingly demonstrating unobvious patterns of phonological variation not totally reducible to interactional factors, Labov broached the issue of how distinct yet interpenetrating interactive and dialectal significances of speech variation are articulated outside of speaker's awareness. His quantitative method puts sociolinguistics on a new footing

2. This point may be clearest in critiques by Bickerton 1971, Romaine 1981, 1982, and sources cited in Irvine's (1985) useful discussion.

insofar as it deals with linguistic variation that speakers are not able to describe (objectify) accurately, or to implement as means to overt, pregiven, describable, interactional ends.[3]

Even though Javanese speech style variation serves primarily to mediate face-to-face interaction rather than to mark the social background of speakers, we saw in Chapter 7 that very real covert dialectal significances do accrue to use of the madya and krama *basa* address styles, which are crucially distinguished by what I have called relatively pragmatically nonsalient elements of the system. Native speakers are neither highly aware of nor able to report accurately on variation within and across these *basa* registers—between formal and informal krama on the one hand, or between krama and madya on the other. Although variation in the grammatico-syntactic and deictic apparatus is overtly stylistic, speakers of different subgroups perceive and report on it in sociocentric ways as either variation between "good" and "bad" basa—by priyayi for whom madya is a substandard social dialect spoken by those who "know no better"—or as "formal" and "informal" basa styles opposed on a cline of politeness or refinedness (Errington 1985b:84–92). Their statements correspond with covert social allegiances to linguistic subcommunities.

In this respect variation among pragmatically nonsalient style elements resembles phonological variation described by Labov, and morphosyntactic stylistic variation stands at the threshold between dialectal (indicator) and stylistic (marker) variation in the speech style system. At the same time, it stands at the threshold of native speakers' awarenesses of stylistic significances of speech style use as a mediator of face-to-face interaction. It is notable that the Labovian view of social dialect evolution elaborated by Kroch (1978), which deals with effects of covert social ideology on dialect evolution, fits very well the most plausible account of the historical evolution of madya from krama speech styles, touched on in Chapter 7 and dis-

3. This differs from but parallels Brown and Levinson's distinction between "unintended/natural signs," which covers what Labov calls "indicators" and their "intended signs produced in such a way as to appear to be unintended," their partial characterization of what Labov calls "markers." Much more sociolinguistically oriented discussion of the problem of intentionality is needed to clarify the use of such distinctions in order to reconcile Labovian type analysis with descriptions of variation that "appears" to be unintended.

cussed at length elsewhere (Errington 1985b, Poedjosoedarmo n.d.). At the same time, madya/krama address style elements have also been the most stable in the speech style system, because they have historically been least susceptible to strategic interactive use.

Open classes of krama speech style elements dyadically opposed to ngoko variants show still more clearly subcommunity differences in and covert dialectal significances of use. The relative pragmatic nonsalience of krama lexemes has been a factor in the mechanistic extension of sound patterns, which broadly resemble the patterned extensions in phonological change that inform Labov's model of linguistic change. Insofar as phonological variation involves elements that are trivially nonreferential, one might say that they are the least pragmatically salient of all segmentable speech elements, and stand next to grammatico-syntactic elements at the extreme end of a continuum of types of variation as most congenially described as data in inductivist Labovian terms.

From the speaker's point of view, terms for persons, and more specifically terms always and only used for speech partners, are most pragmatically salient. From an interactively instrumental perspective more rides socially on choice between highly salient elements than between any others, and for these elements Labovian analysis is obviously inadequate. Labov's early programmatic claims (e.g., 1972: xiii) about the inseparability of sociolinguistic (variable rule) and linguistic analysis are in fact least plausible when considered in light of personal pronoun variation, which, as Labov has written, can only be studied once quantitative measures of "authority, respect, or intimacy" (1972:284) have been developed. This approach is implausible just because of the fundamental significative difference between dialectal "meanings" of phonological variation and interactive "meanings" of pronominal variation, the latter depending crucially on and realized in intersubjective processes and patterns of exchange that can only be created jointly by speech partners. Such intersubjective meaningfulness simply eludes an inductive description that makes no allowance for interpretation of intrinsically occasional, contextualized, stylistically conveyed intent.

Accounts of variation among relatively pragmatically salient speech style elements require the fundamentally different, participant-oriented perspective on interaction suggested in Chapter 5 as a kind of "speaker's point of view" to describe highly salient speech style elements. Speaker's knowledge of possible and proper style use together with norms and strategies of interaction are then characterized as shared understandings, tacit or explicit, about face-to-face interaction—what Goffman calls "rule[s] of conduct [that] may be defined as guide[s] for action," (1967:48) that "impinge upon the individual ... as obligations ... and expectations." (1967:49) Shared normative knowledge of what speech style variants presuppose as recurring social features of contexts must be assumed at least operationally if one is to make principled use of the same kinds of self-reported "data" on which Brown and Gilman's famous analysis (and others stimulated by it) depends.[4] That personal pronoun, proper name, kin term, and title use are natural interactive foci for linguistic usage bespeaks their pivotal role and privileged instrumental nature as mediators of linguistic interaction—that is, their high pragmatic salience.

Friedrich (1972) for instance is able to treat authors as special informants who characterize plausible strategic uses of pronominal repertoires to socially expressive ends;[5] with this approach he vividly illustrates the mediative capacities, latent communicative power, and potentially intention-laden significance of second-person pronoun usage. Statistically rare cases of ambiguous and strategic usage are crucial clues to second-person pronoun use, implemented and interpreted with crucial recourse to biographical and contextual particulars. Creative uses of second-person pronouns are particularly clear examples of the dynamic interplay between rule (or convention or system) and context (of use) that obtrudes precisely through tension between communicative intention imputable to someone in a given interactive context, and some conventionally significant style they implement or enact.

However one chooses to contrast "exceptional" and "ordinary"

4. Brown expanded this approach with Ford (1964) to other referential expressions for persons (titles and names) and formulaic locutions (greetings) in English, and with Raghavan and Iritani (Brown 1965) to Hindi and Japanese usage. The huge literature that has followed can hardly be summarized here. This latter research is unmentioned in Brown and Levinson's criticism (1978:310 n. 98) that the Brown and Gilman model is inapplicable in non-Western societies and languages.

5. Compare in this regard Labov's rhetorical question: "What is the relation between the novelist's stereotype and the language behavior of the people in question?" (1972:201).

cases—as creative and prototypical, strategic and normative, marked and unmarked—one allows for the same kind of interpretive ability, in Ricouer's (1982) sense of the word, that informs construal of conventional behavior as a possible vehicle of interactionally oriented and realized intention. Although it is dangerous to conceive of language as a tool and object of use (Benveniste 1971:223), the pragmatically salient elements of Javanese linguistic etiquette, and of other languages which have been similarly described in the literature, do manifest an overt, interactively instrumental importance as mediators of social relations.

One final basic difference between Labov's and Brown and Gilman's approach needs to be noted. Where stylistic concerns are residualized in Labov's schema, Brown and Gilman present intracommunity variation in normative use as evidence of "group styles" (1960:253), interactive norms informed by social ideologies that may differ across socioeconomic lines and are in effect dialectal insofar as they are indirectly indicative of class status of a speaker. In this respect variation in address style use within the highly stratified courtly elite community considered in Chapter 3 parallels also the broadest lines of Brown and Gilman's approach.

These complementarities between two paradigms—in descriptive foci, methods, operational assumptions (tacit or explicit), and social significances of linguistic variation congenially described—are fairly obvious but are not trivial, and deserve to be considered in light of Greenberg's advice. The Javanese case suggests that structurally and semantically specifiable classes of segmentable speech elements vary intrinsically in their relative susceptibilities to interactively keyed stylistic elaboration, and that they are thus more or less crucial linguistic means for mediating face-to-face interaction, and perhaps expressing nonreferential interactive intentions. It suggests too that segmentable speech elements are more or less salient from a speaker's interactively oriented, instrumental point of view on linguistic codes as mediators of face-to-face conduct and vehicles of referential meaning.

Insofar as I have argued that speakers' awareness of linguistic variation correlates with lexical content and morphosyntactic functions of variants, I have adopted the subjectivist stance implicit in Brown and Gilman's approach and the phrase "native speaker's point of view." The same point of view is implicit in the remark of the priyayi (quoted in Chapter 1) who said that linguistic etiquette (the *unggah-ungguh ing basa*) is about the questions "Who is this person? Who am I? Who is this person to me?." Variation in use of highly salient elements significative of judgments on relations between speech partners are relatively transparent as mediators of social relationships. Less salient variation may be construed as overtly or covertly significative of a user's social background, and so be described as subject to noninteractive social forces of the sort Labov has considered.

Pragmatic salience reflects the Javanese speaker's point of view insofar as it presupposes no analytic line between stylistic and dialectal variation, which we have seen interpenetrate in ways not fully dealt with in the literature. The notion is as abstract as the concept of indexicality on which it is based, used to distinguish referential significances accruing to personal and demonstrative pronouns and performative utterances, conative and emotive meanings of psycho-ostensive particles, and generally interactional significances accruing to use of the entire speech style system. Indexical significances of use of each type of linguistic sign derive from different types of metonymic links between tokens and contexts of use, joined by speech style elements' normative but mutable values in stylistic oppositions.

Styles and Strategies

Fillmore (1975a) identifies this underlying significative commonality between referential and nonreferential "meanings" of speech with the term "social deixis," since developed by Penelope Brown and Steven Levinson (1978) and Levinson (1979, 1983) as a major rubric in pragmatics and a theory of universals of linguistic politeness. They develop plausible, remarkably specific hypothetical universal correlations between politeness and linguistic variation of virtually every sort, extending from voice pitch to code-switching, from syntax to referential deictic usage, from use of compliments to double negative constructions. There is a convergence between their theoretical concerns and particulars of the Javanese case, especially with respect to what I have called normative and strategic use, and the ways that social deixis (as they call it) is so elaborately encoded in Javanese speech styles. The theoretical implications of their model and the wide range of elaborating examples and evidence that they adduce cannot be discussed comprehensively, but some of their arguments and assumptions can be presented and reviewed with an eye to the Javanese case.

Their theory of universals is sketchy in the area of social deixis because (as they say) they lack systematic accounts of complex systems of social deixis (such as this one pretends to be); thus, it is worth reconsidering some specifics of this account in light of their approach. They base their theory on Goffman's notions of face and face work (1967) on one hand, and Grice's very different theory of conversational maxims and implicature (1971, 1975) on the other. Both paradigms inform their analysis of the linguistic side of Goffman's postulated "single logically coherent framework" or "matrix" of face-saving practices (1967:13). An important expository means to their descriptive and theoretical ends is what they call a "Model Person,"[6] an automaton that they construct "almost tongue in cheek" and endow with what they call face wants, knowledge of Gricean maxims, and the ability to work out quasi-deductively a wide variety of face-redressive strategies. Features of speech count as relatively polite insofar as they are face-redressive deviations from maximally efficient speech behavior as defined by Grice, and count as instrumental and "rational" means for redressing a priori, explanatorily primitive face wants. Face wants are threatened by speech acts that impinge on freedom (negative face) or deny commonality and shared values (positive face) and are redressed on the same basis. Brown and Levinson trace many face-redressive strategies to the exploitation of Gricean maxims to invite conversational implicatures, and argue that apparently normative, rule-like features of linguistic politeness can be reduced or traced to such strategies, of which they are "frozen outputs."

Obvious theoretical and empirical points are at issue in differences between the notions of "norm" and "strategy" used in their work and this, differences in both being related in turn to a more fundamental skewing between their Model Person's highly abstract point of view (if it is fairly characterized as having one) and the instrumental, sub-

---

6. This is apparently related to what they later call a "reference model of politeness," although the relation is not entirely clear to me.

jectivist speaker's point of view developed here. There are several points to which a face-oriented analysis can not be easily extended.

Consider first the history of personal pronouns in Javanese, instances of linguistic variation important to any theory of social deixis. Brown and Levinson describe polite personal pronouns as lexicalized rituals of avoidance (1978:195) that serve the negative face-redressive strategy summed up by their mini-maxim "give deference" (1978:183), and that make "special attestations . . . concerning how [speaker] regards [addressee]" (Goffman 1967:71). Brown and Levinson would trace the grammaticalization of indefinite descriptions into polite pronominal forms as a transition from Gricean conversational to conventional implicatures, the former available to construe use of nonpronominal forms as referential of persons by whom and to whom they are used to redress negative face. Their implicature-driven scheme (1978:264) of the dynamic relation between code (what they call form and meaning) and use is, as they admit (1978:309, n. 87) crude, but as it stands obviously bears on the evolution of any of the Javanese personal pronouns that evolved from indefinite referential expressions discussed in Chapter 5.

It is unclear, though, how Brown and Levinson's model could account for the ongoing devaluation and coining of new personal pronouns, cycled down from the "top" of the social hierarchy and the "top" of the stylistic paradigms. The social and linguistic dynamics that have been involved in this ongoing process during the last 150 years, together with the complex personal pronoun repertoires that have resulted, require different notions of strategic and normative use, such that the latter is available as relevant for construal of the former. If strategies oriented essentially to redress of negative face bring about the transformation of indefinite expressions to automatized, negative-face-redressive pronouns as described in Chapter 5, it is unclear what further face wants, strategic or otherwise, would lead to a recurrence of the process, or why anyone, Model Person or otherwise, would then seek some "higher," somehow more negative face-redressive (and nonpronominal) term.

I argued in Chapter 5 that new basa personal pronouns evolved in priyayi usage as replacements for older, recurringly devalued basa pronouns. Such devaluation was taken to be the result of strategies for which normative stylistic expressiveness was instrumental in other-exalting, self-abasing conduct, which was not just ethically proper but interactively efficacious for achieving one's goals. Emulation and appropriation by progressively larger and lower-status groups of speakers across class lines was taken to be a lagging recurrence of that same kind of strategic usage in urban Surakartan society at large, and likewise had for a symbolic focus normatively deferential personal pronouns. The notion of "strategic use" was intended to link extrinsic social projects to shared norms for interaction, the notion of "norm" thus defined reciprocally and complementarily with "strategy." The interplay between the two was crucial to my account of dynamic relations between contextually realized and conventional significances of pronominal devaluation, and of the effects and symptoms of strategic exploitation of normative deferential values.

These senses of norm and strategy differ from Brown and Levinsonn's as does what I have called a Javanese native speaker's "point of view" from that of their Model Person. Brown and Levinson's notion of strategy covers unproblematically related "innovative plans of action" and "routines whose origin is still preserved in their construction" (1978:90), because norms are for them essentially derivative or residual with respect to strategies redressing highly abstract face wants. The history of pronominal change in Javanese suggests that routinized (automatized) normatively polite forms are themselves objects of "innovative plans of action." "Strategy" is a rubric in both treatments for rational, means-to-ends types of activities, but the means, ends, and agents of "strategic" activities in their theory and this case differ. Without allowing for an explanatorily useful notion of norm, it is difficult to see how the devaluational cycle affecting Javanese personal pronouns could be explained. If a notion of pragmatic salience is universally valid, then a theory of universals of politeness must allow for a less abstract native speaker point of view that complements Brown and Levinson's Model Person, and also for the strategic assimilation of normatively polite usage as "input" to broadly strategic, "innovative plans of action" through which normative social significance is subject to change.

This approach speaks to a question Brown and Levinson invite but do not answer. In the words of their editor (Goody 1978:10), how do "strategic choices become institutionalized [that is, encoded] in the amber of normative usage[?]" This question stems from the problematic relation of abstract Model Personhood to membership in an actual linguistic community (Javanese or otherwise), because social conduct (linguistic or otherwise) presumably counts as normative just insofar as its significance devolves from conventional knowledge shared by members of a community who are able to interpret it. The Durkheimian social facts that Brown and Levinson seek to reduce to strategies are in this sense strategically usable as such because they are shared by members of a community. Aspects of linguistic politeness that are normative and shared within a community are easily residualized in a theory elaborated through a homuncular Model Person whose logic is not easily transposable to anything like a community, model or otherwise.

Brown and Levinson do allow for a notion of norm-dependent strategic use in the guise of "marked usage" (1978:235), and this accords with implicit and explicit allusions to normative use in their respective ethnographic descriptions of Tenajapan and Tamil speech communities. Levinson (1982:111) for instance speaks of "normative" and "unmarked" usage, the latter defined elsewhere (Brown and Levinson 1979:333) as "unexpected usage that contrasts with the basic or fundamental usage." If this description of "unmarked usage" is as close to what Goffman calls a rule of use as it seems—"[i]mpinging on consciousness as an expectation or obligation"—then it is also normative and seems to accord with the strategic/normative distinction used here.

So aside from the descriptive utility of what Brown and Levinson call a "normative overlay on strategically coherent patterns of speaking," (1978:287) the notion of "norms for use" has an explanatory role for the Javanese case, and perhaps more generally if other personal pronouns are relatively susceptible to and mutable through similarly strategic use. In this respect the Javanese case shows by its structural elaborateness a general, perhaps universal relation between terms' semantic functions by mode and object of reference, and their social functions as mediators of social relations.

In Brown and Levinson's terminology (1978:281) all speech style elements count as "honorifics" insofar as they are "direct grammatical encodings of relative social status between participants, or between participants and things referred to in the communicative event." This sense of honorifics is obviously and only trivially broader than mine. Two types of krama inggil and krama andhap vocabulary usage appear to elude a face-want oriented account: acts of honorific reference to non-speech participants, and differentially polite, curiously deferential acts of face-threatening performative directive use.

Use of the krama inggil and krama andhap lexicons for speech partners could be construed as redressive of negative face in accordance with Brown and Levinson's mini-maxim "give deference," and acts of honorific reference to non-speech partners in enduring status relations to speaker or addressee might similarly be redressive or threatening of addressee's face wants, as Brown and Levinson's simple diagram (1978:187) suggests. Acts of *mbasakaké* 'speaking the speech of the children' described in Chapter 6, for instance, may impose speaker's view of addressee's social relationship with and style of speech to some non-speech partner referent. Other honorific acts of reference to non-speech partners may conversely redress addressee's negative face by giving them deference via some non-speech partner referent to whom they stand in an enduring social relation. Such acts would be construable as face-redressive by the same logic that informed honorific use of *ijengandika* to refer to kin of high status addressee.[7]

But acts of honorific reference to non-speech partners to whom neither speech partner has an enduring or interactively relevant social relationship cannot be readily incorporated into Brown and Levinson's schema. Notable among these are acts of predication of exchange or coordinate action, agents and recipients of which are not speech partners. For one office worker to use a krama inggil verb to tell a deskmate that their boss has given a report to another employee will redress neither speech partner's face, at least not in any way clear enough even to say whether it redresses positive or negative face. Such occasions of use rather mark an enduring status inequality between agent and recipient of action spoken of, a relationship intrin-

---

7. Brown and Levinson's model could account for choice of styles of reference for bystanders who are audience to but not partners in speech, and could presumably develop a fairly complex calculus for deciding between honorific and nonhonorific use in terms of face wants of bystanders as opposed to addressees. But this is a different category of referent from the absent referents who are at issue here.

sically independent of the status relation between speech partners, as is the motivation for choosing an honorific or nonhonorific verb of exchange. Brown and Levinson might treat such use as historically derivative of face-redressive reference to speech partners, according such ostensibly peripheral usage a historically secondary place. But it is difficult to see how it can be reduced wholly or in many cases even partially to the outcome of redressive strategies or face wants that are intrinsic to face-to-face interaction.

Brown and Levinson's account suggests that encoded semantic indeterminacy of honorifics discussed in Chapter 6 be treated as the "frozen output" of the negative face-redressive strategy "Be vague" (1978:228–32), lexical avoidance of what Goffman (1959:69), citing Simmel (1950:321), calls the "ideal sphere" around persons. If honorific elaboration in other languages and cultures has similar semantic foci and is similarly semantically indeterminate, some implicational array of semantic domains might be grafted onto their scheme. But it is difficult to see how it could account for the differential politeness of the two bald on record directive formulas performed with verbs of speaking *aturi* 'say to' and *suwun* 'request'.

I argued in Chapter 6 that the relative politeness of directive performative use of *aturi* is a function of that lexeme's semantic indeterminacy in an idiomatic construction that configuratively signals its directive force. *Suwun*, glossable as 'request', was less polite because it is lexically determinate, and has just that meaning. This fact was taken as evidence that the lexicon counts as a privileged focus of stylistic elaboration and evaluation relative to syntax: what is unambiguously conveyed by syntactic configuration is more refined and polite than what is unambiguously conveyed by a highly specific lexeme. The greater face-threateningness of *suwun* (as Brown and Levinson would put it) can be explained, it seems, only by incorporating into a calculus of face-redressive strategies a ranking of linguistic structural levels vis-a-vis the relative face-threateningness of stylistic, socially deictic variation that marks "unequivocal, categorical, determinate" evaluations of aspects of social relations (1979:317–21). Segmentable linguistic elements would be accorded more importance or salience, and so would allow, like the notion of pragmatic salience, for correlations between speech elements' lexical and morphosyntactic characteristics and their more or less privileged status in interaction, albeit to specifically face-redressive ends. The tremendous breadth of Brown and Levinson's claims stems in part from their Model Person's ability to manipulate strategically variation of virtually every sort, each equally susceptible or transparent with respect to face-redressive strategies. The Javanese case suggests that a less abstract point of view, such as that developed here, is needed to privilege some types of variation over others.

Because manipulation of topic can serve face-redressive strategies, Javanese further suggests that one must allow for the possibility that positive and negative face-redressive strategies can be implemented simultaneously in different ways through the styles and content of speech. Newly acquainted Javanese, for instance, will often inquire in highly honorific basa about each other's parents, siblings, marital status, children, and so on. They thus introduce the universal topic of kinship, what surely counts as a positive face-redressive strategy, while speaking and referring to each other with style variants that presumably redress negative face. Insofar as these are complementary, co-occurring face-redressive strategies, Brown and Levinson must allow not just for "linguistic realizations of positive- and negative-politeness strategies [which] operate as a social accelerator and a social brake, respectively" (1978:236) in sequential alternation, but also operate concurrently. What they would call the face-redressing function of basa style usage, and the potential face-threatening or face-redressing nature of topics of speech, appear to be relatively independent and perhaps mitigating of each other.

In Chapter 7 I argued that a wide variety of indexically significant speech elements were muted or avoided in relatively polite basa: in the encoded collapse of demonstrative resources, negative imperative or propositive utterances, as well as the nonobligatory suppression of psycho-ostensive particles. Each was taken as a different facet of the relative refinedness of speech style use, but also of self-presentation generally.

The significative unity of these variously muted, indexically significant aspects of behavior is not clearly addressed in a face-redressive theory of politeness. The impoverishment of krama forms that are used as negative and propositive formulas could be attributed to the potential threateningness of both sorts of acts to an addressee's negative face, insofar as the former quite directly impedes his or her

Signs of politeness 245

future action, and the latter may promote a speaker's project over an addressee's. One might argue that psycho-ostensive particles serve to intensify addressee's interest (Brown and Levinson 1978:111) and so redress positive face, even if it is germane for Javanese that such particles are intrinsically unrefined and perhaps indicative of lack of self-control. The collapse of tripartite deictic distinctions might less plausibly be called another grammaticalized outcome of the strategy "Be vague," or perhaps a "point of view" operation (1978:123–27), which redresses negative face by impersonalizing demonstrative reference in ways analogous to impersonalizing strategies Brown and Levinson deal with under the rubric of modal and passive usage (1978:278–81).

But such an explanation will not extend to the complementary collapse of the distal deictic member in the king's presence, presumably another example of bystander honorific usage. It will also not explain why the structural muting of demonstrative pronouns occurs just in those series whose members are necessarily accompanied in use with a physical indexing act, a finding I argued to be consonant with all these other gesturally muted aspects of face-to-face conduct. That the collapse is partial in just this way strongly suggests an underlying significative fit or parallel between linguistic (referential) and nonlinguistic (nonreferential) aspects of polite conduct. The notion of indexical significance, applied broadly to other classes of variants that have special structural characteristics—for pronominal reference to persons, performative imperatives, propositive and negative imperatives, psycho-ostensive particles—has served just this purpose. Taken together, they show how polite Javanese speech is muted gesturally in its indexically significative aspects, referential and otherwise.

This natural conclusion speaks to the broad significative unity underlying conduct, socially and linguistically indexical, that Javanese allude to with the rubric 'ordering of behavior' (*tata-krama*). The Javanese case suggests another, very different sort of maxim: "Avoid or mute indexical aspects of your conduct." This maxim might have, to mention an obvious, concrete subcase, the admonishment sometimes made to children in Java and the United States alike: it is not polite to point at others (and especially, one might add, one's speech partner). This is a very different claim for a universal of politeness, based on a much simpler set of assumptions about speech. It presupposes neither a primitive universal set of face wants nor an abstract ability to calculate threats to face. It depends rather on assumptions about significative commonalities of semiotic process.

This last point is perhaps the most obvious symptom of basic differences between congenial foci and theoretical implications of Brown and Levinsons's approach to linguistic politeness and my approach to Javanese. Where I allow for an abstract notion of indexicality, referential or nonreferential, Brown and Levinson's "social deixis" counts as a descriptive rubric within a Gricean calculus of communicative intent and face-oriented strategies. Where I allow for an instrumental speaker's point of view that accepts normative social meaning as input to broadly social strategies, they postulate a Model Person that calculates universal face-redressive strategies pregiven to interaction.

Rather than pursue the complexities of a Gricean treatment of deixis[8] developed by Levinson 1979, it is more appropriate here to reconsider indexicality as a broadly semiotic rubric that subsumes all deixis, linguistic and social, and that helps explicate what priyayi, at least, perceive to be the underlying unity of all etiquette. Recalling again Pike's remark, we can broach finally the reasons why indexical signs (linguistic or not, referential or not) are liable to diverse stylistic treatments. Put in more explicitly semiotic terms: what peculiar qualities accrue to the indexically significant aspects of conduct that are given such various treatments in Javanese speech and conduct? Why are they relatively muted in what native speakers regard as polite behavior?

Indexicality from the Native Speaker's Point of View

When asked appropriately framed questions, priyayi describe speech styles sociocentrically in terms of their dialectal features, contextu-

---

8. He addresses the conceptual gap between an intuitively obvious notion of "social deixis" and the highly abstract Gricean schema, which accords no clear place to social "meanings" of these kinds of lexical variation, by generalizing the notion. He argues by elimination that social deixis is part of a residual class of nontruth conditional, noncancellable conventional implicatures that evolve out of (are grammaticalized from) conversational implicatures. He thus inverts the terms of discussion by treating conventional

ally in terms of their appropriate use, and sometimes structurally in terms of their system-internal contrasts. But they spontaneously speak of the styles, content, and users of linguistic etiquette far more often as relatively *alus* 'refined, polished' or *kasar* 'crude, coarse', broad enough terms to apply to virtually all affective qualities of experience. Virtually anything with perceptual impact on or realization in 'feeling' (*rasa*) can be qualified as *alus* or *kasar*. These terms have little in common with sign theoretic notions, or a structural linguist's abstract view of language codes except conceptual breadth. The Javanese idiom need not seem exotic, given intuitively similar English ways of speaking of "polished" and "coarse" persons and performances alike, but it remains to reconsider this account as a description of polite conduct as *alus* conduct, possessing what Geertz (1960:240) usefully calls "flatness of affect." One way to do this is with Peirce's semiotic and logic ("the general necessary laws of signs" 2.93), which is based on his three phenomenological categories of experience (data of consciousness, or phanerons). By briefly reviewing his theory of signs and notion of "indexicality" in light of his phenomenology, we can develop another consonant notion of "flatness of affect" which is suggested by Peirce's remarks on qualities of feeling intrinsic to indexical semiotic processes.

Peirce's best known trichotomy of signs—icon, index, and symbol—is the most accessible and what he sometimes called the most fundamental divison of signs (2.275, 4.448), but it hardly captures the subtlety and breadth of his writings on semiosis. Semiosis is for Peirce crucially *processual*, and only analytically reducable to these and other *entities*. Signs, like moments of sign processes, are inherently triadic, involving a sign vehicle (representamen, a first) standing for something (an object, a second) in some respect or capacity to something else (an interpretant, not an interpreter, *pace* Charles Morris).[9] The interpretant is the mediating third through and in

---

implicatures as deictic, expanding and abstracting the latter notion far beyond its primary or obvious sense developed by Fillmore 1975b to deal with social "meanings" of speech.

9. It is unfortunate that Levinson (1983) overlooks the implications of Peirce's semiotic by mentioning instead work by Morris that is derivative of it and has long recognized to be at odds in its behaviorism with the basic themes of Peirce's semiotic; see, e.g., Dewey 1946.

which representamen and object are bound in representative unity.

Peirce distinguished signs (representamina) as icons, which are potentially representative by virtue of their characters in and of themselves (2.247); indexes, which are actually representative of objects by virtue of "being really affected" through a dynamic or causal relation to objects (2.248); and symbols, which are conventionally representative of objects "by virtue of a law, usually an association of general ideas, which operates to cause the sign to be interpreted as referring to that Object"(2.249). This is the second of Peirce's three trichotomies of signs; it rests on a first division between signs (representamina) with respect to their qualities in and of themselves, and is itself in turn presupposed together with the first by the third trichotomy of signs according to the respects in which signs represent objects for interpretants.[10]

The adjectival "indexical" and nominal "indexicality" have been used here to describe linguistic signs that count in Peirce's terminology not as indexes but symbols whose tokens (what Peirce called replicas) stand in dynamic, part/whole relations to their objects. Indexically referential linguistic signs represent (serve to refer to) things presupposed in context—with which, as Peirce puts it, "the interpreting mind is already acquainted"—and belong to the subclass of linguistic signs called designations: "personal, demonstrative, and relative pronouns, proper names . . . [that] act to force the attention to the thing intended "(8.368, n. 23). All of these kinds of linguistic expressions, we have seen, are subject to special treatment in Javanese linguistic etiquette: they are stylistically elaborated and strategically used, structurally muted, or avoided. Personal and demonstrative pronouns have been called indexical here to identify the aspect of their significative nature shared with other, nonlinguistic representamens that stand in dynamic existential relations to their objects.

Indexical linguistic signs are existentially bound to their objects in ways that make likewise for distinctive relations to their interpretants. The nature of these indexical sign/interpretant relations are suggested by Peirce's use of the verb "force" in the passage quoted above, which is neither isolated nor accidental. It appears in Peirce's

---

10. For a convenient overview, see Shapiro 1983.

later characterizations of interpretants as "proper significate effects" of signs, which foreground the notion that signs *determine* their interpretants,[11] these latter facets of or moments in the semiotic process reciprocally representing the relation between that representamen and the represented object in a unitary whole. Part of the "proper significate effect" of an indexical sign may be a feeling "forcibly intruding upon the mind, quite regardless of its being interpreted as a sign" (4.447)—that is, furnishing or forcing acquaintance with entities exterior to semiotic process through an experience of disjunction between disparate experiences. "A rap on the door is an index. Anything which startles us is an index in so far as it marks the junction between two portions of experience. . . . [It] may be expected to connect itself with some other experience" (2.286).

In this respect semiosis involving indexical signs partakes of an experiential quality elaborated in Peirce's phenomenological category of Secondness—diagrammatically related through his architectonic to the second element of the second trichotomy of signs, the index—which he appropriately called *hecceity* or "thisness," a force felt to direct attention by "blind compulsion" (2.306) to an object in immediate experience. "The index asserts nothing; it only says 'There!' It takes hold of our eyes, as it were, and forcibly directs them to a particular object, and there it stops"(3.362). An experience of "intrusion upon the mind" may be intrinsic to the proper significative effect of indexical signs—a mode of acquaintance with some "real thing or fact" in the *hic et nunc* of experience indexically represented.

Now persons' behavior and appearances, purposeful or not—what Goffman calls their "guided doings" and "exuded expressions"—can serve as indexical signs of their states and qualities. Gestures (paradigmatically, acts of pointing), facial expressions, body posture, intonation and loudness of speech all indexically furnish acquaintance with that to which they are dynamically and causally connected. Speech, one facet of behavior, itself contains and constitutes indexically significant speech behavior, referential and nonreferential, in-

---

11. See, e.g., 5.476. On Peirce's choice of terms to describe the processual relation between sign and representamen, see Greenlee (1973:100). On the mediative properties of interpretants, see Parmentier 1985.

sofar as it draws (or forces) attention to aspects of experientially immediate users and contexts of use, referential or otherwise. In this respect psycho-ostensive particles may stand at the threshold between the semantico-referential significances of speech and the psychological states of speakers, conventionally and indexically significant as they are of subjective, occasional psychological states.

For priyayi, at least, modulation of all these experientially direct, indexically significant aspects of self-presentation serves to modulate also the experiential qualities of behavior, the kinds of "proper significate effects" we have seen to be characteristic of the refined, affectively flat, indexically muted linguistic conduct that Javanese call *alus*. Polite speech can be muted not just with respect to its referential indexicality, but its relative specificity in acts of lexical reference to deferred to persons. The preference for indefinite expressions, the collapse in *alus* speech styles of indexically significative speech act formulas and deictic resources, the prescribed abstinence from use of psycho-ostensive particles, all can be seen as linguistic facets of a broader significative difference between relatively coarse (that is, indexically unmuted) and refined behavior.

Such appeals to experiential, qualitative affect of semiotic process might be dismissed as having no empirical basis, although Peirce would say that they do insofar as they partake of his phenomenological categories. Still, it is difficult to imagine how an integrated account of polite linguistic and nonlinguistic conduct could be developed without at least covert recourse to the broadly experiential if not semiotic aspects of personal appearance and conduct that Javanese tacitly assume when they call various styles of conduct *alus* and *kasar*. Claims about affective qualities intrinsic to indexical signs might be dismissed as having no demonstrable relation to native speakers' evaluations on the one hand, or structural descriptions of speech on the other.

But broad claims about the fit between linguistic and nonlinguistic indexical significances of speech have been developed here out of evidence of structural contrast and change in Javanese usage, which is itself directly affected by patterns that recur in particular acts of use by native speakers, as we saw in Chapter 5. Evidence of change in relative pragmatic salience is also evidence of broad significative contrasts of conventional linguistic signs as contextually embedded mediators of social relations. Claims about pragmatic salience are claims about linguistic signs' usefulness as mediators of interaction, a function of speech quite different from that at the base of classic Saussurean conceptions of language use as code-governed, propositionally significant behavior. Insofar as pragmatic salience links descriptions of features of codes to descriptions of use, it suggests a way of recasting the most basic concepts of structure and convention in interactively oriented ways, by qualifying the doctrine of the arbitrariness of the linguistic sign.

None of Saussure's theoretical statements has been more controversial or less amenable to generally acceptable revision than the doctrine of *l'arbitraire du signe*. The large literature spawned by the brief remarks attributed to him support two of his other famous dicta: that the viewpoint creates the object, rather than the reverse (1966:8), and that "it is often easier to discover a truth than to assign to it its proper place" (1966:68).

Linguistic signs (what Peirce calls legisigns) signify conventionally through their tokens (or replicas) by virtue of shared conventional knowledge (what Peirce would call some habit or predisposition to be so interpreted). For Saussure this is knowledge of a dyadic, system-internal bond between signifier and signified.

> The bond between the signifier and the signified is arbitrary.... In fact, every means of expression used in society is based, in principle, on collective behavior or—what amounts to the same thing—on convention. Polite formulas, for instance, though often imbued with a certain natural expressiveness (as in the case of a Chinese who greets his emperor by bowing down to the ground nine times), are nonetheless fixed by rule; it is this rule and not the intrinsic value of the gestures that obliges one to use them (1966:68).

For Saussure the principle of arbitrariness is important outside of linguistics because signs that are "wholly arbitrary ... that actually have have no natural connection with the signified" (1966:69) realize better than any others the ideal of all semiological systems. Arbitrariness of the linguistic sign thus bears on linguistics as a semiological discipline, radically set off from others as is the linguistic sign set off from other signs.

> Unlike language, other human institutions—customs, laws, etc.—are all based in varying degrees on the natural relations of things; all have of necessity adapted the means employed to the ends pursued.... Language is

252   Signs of politeness

limited by nothing in the choice of means, for apparently nothing would prevent the associating of any idea whatsoever with just any sequence of sounds (1966:75–76).

The essential and distinctive conventionality of the signs and systems of language makes linguistics a potential master-pattern for all branches of semiology. The doctrine of arbitrariness is so central to Saussure's linguistic and semiological program that he credited Whitney, from whom he adopted it, with having placed linguistics "on its true axis" (1966:76).

From Whitney (1979) Saussure also borrowed crucial evidence for linguistic arbitrariness—the fact of linguistic change. Historical process, accidental and contingent with respect to the system, may lead to "a shift in the relationship between the signified and the signifier" against which "language is radically powerless to defend itself ... this is one of the consequences of the arbitrary nature of the sign (1966:75)." Change in the Javanese speech styles, however, is patterned in ways that suggest another conclusion: relative to their functions as interactively embedded stylistic mediators of social relations, some types of linguistic signs are relatively more important mediators of face-to-face interaction than others, that is, are more pragmatically salient than others. In Chapter 5 we saw how linguistic signs that once served as honorific nonindexical expressions evolved into distinct indexical referential expressions. Once assimilated to pronominal paradigms, they rapidly changed in pragmatic value not as the result of random factors contingent to the system *(la langue)* but creative awareness and strategic implementation in socially contextualized use *(la parole)*. In Chapter 7 we saw how other covert dialectal symbolic significances of less salient speech style elements stimulated the system-internal extension of semiregular, patterned correspondences between sound and social meaning.

Such contrasting patterns of change in the speech style code (in the Saussurean sense) thus suggest a way to recast the notion of the relative nonarbitrariness in ways that converge with some of the most cogent criticisms of that doctrine. The statement of the doctrine of arbitrariness attributed to Saussure does not so much describe an empirical state of affairs as establish a linguist's analytic point of view. To analytically dissociate acoustic images from concepts, viewing them as contingently and merely conventionally related entities, presupposes and partially constitutes the code-oriented view of language (*la langue*) as object of description, adopting not just what Benveniste rhetorically calls the "impassive gaze of Sirius" (1971:44) but the objective view of the linguist. For the speaker there is an inseparable union between the two: "the concept . . . is perforce identical in my consciousness with the sound sequence. . . . how could it be otherwise? (Benveniste 1971:45)."

Benveniste's argument that the doctrine of arbitrariness is less a statement of fact than an analytic, heuristic position for code-oriented description[12] rests on the same dual view of the "two different universes" of code and discourse which he explored in his later explicitly sign-theoretic writings, as has Ricouer from an explicitly hermeneutic point of view (1974, 1976, 1982, and elsewhere). Benveniste shows how the doctrine of arbitrariness is, as Friedrich (1979) also argues, not disprovable so much as qualifiable in as many ways as there are significative aspects of use; denying the doctrine of arbitrariness has as many consequences as does affirming it. Put simply, it is less misleading to say that the linguistic sign is nonarbitrary relative to particular aspects of its significative value, notable among them for present purposes being their significance as stylistically opposed markers of evaluations and mediators of social relations.

Now if this double perspective on arbitrariness and conventionality helps articulate what is at stake in Saussure's dictum, it also helps elaborate the notion of relative pragmatic salience, which has been developed as correlative between features of a linguistic system (manifested in structural contrasts between linguistic elements with

---

12. An analogy can be drawn with Peirce's characteristically broader distinction between two perspectives on laws and conventions, concepts that for him extended to the semiotic class of legisigns. Individual occasions of sign use that determine particular, occasional interpretants are experienced as active forces, what Peirce calls Law as a Second (1.337). This is the perspective of Jakobson's German peasant who contrasted the German and French words for cheese by saying "*Káse* is so much more natural!" But as "order or legislation," that convention is describable and objectifiable with external metalinguistic statements—that is, propositions significative of conventions. From the viewpoint of *parole* and communicative immediacy, the sound-image and concept are experientially immediate and a necessary, immediate cause. When objectified as conventional generality partaking of the code, it is a conventional and final cause.

different modes and objects of reference) and a speaker's awareness of speech in interaction (manifested in structural mutability brought about through strategic use, and terms' metalinguistic usefulness). Because it is at once conventional and interactional, Javanese speech styles, and linguistic etiquette in general, have a place in both of Benveniste's "two distinct universes:" the "ensemble of formal signs" that is the structured yet dynamic code, and the the manifestation of language "in living communication" (1971:110).

From a sign-theoretic viewpoint, this argument that classes of linguistic signs are relatively nonarbitrary as mediators of social relations is an argument about a semiotic fit between all indexically significant aspects of interaction, linguistic and otherwise. If etiquette's interactional significativeness shares a semiotic basis with language's referential meaningfulness in indexicality, then there is an underlying semiotic feature that happens to be highly elaborated and to have conspicuous, structural linguistic reflexes in Javanese linguistic etiquette. It is this highly developed nature, recalling Pike's comment, that suggests some general if not universal properties of linguistic politeness.

It is unfortunate that Benveniste articulated Saussurean semiology in his later writings (1974) with only limited access to Peirce's writings (Jakobson 1980:34). Had he been able to look beyond what appeared to him as semiotic's debilitating universality (1974:45) to its descriptive particulars, he might have postulated relations between linguistic systems and etiquette systems like the one discussed here. Benveniste's argument that etiquette stands to language as an interpreted to an interpreting sign system, because it is protocol (stated in language) that "produces and interprets etiquette" (1979:50), presumably applies to exotic languages like Javanese, in which etiquette interpenetrates with the semantico-referential system. We have seen that complex stylistic distinctions superimposed on linguistic systems may condition the conventional means for the "said" of speech, and this to the end of developing very broad interactive qualities and informing particular interactive projects.

As a characterization or qualification of relative nonarbitrariness, the notion of pragmatic salience suggests what Javanese speakers assume: that there is an underlying significative commonality to linguistic and nonlinguistic etiquette that cannot be wholly reduced to either significative sphere. Benveniste likewise suggests that very abstract relations exist between linguistic signs and nonlinguistic signs, other "orders of human and social facts" (1971:49). Language and etiquette share indexical significances as species of contextually dependent and interactively significant conduct. This Peircian claim that interpenetrating sign systems share underlying indexical attributes and qualities[13] suggests a very abstract and general basis for the encoded refinedness of, change in, and general structure of Javanese speech styles as one part of Javanese linguistic etiquette.

To conclude that one need not abuse Saussure's notion of code to speak of a Javanese "code of etiquette" is to recast in technical terms what Javanese say: there is a basic unity of, a fit between all the aspects of politesse called the 'ordering of behavior' *(tata-krama)*. The unity of these different faces of etiquette devolves from their common significative basis. Affective qualities of conduct, the ultimate focus of priyayi evaluations of etiquette, turns out finally to fit with modes and objects of signification, and to reflect a very general if not universal principle of politeness clear in the Javanese case just because it is so highly and systematically developed.

* * *

Javanese who helped me learn about Javanese would have trouble recognizing their "point of view" in this long-winded discussion. Partly by design, partly by necessity, I have provided here a simplified picture of what they call *unggah-ungguh ing basa*. I mentioned earlier one priyayi's remark that using and understanding etiquette is like skillful painting, in which shadings are plentiful, hard and fast lines few. There are subtle (*alus*) connections, he was saying, between different aspects of behavior, and between impressions people intentionally and unintentionally convey about who they are in their conduct. To learn to use etiquette properly, he said, I would have to learn how such pictures are painted in interaction.

13. I avoid lengthy discussion of whether or not this claim might count as one of Benveniste's postulated homological relations between sign systems (1974:60), which would require extensive discussion of his terminology, including senses of the words "semiotic" and "semantic" very different from those used here, but found also in Ricouer 1974:79–86.

I have described basic, structurally conspicuous aspects of etiquette by working less with a palette than a paint-by-numbers kit: lines are artificially simplified in part for lack of descriptive skill, but also for the sake of descriptive clarity and relative conciseness. The strategy's strengths are its weaknesses, and if I portray conventions and structures of linguistic etiquette overcategorically and unsubtly, I like to think that I also incorporate something of the views on linguistic etiquette I learned. This work suggests one way their point of view bears on the study of linguistic communication, and how sociolinguistics may be more of a unitary field within which analytic perspectives naturally and explicitly complement each other.

The last word is not from Javanese, or by them, but for them: my patient friends and teachers, and others who may come across this curious account of a part of their culture. *Nyuwun pangapunten sedaya kelepatan kula.*

Bibliography

Adatrechtbundels
    1931   De positie der selir in Middel Java. Series C 34:191.

Anderson, Benedict R. O'G.
    1966   The languages of Indonesian politics. *Indonesia* 1:89–116.
    1972   The idea of power in Javanese culture. In *Culture and politics in Indonesia.* Edited by Claire Holt, B. Anderson, and J. Siegel. Ithaca, N.Y.: Cornell University Press, 1–69.

Bachtiar, Harsja
    1973   *The religion of Java*: a commentary. In *Majalah ilmu-ilmu sastra Indonesia* 5 (1):85–115.

Baugh, John and Joel Sherzer, editors
    1984   *Language in use: readings in sociolinguistics.* Englewood Cliffs, N.J.: Prentice-Hall.

Bax, Gerald W.
    1974   *Language and social structure in a Javanese village.* Ph.D. dissertation, Tulane University.
    1975   Urban-rural differences in speech level usage in Java. *Anthropological Linguistics* 17 (1):24–32.

Becker, Alton L.
    1977   Text-building, epistemology and aesthetics in Javanese shadow theatre. In *The imagination of reality: essays in Southeast Asian coherence systems.* Edited by A. L. Becker and A. Yengoyan. Norwood: Ablex, 211–243.

Benveniste, Emile.
    1971   *Problems in general linguistics.* Translated by Mary E. Meek. Miami Linguistics Series. Coral Gables, Fl.: University of Miami Press.
    1974   *Problèmes de linguistique générale II.* Paris: Gallimard.

van den Berg, L. W. C.
  1902 *De inlandsche rangen en titles op Java en Madoera.* s'Gravenhage: Martinus-Nijhoff.

Bickerton, Derek.
  1971 Inherent variability and variable rules. *Foundations of language* 7:457–92.

Binnick, Robert I.
  1970 Ambiguity and vagueness. In *Papers from the sixth regional meeting of the Chicago Linguistics Society.* Chicago: CLS, 147–53.

Bonneff, Marcel
  1981 Un aperçu de l'influence des aspirations democratiques sur la conception et l'usage des nivaux de langue en Javanais: le mouvement Djowo-Dipo et ses prolonguements. In *Papers on Indonesian languages and literatures.* Edited by Nigel Phillips and Khaidir Anwar. Cahiers d'Archipel 13. London: School of Oriental and African Studies, Paris: Ecole des hautes études en sciences sociales.

Brakel, Lode.
  1969 Korte mededelingen: a note on the importance of the Ngoko-Krama distinction for the determination of Javanese language structure. *Bijdragen tot de taal-, land-, en volkenkunde* 125:263–66.

Brandes, J. L.
  1889 Een Jayapattra of acte van eene rechterlijke uitspraak van Caka 849. *Tijdschrift van het koninklijk Bataviaash Genootschap van Kunsten en Wetenschappen* 32:98–149.

Brown, Penelope and Steven Levinson
  1978 Universals in language usage: politeness phenomena. In *Questions and politeness: strategies in social interaction.* Edited by E. Goody. Cambridge: Cambridge University Press, 56–310.
  1979 Social structure, groups, and interaction. In *Social markers in speech.* Edited by K. R. Scherer and H. Giles. Cambridge: Cambridge University Press, 291–341.

Brown, Roger
  1965 *Social psychology.* New York: The Free Press.

Brown, Roger, and Albert Gilman
  1960 The pronouns of power and solidarity. In *Style in language.* Edited by Thomas Sebeok. Cambridge, Mass.: MIT Press, 253–76.

Brown, Roger, and Marguerite Ford
  1964 Address in American English. In *Language in culture and society.* Edited by Dell Hymes. New York: Harper and Row, 233–244.

Cedergren, Henrietta and David Sankoff
  1974 Variable rules: performance as a statistical reflection of competence. *Language* 50 (2):333–55.

Cohen Stuart, A.B.
1880 *Adellijke titels bij de Javanen.* Batavia: Landsdrukkerij.

Comrie, Bernard
1976 Linguistic politeness axes: speaker-addressee, speaker-referent, speaker-bystander. *Pragmatics microfiche* 1.7:A3. Cambridge: Department of Linguistics, University of Cambridge.

Dewey, Alice.
1978 Deference behavior in Java: duty or privilege. In *Spectrum: essays presented to Sutan Takdir Alisjahbana on his seventieth birthday.* Edited by S. Udin. Jakarta: Dian Rakyat, 420–29.

Dewey, John
1946 Peirce's theory of linguistic signs, thought, and meaning. *Journal of Philosophy* 43:85–95.

Dirdjosiswojo
1957 *Krama inggil.* Yogyakarta, Indonesia: Kalimosodo.

Dixon, R. M. W.
1971 A method of semantic description. In *Semantics: an interdisciplinary reader in philosophy, linguistics, and psychology.* Edited by D. D. Steinberg and L. S. Jakobovits. Cambridge: Cambridge University Press, 436–71.

Dunbar, E. N.
1973 *How to say 'give' and 'receive' in Japanese: a preliminary study.* Department of Linguistics Working Papers (5:11). Honolulu: University of Hawaii.

Dwidjosusana, R.I.W., et al.
n.d. *Paramasastra Jawi enggal* [New Javanese grammar]. Sala, Indonesia: Fadjar.

Errington, J. Joseph
1982 Speech in the royal presence: Javanese palace language. *Indonesia* 34:89–101.
1984 Self and self-conduct among the traditional Javanese. In *American Ethnologist* 11:275–90.
1985a On the nature of the sociolinguistic sign: describing the Javanese speech levels. In *Semiotic mediation: psychological and sociocultural perspectives.* Edited by E. Mertz and R. Parmentier. New York: Academic Press, 287–310.
1985b *Language and social change in Java: linguistic reflexes of modernization in a traditional royal polity.* Monographs in International Studies, Southeast Asia series no. 65. Athens, Oh: Ohio University Center for International Studies
1986 Continuity and change in Indonesian language development. *Journal of Asian Studies* 45 (2):329–53.

260 Bibliography

Fillmore, Charles J.
- 1982 Towards a descriptive framework for spatial deixis. In *Speech, place and action: studies in deixis and related topics.* Edited by R. J. Jarvella and W. Klein. New York: John Wiley & Sons, 31–60.
- 1975a *Santa Cruz lectures on deixis, 1971.* Bloomington: Indiana University Linguistics Club.
- 1975b An alternative to check-list theories of meaning. In *Proceedings of the first annual meeting of the Berkeley Linguistics Society.* Berkeley, Calif.: BLS, 123–31.

Fishman, Joshua
- 1972 Domains and the relationship between micro- and macrosociolinguistics. In *Directions in sociolinguistics.* Edited by John J. Gumperz and Dell Hymes. New York: Holt, Rinehart, and Winston, 437–53.

Frake, Charles
- 1980 *Language and cultural description.* Edited by Anwar S. Dil. Stanford, Calif.: Stanford University Press.

Friedrich, Paul
- 1972 Social context and semantic feature: the Russian pronominal usage. In *Directions in sociolinguistics.* Edited by John J. Gumperz and Dell Hymes. New York: Holt, Rinehart, and Winston, 270–300.
- 1979 The symbol and its relative non-arbitrariness. In *Language, context, and the imagination.* Edited by Anwar Dil. Stanford, Calif.: Stanford University Press, 1–61.

y Gasset, Ortega
- 1959 The difficulty of reading. *Diogenes* 28:1–17.

Geertz, Clifford
- 1960 *The religion of Java.* Chicago: University of Chicago Press.
- 1973 *The interpretation of cultures.* New York: Basic Books.
- 1980 *Negara.* Princeton, N.J.: Princeton University Press.

Geertz, Hildred
- 1961 *The Javanese family: a study of kinship and socialization.* Glencoe, Ill.: The Free Press.

Gericke, J. F. C. and T Roorda.
- 1901 *Javaansch-Nederlandsch handwoordenboek.* Amsterdam: Johannes Muller.

van Goens, Ryckleff
- 1856 Corte beschrijvinge van 't eijland Java. *Bijdragen tot de Koninklijk Instituut voor de taal-, land- en volkenkunde* 4:351–67.

Goffman, Erving.
  1959 *The presentation of self in everday life.* Garden City, N.Y.: Doubleday and Co.
  1967 The nature of deference and demeanor. In *Interaction Ritual: essays on face-to-face behavior.* New York: Pantheon, 47–96.
  1974 *Frame analysis: an essay on the organization of experience.* Cambridge, Mass.: Harvard University Press.

Gonda, J.
  1948 The Javanese vocabulary of courtesy. *Lingua* 1:333–76.

Goody, Eleanor, editor
  1978 *Questions and politeness: strategies in social interaction.* Cambridge: Cambridge University Press.

Greenlee, Douglas
  1973 *Peirce's concept of sign.* The Hague: Mouton.

Grice, H. P.
  1971 Meaning. In *Semantics: an interdisciplinary reader in philosophy, linguistics, and psychology.* Edited by D. D. Steinberg and L. S. Jakobovits. Cambridge: Cambridge University Press, 53–59
  1975 Logic and conversation. In *Syntax and semantics vol. 3: speech acts.* Edited by Peter Cole and J. L. Morgan. New York: Academic Press, 41–58.

de Groot, A. D. Cornet
  1843 *Javaansche spraakkunst.* Uitgegeven in naam en op verzoek van het Bataviaasch Genootschap van Kunsten en Wetenschappen door J. F. C. Gericke. Amsterdam: Johannes Müller.

Gumperz, John J. and Dell Hymes, editors.
  1972 *Directions in sociolinguistics.* New York: Holt, Rinehart, and Winston.

Haas, Mary
  1951 The declining descent rule for rank in Thailand. *American Anthropologist* 53:585–87.

Halliday, M. A. K., Angus McIntosh, and Peter Strevens
  1972 The users and uses of language. In *Readings in the sociology of language.* Edited by Joshua Fishman. The Hague: Mouton, 139–69.

Harris, Roy
  1978 The descriptive interpretation of performative utterances. *Journal of Linguistics* 14:309–10.

van den Haspel. C.C.
  1985 *Overwicht in overleg: hervormingen van justitie, grondgebruik en bestuur in de vorstenlanden op Java 1880–1930.* Verhandelingen van het Koninklijk Instituut no. 111. Dordrecht: Foris Publications

Bibliography

Haviland, John B.
  1978 Guugu-Yimidhir brother-in-law language. *Language in Society* 8:365–93.

Head, Brian
  1978 Respect degrees in pronominal reference. In *Word structure*, Vol. 3 of *Universals of human language*. Edited by Joseph Greenberg. Stanford, Calif.: Stanford University Press, 151–211.

Horne, Elinor Clark
  1974 *Javanese-English dictionary*. New Haven. Conn.: Yale University Press.

Householder, Fred W.
  1983 Kyriolexia and language change. *Language* 59 (1):1–17.

Husserl, Edmund
  1970 Investigation I: Expression and meaning. In *Logical investigations*. Vol. 1. Translated by J.N. Findlay. London: Routledge & Kegan Paul, 269–333.

Ikranegara, Kay
  1975 Lexical particles in Betawi. *Linguistics* 165:93–108.

Indonesia Reports
  1985 Culture and society supplement—May 25, no. 7. College Park, Md.: Indonesia Publications.

Irvine, Judith T.
  1979 Formality and informality in communicative events. *American Anthropologist* 81:773–90.
  1985 Status and style in language. *Annual Review of Anthropology*. 14:557–81.

Jackson, Karl D.
  1978 Urbanization and patron-client relations: the changing quality of interpersonal communication in the neighborhoods of Bandung and the villages of West Java. In *Political power and communications in Indonesia*. Edited by Karl D. Jackson and Lucian W. Pye. Stanford, Calif.: Stanford University Press, 343–92.

Jakarta, Arsip Nasional
  1918 *Memorie van overgave opgemaakt door den Resident van Soerakarta, F. P. Sollewijn Gelpke*.

Jakobson, Roman
  1960 Closing statement: linguistics and poetics. In *Style in language*. Edited by T. Sebeok. Cambridge, Mass.: MIT Press, 350–77.
  1971 Quest for the essence of language. In *Selected writings II*. The Hague: Mouton, 345–59.

1980   A few remarks on Peirce, pathfinder in the science of language. In *The framework of language*. Ann Arbor: Michigan Studies in the Humanities, 31–38.

Jarvella, R. J., and W. Klein, editors
1982   *Speech, place and action: studies in deixis and related topics.* New York: John Wiley & Sons.

Jasawidagda
1957   Wawasan bab mekaripun basa Jawi. In *Medan bahasa, basa Jawi* 8:21–32.

Jespersen, Otto
1964   [1921] *Language: its nature, development and origin.* New York: W. Norton and Co.

Keeler, Ward
1984   *Javanese: a cultural approach.* Monographs in International Studies, Southeast Asia Series no. 69. Athens, Oh.: Ohio University Center for International Studies.

Kern, H.
1917   Woordverwisseling in het Galelareesch. In *Verspreide Geschriften* vol. 6. s'Gravenhage: Martinus Nijhoff, 198–206.

Kiparsky, Paul
1968   Linguistic universals and linguistic change. In *Universals in linguistic theory*. Edited by E. Bach and R. T. Harms. New York: Holt, Rinehart, and Winston, 171–202.

Koentjaraningrat
1957   *A preliminary description of the Javanese kinship system.* Southeast Asia Studies Cultural Report Series, IV. New Haven, Conn.: Yale University.
1963   Review of *The religion of Java*. In *Majallah Ilmu-Ilmu Sastra* I(1/2):188–91.
1985   *Javanese culture.* Singapore: Institute of Southeast Asian Studies and Oxford University Press.

Kroch, Anthony
1978   Toward a theory of social dialect variation. *Language in Society* 7:17–36.

Labov, William
1971a Some principles of linguistic methodology. *Language in Society* 1:97–120.
1971b The notion of 'system' in creole languages. In *Pidginization and creolization of languages.* Edited by Dell Hymes. Cambridge: Cambridge University Press, 447–72.

264   Bibliography

- 1972 *Sociolinguistic patterns.* Philadelphia: University of Pennsylvania Press.
- 1973 The boundaries of words and their meanings. In *New ways of analyzing variation in English.* Edited by C.J. Bailey and Roger Shuy. Washington, D.C.: Georgetown University Press, 340–373.
- 1978 Denotational structure. *Papers from the parasession on the lexicon.* Edited by D. Farkas, W. Jacobsen, and K. Todrys. Chicago: Chicago Linguistic Society, 220–60.
- 1984 Field methods of the project on linguistic change and variation. In *Language in use: readings in sociolinguistics.* Edited by John Baugh and Joel Sherzer. Englewood Cliffs, N.J.: Prentice-Hall, 28–53.

Lansing, J. Stephen
- 1983 *The three worlds of Bali.* New York: Praeger.

Lavandera, Beatriz
- 1978 Where does the sociolinguistic variable stop? *Language in Society* 7:171–83.

Leach, Edmund
- 1964 Anthropological aspects of language: animal categories and verbal abuse. In *New directions in the study of language.* Edited by Eric Lenneberg. Cambridge, Mass.: MIT Press, 23–63.

Levinson, Steven
- 1979 Pragmatics and social deixis: reclaiming the notion of conventional implicature. *Proceedings of the Fifth Annual Meeting of the Berkeley Linguistics Society.* Edited by C. Chiaraello, J. Kingston, et al. Berkeley, Calif.: BLS, 206–23.
- 1982 Caste rank and verbal interaction in western Tamilnadu. In *Caste ideology and interaction.* Edited by D. McGilvray. Cambridge: Cambridge University Press, 99–124.
- 1983 *Pragmatics.* Cambridge: Cambridge University Press.

Lyons, John
- 1977a *Semantics I.* Cambridge: Cambridge University Press.
- 1977b *Semantics II.* Cambridge: Cambridge University Press.

McCawley, James D.
- 1981 *Everything that linguists have always wanted to know about logic * * but were afraid to ask.* Chicago: University of Chicago Press.

McGillavry, H.
- 1836 Eene korte verhandeling of aanteekeningen omtrent den Adelstand der Javanen. *Verhandelingen van het Bataviaasch Genootschap van Kunsten en Wetenschappen* Batavia: Landsdrukkerij, 29–62.

Mertz, Elizabeth and Richard J. Parmentier, editors.
- 1985 *Semiotic mediation: psychological and sociocultural perspectives.* New York: Academic Press.

Miller, George A.
  1982 Some problems in the theory of demonstrative reference. In *Speech, place and action: studies in deixis and related topics*. Edited by R. J. Jarvella and W. Klein. New York: John Wiley & Sons, 61–72.

Moertono, Soemarsaid
  1963 *State and statecraft in old Java: a study of the later Mataram period, 16th to 19th century*. Ithaca, N.Y.: Modern Indonesia Project.

Nothofer, Bernd
  1981 *Dialektatlas von Zentral-Java*. Weissbaden: Otto Harrassowitz.

Padmasusastra
  1896 *Urapsari*. Betawi: G. Kolff.
  1900 *Warnabasa*. Surakarta.
  1905 *Layang basa Jawa* [Treatise on Javanese]. Betawi: Landsdrukkerij.
  1907 *Serat Tatacara: ngadat sarta kalakuwanipun tetiyang Jawi ingkang taksih lumengket dhateng gugon-tuhon* [Treatise on custom: together with practices of Javanese who still adhere to traditional beliefs]. Betawi: Kanjeng Gupermen.
  1911 *Layang basa Solo-Javaansche samenspraken* [Treatise on Solonese language: Javanese conversations]. Met eene inleiding door Dr. D. A. Rinkes. Betawi: Pirmah Papirus.
  1912 *Serat Pathibasa-Javaansche synomiemen* [The *Pathibasa* treatise-Javanese synonyms]. Semarang Drukkerij en boekhandel H. A. Benjamins.

Pakubuwana X
  1900 *Serat Pranatan Adhel* [Treatise of rules nobility]. Eastern Manuscript Collection, Leiden University. Cod. Or. 6421.

Parmentier, Richard J.
  1985 Signs' place in Media Res: Peirce's concept of semiotic mediation. In *Semiotic mediation: psychological and sociocultural perspectives*. Edited by Elizabeth Mertz and Richard J. Parmentier. New York: Academic Press, 23–48.

Paulston, Christina Bratt
  1984 Pronouns of address in Swedish: social class semantics and a changing system. In *Language in use: readings in sociolinguistics*. Edited by John Baugh and Joel Sherzer. Englewood Cliffs, N.J.: Prentice-Hall, 268–91.

Peacock, James.
  1975 *Consciousness and change: symbolic anthropology in evolutionary perspective*. New York: John Wiley & Sons.

Peirce, Charles Sanders.
  1960 *Collected Papers*. In 8 volumes. Edited by C. Hartshorne, P. Weiss, and A. Burks. Cambridge, Mass.: Harvard University Press.

Pike, Kenneth
    1975   On describing languages. In *The scope of American linguistics: papers of the first golden anniversary symposium of the Linguistics Society of America*. Edited by R. Austerlitz. Lisse: Peter de Ridder, 9–30.

Poedjosoedarmo, Soepomo
    1968a Javanese speech levels. *Indonesia* 6:54–81.
    1968b Wordlist of non-ngoko vocabularies. *Indonesia* 7:165–90.
    n.d.   Perkembangan madya. Photocopy.

Poedjosoedarmo, Soepomo, Th. Koendjono, Gloria Poedosoedarmo, and A. Sukarso
    1979   *Tingkat-tutur bahasa Jawa*. Jakarta: Pusat Pembinaan Pengembangan Bahasa, Department Pendidikan dan Kebudayaan.

Poerwadarminta, W. J. S.
    1939   *Baoesastra Djawa* [Javanese dictionary]. Batavia: J. B. Wolters

Prawirohardja, Dalil.
    1958   Mingsad-mingseding basa [Changes in language]. *Medan bahasa, basa Jawi* 8:21–26.

Ras, J. J.
    1982   *Inleiding tot het modern javaans*. The Hague: Koninklijt Instituut voor taal-, land-, en volkenkunde.

Rickleffs, M. C.
    1974   *Jogjakarta under Mangkubumi, 1742–1792: a history of the division of Java*. London Oriental Series, no. 30. Oxford: Oxford University Press.
    1983   The crisis of 1740–41 in Java: the Javanese, Chinese, Madurese, and Dutch, and the fall of the court of Kartasura. In *Bijdragen tot de taal-, land-, and volkenkunde* 139 (2):268–90.

Rickleffs, M. and Soepomo Poedjosoedarmo
    1967   The establishment of Surakarta: a translation from the Babad Gianti. *Indonesia* 4:88–109.

Ricouer, Paul
    1974   Part I: Hermeneutics and structuralism. In *The conflict of interpretations*. Edited by Don Ihde. Evanston: Northwestern University Press, 27–96.
    1976   *Interpretation theory: discourse and the surplus of meaning*. Fort Worth, Tex.: The Texas Christian University Press.
    1982   The model of the text: meaningful action considered as a text. In *Hermeneutics and the human sciences*. Edited and translated by John B. Thompson. Cambridge: Cambridge University Press, Paris: Editions de la Maison des Sciences de l'Homme, 197–221.

Robson, Stuart O.
1976 An elementary reference grammar of Javanese. Manuscript

Romaine, Suzanne
1981 The status of variable rules in sociolinguistic theory. *Journal of Linguistics* 17:93–119.
1982 Socio-historical linguistics: its status and methodology. Cambridge: Cambridge University Press.

Roorda, T.
1855 *Javaansche grammatica benevens een leesboek tot het oefening in de Javaansche taal.* Vol. 1. Amsterdam: Johannes Muller.

Rouffaer. G. P.
1921 Vorstenlanden. *Encyclopadie van Nederlands-Indies* IV:586–653. Leiden: Brill.

Sapir, Edward.
1921 *Language.* New York: Harcourt, Brace, and World.

Sastrasubrata
1912 Personal letter to G. A. Hazeu. Manuscript at the Royal Institute of Linguistics and Anthropology, Leiden University OR H1083.

Sastrawirya, M.
1931–1932 Surakarta. Tata-krama Jawi [Javanese etiquette]. In *Pustaka Jawi.*

de Saussure, Ferdinand
1966 [1915] *Course in general linguistics.* Translated by Wade Baskin. New York: McGraw-Hill.

Schrieke, B. J. O.
1957 *Indonesian sociological studies,* Vol. 2. The Hague: W. van Hoeve.

Scott, James C.
1972 Patron/client politics and political change in Southeast Asia. *American Political Science Review* 66(1):91–113.

Searle, J.
1969 *Speech acts: an essay in the philosophy of language.* Cambridge: Cambridge University Press.
1979 *Expression and meaning: studies in the theory of speech acts.* Cambridge: Cambridge University Press.

Seto, B. M.
1958 Urun rembag: bab mekaring basa Djawi. [Discussion: about the development of Javanese]. *Medan bahasa, basa Jawi* 8:33–42.

Shapiro, Michael
1983 *The sense of grammar: language as semeiotic.* Bloomington: Indiana University Press.

Shaw, W.
  1971 Mining superstitions, magic, and taboos. *Federation Museum Journal* 61 (n.s.): 31–50.

Siegel, James T.
  1986 *Solo in the new order: language and hierarchy in an Indonesian city.* Princeton, N.J.: Princeton University Press.

Silverstein, Michael
  1976 Shifters, linguistic categories, and cultural description. In *Meaning in anthropology.* Edited by K. H. Basso and H. A. Selby. Albuquerque: University of New Mexico, 11–56.
  1977a The limits of awareness. Transcript of a lecture given to the Harvard Anthropology Seminar, Cambridge, and the Penn Anthropology Colloquium, Philadelphia.
  1977b Cultural prerequisites to grammatical analysis. In *Linguistics and Anthropology.* Edited by M. Saville-Troike. Washington, D.C.: Georgetown University Round Table on Languages and Linguistics, 139–151.

Simmel, Georg
  1950 *The sociology of Georg Simmel.* Translated and edited by K. H. Wolff. Glencoe, Ill.: The Free Press.

Skeat, Walter W. and Charles O. Blagden.
  1906 Taboos and other special forms of speech. In *Pagan races of the Malay peninsula,* vol. 2. London: Macmillan, 414–431.

Soebroto, T.
  n.d. *Unggah-ungguh ing basa* [Speech styles]. Surakarta, Java: Empat Serangkai.

Soeradipoera, R. Ng.
  1913 *Serat Bedhahipun Kraton nagari Ngajogjakarta, saha kendhangipun ingkang Sinuhun Kangjeng Susuhunan Pakubuwana Ingkang Kaping VI Narendra negara Surakarta Adhiningrat* [Treatise on the division of the kingdom of Jakarta, together with the exile of Pakubuwana VI of Surakarta]. Batavia: Pirmah Papirus.

Spielmann, Roger W.
  1980 Performative utterances as indexical expressions—comment on Harris. *Journal of Linguistics* 16:89–94.

Steinberg, D. D., and L. A. Jakobovits, editors
  1971 *Semantics: an interdisciplinary reader in philosophy, linguistics, and psychology.* Cambridge: Cambridge University Press.

Subalidinata, R.S. and Nartoatmojo, Marsono
  1975 *Sejarah ejaan bahasa Jawa dengan huruf Latin—dan ejaan ba-*

hasa Jawa yang disesusaikan dengan ejaan bahasa Indonesia yang disempurnakan [History of the spelling of Javanese with Latin letters, and the spelling of Javanese made to fit with the perfected spelling of Indonesian]. Widyaparwa no. 12. Yogyakarta: Balai Penelitian Bahasa.

Surakarta, Radyapustaka Museum
    n.d.   *Serat wewaton tata-krami kedhaton pisusungipun Radèn Ngabéhi Jayadarsana* [Treatise on etiquette, an offering by Radèn Ngabéhi Jayadarsana]. No. 74, Handwritten Mansucript Collection.

Sutherland, Heather
    1975   The priyayi. *Indonesia* 19:57–80.
    1979   *The making of a bureaucratic elite*. ASAA Southeast Asia publications series. Singapore: Heinemann.

Tambiah, Stanley J.
    1976   *World conqueror and world renouncer*. Cambridge: Cambridge University Press.

Tanner, Nancy
    1967   Speech and society among the Indonesian elite: a case study of a multilingual community. *Anthropological Linguistics* 9:15–39.

Uhlenbeck, E. M.
    1978   *Studies in Javanese morphology*. Translation series no. 19. The Hague: Koninklijk instituut voor taal-, land-, en volkenkunde.

Walbeehm, A. H. J. G.
    1896   *De taalsoorten in het Javaansch*. Batavia: Albrecht and Co.

Welsh, C, and R. Chametzky
    1983   Performatives as indexicals: resolving the performadox. *Proceedings of the Ninth Annual Meeting of the Berkeley Linguistics Society*. Berkeley, Calif.: BLS, 266–280.

Whitney, William D.
    1979   [1875] *The life and growth of language*. New York: Dover.

Winter, C.F., Sr.
    1843   Instellingen, gewoonten, en gebruiken der Javanen to Soerakarta. *Tijdshrift voor Nederlands Indie* 4, part 1.
    1844   Regstpleging over de onderdanen van Z.H. der Soesoehoenan van Soerakarta. *Tijdschrift voor Nederlands Indie* 6, part 1.
    1846   Javaansche titels. *Tijdschrift voor Nederlands Indie* 8, part 4.
    1848   *Javaansche zamenspraken, uitgegeven met een bijvoegsel bij het Javaansche woordenboek door T. Roorda*. Amsterdam: Johannes Muller.

Wolff, John U.
　1976　The functions of Indonesian in central Java. In *Pacific linguistics*. Edited by Nguyen Dang Liem. South-east Asian linguistic studies, Series C, no. 42. Canberra: School of Pacific studies, Australia National University, 219–35.

Wolff, John U., and Soepomo Poedjosoedarmo
　1982　*Communicative codes in central Java*. Linguistics series VIII, data paper no. 116. Ithaca, N.Y.: Southeast Asia program, Department of Asian Studies, Cornell University.

Index of Javanese Words

The nasal active verb marker is represented here as *N-*. It is realized as a velar before root initial vowels and liquids, a palatal before /c/ and /s/, and otherwise assimilates place of articulation of root initial consonants and glides. It coalesces with root initial /w/, /c/, and voiceless stops. Nasals epenthetically inserted between root final vowels and verbal suffix *-i* or possessive suffix *-é* (*-ipun* in krama) are represented here as *(n)*. Glottal stops epenthetically inserted between root final vowels and verbal suffix *-aké* (*-aken* in krama) are represented as *(k)*. Vowel sandhi represented orthographically in the text are not indicated in this index.

abdi, 118; —— dalem, 66n, 118, 119, 120n, 127, 128; —— dalem kula, 118–19, 127, 129. See also abdidalem, dalem ki of omah
abdidalem, 119–20, 122–23, 125, 126, 127, 129, 228. See also abdi, adalem, dalem ka of aku
adalem, 119–20, 129
adhel, 47 n.1
adhi, 137, 145; —— mas, 145, 146–47. See also dhi(k)
adipati, 25, 26; ka-——-an, 44, 61; —— anom, 59
agung, 25. See also negara.
aja, 213–15; —— lho, 222
ajeng, 66, 67, 67 n.23, 135n; bendara radèn, —— 80; N-——, 57 n.12, 125 n.14. See also radèn.
aji, 49; N-——-(n)i, 49
akrab, 49
aku, 50, 62–63, 71, 216
alun-alun, 32–33
alus, 2, 3, 11, 35, 50, 96–97, 150, 176, 192–94, 217, 220, 247, 250; ngoko ——, 50, 75, 102, 177;

ka-——-en, 138, 147
ampéyan, 57
ampil, 61
ampun, 215
anak, 28, 72, 119, 122 n.12, 135, 137; —— mas, 145
andhap, 38, 99; ——-asor, 38, 40, 42, 64, 99, 129, 156
anom, 59
apa, 95
ara, 220n
aran, 126 n.17, 203
arang, 201
arep: N-——, 125 n.14
arya: bendara pangéran ——, 60, 78, 80 n.33; kangjeng gusti pangéran ——, 60, 78; kangjeng pangéran ——, 60; kangjeng radèn mas ——, 80 n.33
asma, 126
asor, 38, 99; andhap-——, 38, 40, 42, 64, 99, 129, 156
asta, 171; di-——, 172, 173; N-——, 171, 172
athik, 220n

272 Index of Javanese words

atur, 179, 180, 185, 189; ———-i, 180–86, 188–90, 243; ———-aké, 181, 182; ———-ana, 182; N-———-i, 185, 190; (u)m-———, 179–80; ———-i priksa, 182–83
awis, 201
awu, 70–72, 70n
ayo, 218
ayu: dèn ———, 82; mbok ———, 138; ndara ———, 68, 81–82; ndara dèn ———, 68, 81–82; radèn ———, 59, 67, 67 n.23, 78, 81, 82

baku, 172
bakul, 147
bapak, 28, 113, 135, 136–38, 143, 144, 147–48, 181; panjenenganipun ———, 128. See also pak
basa, 40, 87–88; ———-(k)aké, 88; N-———-(k)aké, 160–62, 242; ——— désa, 144; ——— kedhaton, 125 n.5, 166n; ——— niki-niku, 205. See also subject index
bathik, 47
bécak, 138, 146
béda, 201–02
béhi, 137 n.26, 145 n.34. See also ngabéhi
bendara, 55, 56, 59, 61, 67, 68, 78, 80, 82; ——— pangéran arya, 78, 80 n.33.; ——— radèn ajeng, 61, 80; ——— radèn mas/ayu, 61, 64, 78. See also ndara
bènten, 201–02
besut, 195, 220
bibi, 62n.
biyung, 142 n.29
bojo, 57 n.9
bu, 144. See also ibu
buku, 181
bupati, 26, 120; ke-———-an, 201
buyut, 55, 65, 68; ——— dalem, 54, 71, 74, 80

cahya, 29–30
canggah, 55, 65, 68; ——— dalem, 54, 68, 71, 82
cangking, 173n
caos, 157, 177–78; ———-i, 181; ———-aké, 181; N-———-i, 159; ———-i priksa, 181–82;
cara: ——— désa, 146; ——— Jawa, 1, 3; ——— ndara-ndara, 76, 81
cawik, 165; ———-i, 166

cawok, 165
cecèkèr, 39
cekap, 200
cekel, 173; di-———, 172; N-———, 172
celuk, 180, 183; N-———, 184; tak-———, 184
cilik: wong ———, 55; priyayi ———, 67, 75
ciritan: putra ———, 59
coba, 202
cobi, 202
cocok, 183
crita, 179, 180; ———-(n)i, 180; ———-(k)aké, 180
cukup, 200

dalem ka of aku, 51, 62–63, 65, 67–68, 71–73, 75, 76, 77, 103–105, 117–24, 127, 129–31, 143, 155, 162; ———-dalem, 62, 71, 72; ———-daleman, 63, 71; di-———-dalemi, 122; in imperatives, 186; in possessive constructions, 123–24. See also abdidalem, adalem, dalem ki of omah
dalem-daleman. See dalem ka of aku
dalem ki of omah, 31, 37, 54–55, 88, 119, 120; abdi ———, 66n, 118, 119, 120n, 127–28; buyut ———, 54, 71, 74; canggah ———, 54, 68, 71, 82; garwa ———, 57, 59, 64, 79; ing ngarsa ———, 34; kawula ———, 117, 118; panjenengan ———, 127–28, 130, 133; in possessive constructions, 123–24; pranatan ———, 79 n.31; priyantun ———, 57, 61–62; putra ———, 55, 59, 61–62, 64, 70, 73, 80, 123; putra sentana ———, 55; sampéyan ———, 125, 126 n.16; sentana ———, 55, 67; wayah ———, 54, 65–67, 70, 73, 79, 80, 82, 120, 130, 140, 142; waréng ———, 65. See also abdi, buyut, canggah, putra sentana, waréng, wayah, pranatan, priyantun
dedeg: N-———-i, 126
dèn: ——— béhi, 68, 137 n.26, 145 n.34; ——— mas/ayu, 82; ndara ——— mas/ayu, 81; ——— masan, 67, 82. See also radèn, ndara, mas, ayu
dèrèng, 100
désa: basa ———, 144; cara ———,

Index of Javanese words 273

146; krama ———, 200, 201, 202;
wong ———, 200
dhi, 135, 145; ——— mas, 145. See
also adhi, dhik
dhik, 145. See also adhi, dhi
dhing, 220n
dhisik, 214
dhuwur, 98
digsura, 64, 100, 156
dika, 124–25, 131, 144. See also
ijengandika
dina, 63 n.20; pa-———-an, 63
dinten, 63 n.20; pa-———-an, 63
dokok, 178
duka, 218; di-———-(n)i, 218; nyuwun ———, 218
durung, 100

éyang, 137, 141–43, 147

gamelan, 29n
garwa, 57 n.9; ——— ampéyan, 57;
——— ampil, 57, 61; ——— dalem,
57–59, 61, 62, 64, 79; ——— ngajeng, 57 n. 12; ——— padmi, 57, 61;
——— wingking, 57–58 n.12
gawa, 172–73; di-———, 172–73;
N-———, 172
gawé: N-———, 172
gedhèk, 42
grad, 54, 55
griya, 89
gumedhé, 142
gusti, 28, 55, 63–64, 78, 79–80, 112–
13, 136, 166; ——— kangjeng ratu,
61; kangjeng ——— pangéran, 59,
117; kangjeng ——— pangéran arya,
60, 61, 78; ——— pangéran arya,
60–61; para ———, 55–56, 59;
——— radèn mas/ayu, 60, 78; ———
proper name, 80. See also ti,
pangéran

ibu, 62, 72, 135, 137, 141, 143–44, 147
ijengandika, 124, 129, 139–41, 242.
See also jengandika.
ika, 208n
iki, 206, 208–10; ——— lho, 222
iku, 208
inggil, 98–99
ingkang, 145 n.33, 186n
ipé, 72; ———-an, 72; kangmas
———, 72; mbakyu ———, 72

jaluk, 174–76, 186–90; tak-———,
186–89; N-———, 176, 187 n.24,
188
jangkep, 119
jarwa dhosok, 142 n.30
jeneng, 203; N-———-i, 126;
paN-———-an, 126. See also jumeneng, panjenengan
jeng, 125, 135n
jengandika, 59 n. 14. See also
ijengandika
jumeneng, 126; ———-aké, 126.
See also jeneng
jupuk, 93, 174–75, 178; N-———,
99, 175–76

kabèh, 61 n. 17, 203
kabu, 201
kadipatèn, 44, 61. See also adipati
kaé, 206, 208, 210
kagem, 143
kahyangan, 33
kakang, 137, 138, 144–46; ——— mas,
145–46. See also kang kin term,
mas, kangmas
kakèk, 142
kakung, 81; mbah ———, 142; ndara
———, 81
kalah, 39; N-———, 39–40, 43
kalangan: ——— ningrat, 75, 130 n.21
kalipah, 29
kalung samir, 30
kalusen, 138. See also alus
kampung, 5, 33; krama ———, 199n
kanca, 123; ———(n)é/-(n)ipun,
123–24
kandha, 179–80, 183–84;
———-(k)aké, 179; ———-(n)i,
181–82, 186–87
kang kin term, 144–46, 148; ———
mas, 135, 145. See also kakang,
mas, kangmas
kang relative clause/topic marker, 145
n.33. See also keng, sing, ingkang
kanggé, 143
kanggo, 143
kangjeng, 60, 61 n.16; ——— gusti, 63;
——— gusti pangéran, 59, 60, 117;
——— pangéran arya, 60, 66; ———
radèn mas arya, 80 n.33; ——— ratu
alit, 61; bendara ——— pangéran
arya, 60; panjenengan dalem ———,
128; panjenengan ———, 128
kangmas, 63, 72–73, 135, 137,

274 Index of Javanese words

kangmas (continued)
 145–47; ——— ipé, 72. See also
 mas, kang kin term, kakang
kaprah. See salah
kasar, 3, 11, 96, 110, 165, 194, 247, 250
katut, 122
kawruh, 70
kawula, 28, 30n, 33, 117–19, 121, 126;
 ——— dalem, 118
kebo, 201
kebupatèn, 201. See also bupati
kedhaton, 30n; basa ———, 125 n.15,
 166n
kémawon, 214
kéné, 208, 209
keng: ——— raka/rayi, 145. See also
 kang relative clause/topic marker
keplok, 194
keputrèn. See putri
késah, 100–101
kok, 221–22
kolot, 76, 130
kon, 186–87, 189–90; tak-———,
 186, 189
kono, 208–209
kowé, 50, 62–63, 71, 104
krama, 35, 203; di-———-aké, 201
kramantara, 102
kramat, 31
krami, 30 n.7, 35n, 203. See also tata-
 krami
kraton. See ratu
kris, 31n, 33
kula, 51, 62–63, 65–66, 68, 73, 77,
 104, 116–24, 126, 143, 162, 216;
 abdidalem ———, 127, 129; *———
 dalem, 118; putra ———, 140, 141n
kurang, 183
kuwi, 209–10
kyai lurah, 128

landa, 5
larang, 201, 221
lha, 220n, 222n
lho, 218, 221–22
loro, 221
luhur, 122
lunga, 113
lungguh, 70; pa-———-an, 25
lurah, 128 n.18
luwes, 8

madya, 88
madyakrama, 204

madyangoko, 204
maésa, 201
maésapejahan, 201
mancanegara, 25–26
mandala, 28
mangga, 38, 218–19; di-———-(k)aké,
 219
mangkat, 100
mang, 124. See also samang,
 sampéyan
mas descent title, 67n, 69, 82, 146–47,
 228; (a)dhi ———, 145, 146; (a)nak
 ———, 145; bendara radèn ———,
 60, 64, 78; dèn ———, 67; kakang
 ———, 145–46; kang ———, 145;
 kangjeng radèn ——— arya, 80 n.33;
 mbok ———, 145; ndara ———, 68,
 81–82; ndara dèn ———, 81–82;
 radèn ———, 59, 66, 68, 82. See also
 ayu, dèn, kang, mas kin term, ndara,
 radèn
mas kin term, 44, 146–48, 228. See
 also mas descent title
matur. See atur
mbah, 137, 142–43; ——— kakung,
 142; ——— putri, 142; si ———, 142
mbak, 135, 138–39, 148. See also ayu,
 mbakyu, mbok, yu
mbakyu, 72, 135, 138–39, 148;
 ——— ipé, 72. See also mbak,
 mbok, ayu, yu
mbok kin term, 62, 137, 143–44;
 ——— mas, 145; ——— ayu, 138
mbok optative particle: ——— ya, 214
mboten, 216
mbuh, 217; di-———-i, 217
menapa, 95
mendhet. See pendhet
meneng, 39
menggung, 137 n.26, 145 n.34. See
 also tumenggung
menika, 210, 215
mlaku: ——— ndhodhok, 36
mlayu, 214
mpit, 173
mpu, 31n
mpun, 100, 214–15
mréné, 184
mriki, 184
mriyayèni. See priyayi
mudhakrama, 102
mundhut. See pundhut
munjuk, 177 n.14. See also unjuk

Index of Javanese words

nak, 122; ———-sanak, 134 n.22;
———-misan, 134 n.22. *See also*
anak
nama, 203
nami, 126, 203
nandalem, 51, 62–63, 65–68, 71, 73,
76–77, 103–105, 126 n.16, 130, 155.
See also panjenengan, panjenengandalem, ndandalem
napa, 95
nata, 35
ndandalem, 130 n.20. *See also*
nandalem.
ndara, 55–56, 67–69, 76, 80–82;
——— dèn mas/ayu, 68, 81, 82;
——— kakung, 81; ——— mas/ayu,
68, 81, 82; ——— putri, 81, 161;
para ———, 55–56, 67; rasa ———,
68. *See also* bendara, radèn, mas,
ayu, dèn
ndedegi. *See* dedeg
ndika. *See* dika
negara, 25–26, 75 n.29; ———-agung,
25
negari, 25
nèm, 58
nènèk, 142
nesu, 218
ngabéhi, 69n, 137 n.26. *See also* béhi
ngalah, 39–40, 43. *See also* kalah
ngapurancang, 36
ngendika, 179; ———-i, 179 n.16, 180;
———-aké, 181 n.17
ngga, 219. *See also* mangga
nggèr, 30 n.9
ngoko. *See* subject index
ningrat, 75; kalangan ———, 130 n.21
nini, 142
njaluk. *See* jaluk
njangkar, 112, 135
njenengan, 129, 138. *See also*
panjenengan
njupuk. *See* jupuk
nya, 218, 222
nyambut-damel, 172
nyambut-gawé, 172
nyekel. *See* cekel
nyuwun: ——— duka, 218. *See also*
suwun

omah, 88–89, 118
ombé, 177

padinan. *See* dina

padintenan. *See* dinten
padmi, 65–66. *See also* garwa
pak, 136, 137, 138, 139n, 147–48;
——— bécak, 138; ——— béhi, 137;
——— dhé, 135; ——— lik, 135;
——— menggung, 137, 145 n.34
palungguhan. *See* lungguh
paman, 142 n.29
pancer, 54–55, 70
pandhita, 31
pandonga, 123
pangan, 176
pangéran, 61; ——— putra, 66; ———
sentana, 66, 80 n.33; bendara ———
arya, 78, 80 n.33; bendara kangjeng
——— arya, 60; gusti ——— arya,
61; kangjeng ——— arya, 60, 66;
kangjeng gusti ———, 59, 60, 117;
kangjeng gusti ——— arya, 60, 61
pangèstu, 39
panghulu, 58
pangku, 41
panjenengan, 50–51, 62–63, 65–66,
68, 73, 75, 77, 104, 124, 126–29,
130–31; ——— dalem, 127–28, 130,
133; ———-ipun, 127–28; ———
kangjeng, 128; ——— sampéyan,
127–29, 129; in possessive constructions, 127; in prefatory expressions,
126. *See also* dalem, jeneng, ndandalem, panjenengandalem, penjenengan, sampéyan
panjenengandalem, 62, 104, 130, 228.
See also panjenengan
pantes, 36, 52, 72, 76
para, 55; ——— gusti, 55–56, 59;
——— luhur, 122; ——— ndara,
55–56, 67, 82; ——— yayi, 57 n.11
paring, 157, 177, 178; ———-i, 159,
178, 181; ———-aké, 181; ———-i
priksa, 181–82
pasisiran, 26
pasowanan. *See* sowan
patèn. *See* pati
pati, 201; ———-an, 201
pejah, 201; ———-an, 201
pek mantu, 54
pendhapa, 37
pendhet, 93, 99; N-———, 99
penjenengan, 129. *See also*
panjenengan
penyan, 129 n.19
perintah, 186
pesindhèn, 29n

276　Index of Javanese words

pirsa, 181 n.18. *See also* priksa
pokok, 172
pralambang, 24, 44
pramaiswari, 57, 58
pranatan, 79 n.31, 120
priksa, 181–83; aturi ———, 181–83; caosi ———, 181–82; paringi ———, 181–83; mundhut ———, 183; suwun ———, 183
priyagung, 26
priyantun, 44; ——— dalem, 57, 61, 62; ——— nèm, 58; ——— sepuh, 58
priyayi, 2, 57 n.11; ——— cilik, 67, 75; ——— luhur, 26, 75; N- ———-(n)i, 75
pundhut, 99, 174–75, 183; N- ———, 99, 174, 175; N- ——— priksa, 183
puniki, 210
puniku, 210
pusaka, 31, 37
putra, 54, 137; ——— ciritan, 59; ——— dalem, 55, 59, 61–62, 64–65, 70, 73, 80, 123; ——— jengandika, 59 n.14; ——— kula, 140, 141n; ——— sentana, 55, 61; pangéran ———, 66
putri, 81; ka- ———-an, 58; mbah ———, 142; ndara ———, 81, 161
putu, 137, 140

rada, 203
radèn, 67, 69, 80–82, 146; ——— ajeng, 66; ——— ayu, 59, 67, 81, 82; ——— mas, 60, 66, 68, 81, 82; ——— nganten, 69; bendara ——— ajeng, 80; bendara ——— ayu, 61, 64, 80; bendara ——— mas, 64, 78, 80; kangjeng ——— mas arya, 80 n.33. *See also* dènmasan, dèn
rai, 42
radi, 203
rak, 220n
raka, 137, 144, 145; keng ———, 145
rama, 136–37
rasa, 247; ——— ndara, 68
ratu, 22, 31; ka- ———-an, 22, 25–27, 31–32, 43
rayi, 128, 137, 145; keng ———, 145
rika, 125 n.14
riya: ——— nginggil, 66n; ——— ngandhap, 66n
roroning tunggal, 31
rumiyin, 214

sajèn. *See* saji
saji, 177–78; ———-an, 178
sakti, 29 n.6
salah, 9; ——— kaprah, 9, 143, 146, 201, 202
samang, 124. *See also* mang, sampéyan
sampéyan madya of aku, 104, 124–27, 129–31, 138; ——— dalem, 125, 125–26 n.16; panjenengan ———, 127, 128, 129. *See also* mang, samang
sampéyan ki of sikil, 125
sampun, 100, 214–16
sangga, 219n
saos. *See* caos
sebut: N- ———, 80 n.32
sedanten, 203
sedaya, 203
sega, 92, 93, 96, 106
sekul, 92, 93, 96, 106
sèlèh, 178
selir, 57, 58 n.13, 59, 66
sémah, 57 n.9
semanten, 96
sembah, 33, 42, 64, 67, 71, 142
semono, 96
semonten, 96
sentana: ——— dalem, 55, 65, 67; pangéran ———, 66, 80 n.33; putra ———, 55, 61
sepuh, 58, 69; ——— tuwuh, 70
si: ——— mbah, 142
sikil, 125
sing, 186n
slametan, 33n, 129
sliramu, 50n, 104
sliranè, 50n
sowan: pa- ———-an, 31
suka: N- ———-(n)i, 159
suku, 125
sumanak, 8n
sumangga, 219. *See also* mangga
sumerep, 182 n.19
sumurup, 182 n.19
supados, 186
supaya, 176, 186
suwun, 99, 175, 176, 185–86, 187 n.24, 188–90, 216, 243; N- ———, 99, 175, 176; ——— priksa, 183

ta, 220n
tak-, 216
takèn, 183

Index of Javanese words

takon, 183
taksih pamili, 54
taling-tarung, 41
tampa: ———-(n)ana, 218
tanah sabrang, 26
tangan, 171
tarung, 41
tata, 35
tata-krama, 11, 16, 33–35, 197, 203, 224, 245, 255
tata-krami, 30 n.7. *See also* tata-krama
tedah, 200
tedha: N-———, 176
tengga, 200
teras, 202
terus, 202
ti, 79, 80. *See also* gusti
tindak, 100, 112, 161, 167 n.8, 182
tiyang, 44; ——— dhusun, 200
trah, 66
trap-trapan, 73, 106
tuduh, 200
tuku, 174, 175
tumenggung, 24, 137 n.26
tunggu, 200
turun 54n; ke-———-an, 54n
tuwa, 69
tuwuh, 70

ulem, 183
undang, 183, 184

unggah-ungguh, 11; ——— ing basa, 10, 16, 49, 237, 255
unjuk, 177
upama, 203
upami, 203
urmat, 185
uwa, 142 n.29

waé, 214
wahyu, 29, 30
warana, 29
warèng, 55: ——— dalem, 65, 68
wayah, 120, 123, 137; ——— dalem, 54, 65–68, 70, 73, 75 n.29, 76–77, 79–80, 82, 94, 120, 123, 130, 140, 142
wedana, 25, 26
wedi, 142
welah, 200
wènèh, 177–78, 183–84, 189; N-———-i, 159, 178
wingking, 57 n.12
wis, 100, 213, 214–15
wong, 44; ——— cilik, 55; ——— désa, 200
wringin, 30
wuluh, 200

yu, 138–39, 148. *See also* mbakyu, mbok

Index of Authors

Anderson, B., 7n, 27, 29, 31, 32

Bax, G. W., 74n
Becker, A. L., 142n
Benveniste, E., 15, 103n, 154, 217, 236, 253, 254, 255
van den Berg, L. W. C., 47n, 61n, 66n
Bickerton, D., 232n
Binnick, R. I., 170
Blagden, C. O., 191n
Bonneff, M., 81n
Brakel, L., 208
Brandes, J. L., 203
Brown, P., 15n, 16n, 231–32, 237–44, 246
Brown, R., 19, 48, 74, 93, 94, 227, 230, 235, 236

Cedergren, H., 232
Chametzky, R., 158n
Cohen, Stuart A. B., 47n
Comrie, B., 210n

Dewey, A., 42n
Dewey, J., 247n
Dixon, R. M. W., 170–72

Errington, J., 2n, 8n, 9, 28n, 39n, 45, 52n, 49, 75n, 77, 81n, 95, 97, 98n, 102n, 115n, 124, 125, 128n, 130n, 152n, 166n, 167n, 177n, 199n, 204, 205, 210, 226, 233, 234

Fillmore, C. J., 15, 207, 208, 209, 232, 247n
Fishman, J., 232
Ford, M., 235n

Frake, C., 225
Friedrich, P., 227, 235, 253

y Gassett, O., 196n
Geertz, C., 1, 2, 12, 13, 25n, 28, 33n, 35, 67, 96, 100, 247
Geertz, H., 134n, 146n
Gericke, J. F. C., 70n, 71n, 126
Gilbert, W. S., 83n
Gilman, A., 19, 48, 74, 93, 94, 227, 230, 235, 236
van Goens, R., 47n
Goffman, E., 11, 161, 191, 192, 235, 238, 239, 241, 243, 249
Gonda, J., 10, 197, 199
Goody, E., 240
Greenlee, D., 249n
Grice, H. P., 238, 239, 246
deGroot, A. D., 126, 127

Haas, M., 67
Halliday, M. A. K., 195
Harris, R., 158n
van den Haspel, C. C., 25n, 27, 33, 66n, 196n
Haviland, J. B., 170
Head, B., 227
Horne, E. C., 172n
Householder, F. W., 202n
Husserl, E., 16n, 196n

Ikranegara, K., 220n
Irvine, J. T., 232n

Jackson, K. D., 28
Jakobson, R., 14, 15, 96, 219, 228, 253n, 254

Index of authors

Jespersen, O., 15

Kaplan, D., 209
Keeler, W., 8, 121n, 144n, 146n, 187n
Kern, H., 191n
Kiparsky, P., 109
Koendjono, Th., 159n
Koentjaraningrat, 57n, 70n, 134n, 145n
Kroch, A., 205, 233

Labov, W., 19, 52, 196, 199–205, 230–37
Lansing, J. S., 67
Lavandera, B., 232
Leach, E., 165
Levinson, S., 15n, 16n, 231–32, 237–44, 246
Lyons, J., 14

Marsono, xv
McCawley, J., 187n
McIntosh, A., 195
McGillavry, H., 47n, 61n
Miller, G. A., 209
Moertono, S., 25, 26, 29, 31
Morris, C., 247

Nothofer, B., 146n

Padmasusastra, 42, 43, 52n, 62, 63, 68, 69, 81, 92, 98n, 102n, 117, 125n, 127, 128, 136n, 141n, 179n, 187n
Parmentier, R. J., 249n
Peacock, J., 5, 46
Peirce, C. S., 14, 15, 174, 229, 247–51, 254
Pike, K., 225, 246, 254
Poedjosoedarmo, G., 159n
Poedjosoedarmo, S., 8, 22, 95, 102n, 108, 159n, 165, 169, 172n, 203, 204, 234
Poerwadarminta, W. J. S., 173, 211n, 217n, 218
Prawirohardja, D., 8n

Ras, J. J., 187n
Rickleffs, M., 22, 23, 26
Ricouer, P., 236, 253, 255n
Robson, S. O., 187n
Romaine, S., 232
Roorda, T., 70n, 125, 126, 171n, 211
Rouffaer, G. P., 25, 47n, 82

Sankoff, D., 232
Sapir, E., 195
Sastrasubrata, 129
Sastrawirya, M., 120, 129
de Saussure, F., 15, 106, 251–55
Schrieke, B. J. O., 25, 27, 30n, 47n
Scott, J. C., 28
Searle, J., 185
Shapiro, M., 248n
Shaw, W., 191n
Siegel, J., 2n, 222n
Silverstein, M., 12–13, 15, 107, 158n
Simmel, G., 243
Skeat, W., 191n
Soeradipura, R. Ng., 120n
Spielmann, R. W., 158n
Strevens, P., 195
Subalidinoto, R. S., xv
Sukarso, 159n
Sullivan, A., 83n

Tambiah, S. J., 27n, 28
Tanner, N., 7n

Uhlenbeck, E. M., 11, 88, 92, 100, 103n, 198, 199, 204, 207, 208, 210, 225

Walbeehm, A. H. J. G., 20, 89, 92, 98, 171n, 181n, 197–99, 201–02
Whitney, W. D., 252
Welsh, C., 158n
Winter, C. F., Sr., 47n, 127, 136
Wolff, J. U., 8, 108, 169, 204

Index of Subjects

abusive terms, 165. *See also* krama inggil
address styles: change in, 77, 195; and continuum of refinedness, 194, 224; demonstrative pronouns in, 205; exchange of, 50–51, 74–76, 93–95, 101–02; expressive shading of, 195; and fast-speech processes, 204, 226; and gestures, 217, 222; vs. honorifics, 100–01; and hypercorrection, 229; intralevel variation in, 204; in linguistic etiquette, 194, 223; and modes of lexical reference, 97; and ngoko/krama oppositions, 89–97, 199, 234; and ngoko/madya/krama oppositions, 89, 95–97, 203–04, 229; ngoko vs. basa, 50, 87–88; in other languages, 198; and presentation of self, 88; social meanings of, 13–14; vs. speech styles: 14, 194, 223–24; and status, 74; subcommunity allegiances to, 233. *See also* basa, ngoko, madya, krama, ngoko/krama oppositions, ngoko/madya/krama oppositions
affinal relations, 72–73. *See also* kin terms, status
ambiguity, 170
antyabasa, 102
appanage, 25
arbitrariness of the linguistic sign, 251–53

baby talk, 165
basa, 38, 40, 49–51, 87–89, 226. See also *mbasakaké*

Batavia, 23
bilingualism, 8
Binatara, 30
Brajanala, 33

change from above, 199–202
change from below, 199–203, 205
code switching, 8
concubines. *See* wives
conservative vs. modern use: historical background of, 115; of *éyang*, 142–43; of *kangmas*, 146–47; of kin terms, 142; of krama, 199, 201–03, 205; of madya, 205; of *nandalem*, 130; of *panjenengan*, 129; of possessive constructions, 123–24; of pronominal *dalem*, 120–23; and *salah kaprah*, 9; of *suwun*, 176. *See also* kin term use, personal pronoun use, speech style use, krama inggil, krama, madya
conversational maxims, 238
crown prince, 59
cult of glory, 24, 32

data vs. process of talk, 232
deference: and allusiveness, 154, 174, 191–93; and domain of person, 226; and face wants, 242; and semantic indeterminacy, 226, 228. *See also* etiquette, honorifics, refinedness
deictics. *See* deixis
deixis: vs. indexicality, 16–17, 227; and indexical muting, 209; referential vs. social, 14–15, 237, 246; unrefinedness of, 223. *See also* in-

Index of subjects

deixis (continued)
dexicality, demonstrative pronouns, personal pronouns
delocutive verbs, 217–19
demonstrative pronouns, 205–11; correlational vs. noncorrelational, 208, 223; as designations, 248; and face redress, 245; and gestures, 211, 228; indexicality of, 96, 205, 228, 248; indexical muting of, 228; and indexing acts, 245; in metalinguistic statements, 205; in palace language, 210, 245
derivative krama, 198. See also hyperkrama, krama
designations, 248
descent, 53–69; degrees of, 54–56; distance from a king, 48, 53; and etiquette usage, 61–64; hierarchy of, 48; and kingship, 30; of nomarchs, 26; and relative status, 53; and rights to titles, 46, 54–56, 67. See also priyayi, status, titles
directives: in etiquette, 11; as face-threatening actions, 243–44; with honorifics, 158, 185–90, 243; indexicality of, 190, 196; with interjections, 222; with invitative particles, 218; negative directives, 213–16. See also imperatives, kon, aturi, suwun, aja, wis, ampun, mpun, sampun
duplex structures, 96
Dutch, 7, 23–24, 42, 44
Dyirbal, 170

etiquette, 34–43; as aesthetics and ethics, 3–4, 34–37; changing norms of, 3, 9; conventionality of, 251–52; as diacritic of priyayi status, 34; and directives, 11; during visits, 37–38; and face want analysis, 237–46; and flatness of affect, 35; and gestural muting, 196, 212; and humility, 33, 35–43; and indexical muting, 223a–24, 228, 245; and interactive strategy, 40–42; linguistic vs. nonlinguistic, 3–4, 12–13, 16, 194–97, 211–12, 255; in palace, 24, 33; and presentation of self, 11, 223, 250; priyayi conceptions of, 11–12, 24, 34–35, 224, 246–47; and proximity with the king, 31–34, 36; and refinedness, 11, 35, 194–97, 246–47,
250; significative unity of, 255; vs. speech styles, 11, 223; and status, 46; and titles, 48. See also linguistic etiquette, speech styles
exchange: of address styles, 50–51, 74–76, 93–94, 101–02, 227; and Brown and Gilman model, 93; and honorific idiomaticity, 179; and honorific/non-honorific oppositions, 156–57, 174–85, 192; of honorifics, 101–02; of kin terms, 135; linguistic vs. nonlinguistic, 192; as mediated interaction, 155, 174–75; of personal pronouns, 63, 71–72, 75–76, 93, 105; and pragmatic range, 159–60; predicates of, 155–57, 174–79; as process, 234; and pronominal reference, 155; as semantic domain, 99, 155, 157, 174–85, 227–28; and semantic indeterminacy, 174–79, 191–92, 227; of speech, 179–85; and speech partner roles, 155; of speech styles, 93, 99–103, 227
exclamations, 196

face wants, 237–46
fast-speech processes: and *abdidalem*, 119; and *ijengandika*, 124; and *kula*, 123; and krama, 204, 226; and madya, 129, 204, 226; and *panjenengan*, 129; and *panjenengandalem*, 130; and *sampéyan*, 124; and structural change, 131
figurative expressions: automatization of, 116, 119, 125, 127; combinability with other terms, 114; construal of, 114, 132; evolution into personal pronouns, 114–19, 126–28, 130–33, 228; indefiniteness of, 114; and pragmatic devaluation, 116, 133
formulaic locutions 212–19: and face redress, 244; indexicality of, 212, 223–24, 228; in linguistic etiquette, 224. See also directives

gestures: and demonstrative pronouns, 211, 228; indexicality of, 16, 196, 249; and indexing acts, 208, 211, 224; and interjections, 196, 220, 222, 249; linguistic vs. nonlinguistic, 196, 211; in madya vs. krama, 212; muting of, 196, 209–12, 217, 223; and presentation of self, 211,

223; and propositives, 217; and psycho-ostensive particles, 220; and refinedness, 48, 74, 196. *See also* indexicality, demonstrative pronouns, refinedness
group styles, 48, 73–77
Guugu Yimiddhir, 170

Hamengkubuwana, 54
hermeneutics, 253
honorific/non-honorific oppositions: vs. address style oppositions, 100; and domain of exchange, 155–57, 174–85, 192; and frequency of use, 162–63; intraset vs. interset relations, 153–54, 164, 170–90; among kin terms, 134, 136–37, 139, 144; to *mbasakaké*, 160; among personal pronouns, 102–03, 155–56, 160; in reference vs. address, 98–102, 242–43; and self-reference, 99; and semantic indeterminacy, 153–54, 158, 162, 164, 170–78, 191–93, 243. *See also* honorifics, krama inggil, krama andhap
honorifics: Brown and Levinson's definition of, 242; and communicative indirectness, 191–92; deferential expressiveness of, 153, 167; in exchange, 101–02; and face wants, 242–43; and humility, 99–100, 155–56; idiomaticity of, 157, 179–89; and intimacy, 165–66; and kin terms, 134, 136–37, 139; in physical domain, 158; in possessive constructions, 140; and pragmatic range, 158–60; predicates of acquisition, 174–77; predicates of disposal, 177–78; and presentational rituals, 192, 242; and self-reference, 99, 156, 166; semantic domain, 89, 103, 139, 152; semantic vs. pragmatic significances of, 88–89, 98, 100, 152–53, 192–93; and speech partner reference, 98, 101–02, 242–43; and speech partner roles, 102, 159–60, 190; and taboo vocabularies, 170, 191; and terms of abuse, 165; and verbs of speech, 158, 179–90. *See also* honorific/non-honorific oppositions, krama inggil, krama andhap, exchange
humility, 38–43; conventionality of, 4, 35, 38, 40; and honorific use, 99–100, 155–56; and interactive strategies, 40–43, 108, 131, 239–40; and normative vs. strategic etiquette use, 35, 41–43, 108, 122–23, 131; and pronominal use, 122, 129, 133, 239–40; and proximity with the king, 33; and title use, 64, 83. *See also andhap-asor*, etiquette, normative vs. strategic use
hyper-krama, 203. *See also* krama
hypercorrection, 200, 203
hyponymy, 173

icon, 247
imperatives: with *aturi* vs. *suwun*, 185–90; in madya vs. krama, 214–16; in ngoko, 182, 184, 187, 214; negative imperatives, 213–16; and performativity, 190. *See also* directives
indexicality: and collapse of deictic distinctions, 205–12, 244–45; of deictics, 15; vs. deixis, 15; of demonstrative pronouns, 96, 196, 205, 228, 248; of designations, 248; as duplex structures, 96; in etiquette, 223–24, 228–29, 245, 246–49; and formulaic locutions, 212, 223–24, 228; of gestures, 16, 196, 249; and imperatives, 228, 244; vs. index, 248; and indexing acts, 205–12, 245; of interjections, 16, 218–19, 223–24, 228; of invitative, 196, 218–19; linguistic vs. nonlinguistic, 15–16, 245, 250, 255; of madya elements, 96, 196; as mode of lexical reference, 16, 97, 103, 116, 132, 228, 248; muting of, 132, 149, 208–12, 216, 223–24, 244–46; in ngoko vs. basa speech, 216; of performatives, 190–92, 228; of personal pronouns, 15, 103, 105, 113, 155, 226–28, 245, 248; of pointing, 16, 196; and pragmatic salience, 150, 237; in presentation of self, 223–24, 249–50; proper significate effect of, 249; and propositives, 196, 217, 244–45; of proscriptions, 196; of psycho-ostensive particles, 196, 223, 228; and pure indexicals, 209; qualities of, 133, 246, 248–50; and referential directness, 132–33, 149, 150; and secondness, 247; semantic vs. pragmatic, 14–17, 107–09, 133; in

284   Index of subjects

indexicality (*continued*)
  semiotics, 15–16, 109, 228–29, 246–47; of vocative use, 134, 150, 228; unrefinedness of, 17, 132, 149, 223–24, 244, 246–47, 250
Indonesian, 7–8
Ingkang Sinuhun, 125
interjections, 219–23; emotive vs. conative functions of, 219, 221; as gestures, 196, 220, 222; indexicality of, 16, 219, 223–24, 228; in presentation of self, 223; as subjective and occasional expressions, 219
interpretant, 247–49
intralevel variation, 195, 204, 233
invitative, 196, 218–19

Jakarta, 44
Javanese orthography, xv–xvi, 41

Kartasura, 22, 23, 44
Kemandhungan, 33
king: as definer of official titles, 77, 82; as delegate of God, 29–30; as head of Islam, 58; and local nomarchs, 26–27; as unmoving center, 32; danger of proximity with, 31, 33–34; magical power of, 30; as source of noble status, 53–54, 70; titles of, 58
kingdom: administrative structure of, 25–29; modern irrelevance of, 43–44; and patron-client relations, 27
king's family, 56–64; children in, 59–64; exemplariness of, 56, 64; kin term use in, 63; linguistic etiquette in, 61–63; personal pronoun use in, 62–63; relative statuses in, 59–64; size of, 56–57; speech style use in, 61–63; title use in, 63–64; wives in, 57–58
kingship: and charisma, 28–31; and descent, 30; and etiquette, 31–34; ideology in erosion, 77; and patron-client relations, 28; Javanese conception of power, 29–32; Javanese ideology of, 24; magico-religious implementation of, 28–34; technical implementation of, 25–28
kin terms: and Brown and Gilman model, 235; as collective designations, 113; combinability with honorifics, 142; in complex expressions, 137, 139, 145; and deferential reference, 134; in etiquette, 11, 16, 111, 134; in honorific/non-honorific oppositions, 134, 136–37, 139, 141–44, 158; in other languages, 227; pragmatic salience of, 140, 144, 160; and pronominal change, 148; referential indefiniteness of, 111, 113–14; semantic content of, 134; and seniority, 135; and speech style use, 50, 134–35; in teknonyms, 145; vs. titles, 111, 135–36, 147. *See also* kin term use
kin term use: change in, 18, 76, 135; conservative vs. modern, 142–43; 146; and genealogical seniority, 71–73; and *ijengandika*, 139–40; in king's family, 61–63; to *mbasakaké*, 161; in metapragmatic statements, 50, 53, 72–73, 135–36; among nobility, 71–73, 74, 136–43; 144–48; by nonpriyayi, 144, 145, 147; normative vs. strategic, 140, 144; in patterns of exchange, 135; and pragmatic devaluation, 149; in reference vs. address, 134, 137, 139–41; in vocatives, 114, 134, 137–39, 144–46, 148, 151, 228. *See also éyang, (kang)mas, kang, mbakyu, mbak, yu, mbok,* kin terms
krama: ambiguity of, 88; as basa address style, 88; conservative vs. modern use of, 199, 201–03, 205; deictic distinctions in, 205, 244; delimitation of, 197; derivative vs. nonderivative, 198, 201; dialectal significance of, 196–204; formulaic locutions in, 212–19, 244; frequency of use, 92, 163; growth of, 92, 212–19; interjections in, 220–23; intralevel variation in, 195, 204; vs. *krama désa,* 200–03; vs. madya, 97; mixing with madya, 205; negative directives in, 214–15, 244; optional, 198, 201; phonaesthetic qualities of, 197; pragmatic nonsalience of, 199, 234; propositive in, 212, 216–17, 244; refinedness of, 196, 212; structural peripherality of, 204; words vs. forms, 197–98. *See also* ngoko/krama oppositions, ngoko/madya/krama oppositions, *krama désa*
krama andhap: to *mbasakaké,* 162;

Index of subjects 285

change to krama, 176; definition of, 99; and exchange, 176–85; vs. krama inggil, 99, 152; idiomaticity of, 158, 179–85; and paradigmatic structure, 152–58; in performatives, 158, 179, 183–90, 213; and personal pronouns, 155; pragmatic range of, 159–60, 174; in self-reference, 156; semantic indeterminacy of, 157; semantic and pragmatic significances of, 99; and verbs of speaking, 158. *See also* honorifics, honorific/non-honorific oppositions, krama inggil, performatives
krama désa, 198, 200–03. *See also* krama, madya
krama inggil: definition of, 98–99; and exchange, 101, 174–85; and kin terms, 134, 136–37; vs. krama andhap, 99, 152; to *mbasakaké*, 161; metalinguistic ambiguity of, 98; and paradigmatic structure, 152–58, 163; and personal pronouns, 155–56; and pragmatic devaluation, 139–41; pragmatic range of, 155–60; in self-reference, 99–100, 156, 166; in reference vs. address, 100–02; variable knowledge of, 167. *See also* honorific/non-honorific oppositions, krama andhap, little-known krama inggil, performatives, personal pronouns

lagging emulation, 131
linguistic etiquette, 9–17, 40, 42–43, 223–28; vs. address styles, 194, 223; vs. etiquette, 3–4, 12, 16, 194–97, 211–12, 255; change in, 9, 77, 108; and expressions of humility, 38–40; formulaic locutions in, 224; and humility, 40, 43; and indexicality, 107–09, 246–47; and interjections, 224; in Javanese vs. other languages, 20, 226; and kin term use, 11, 16, 111, 113, 134; and normative vs. strategic use, 40–43, 108; semantico-referential significances of, 12; vs. speech styles, 10–12, 103, 109, 144, 148, 195, 197; and speech topics, 244; universals of: 225; and vocatives, 111. *See also unggah-ungguh ing basa*
linguistic inflation, 83
literary words, 195

literature, 85–86, 153
little-known krama inggil, 153, 165–70, 226

madya, 95–98, 197–219, 226: ambiguity of, 88; and continuum of refinedness, 204; conservative vs. modern use of, 205; demonstrative pronouns in, 205–06, 212; distributional delimitation of, 95; evolution from krama, 95, 233; and fast-speech processes, 129, 204, 226; indexical elements in, 96, 196; intra-level variation in, 96, 205; invitative in, 219; linguistic gestures in, 196, 205, 212; mixing with krama, 205; negative directives in, 214–15; propositive in, 212, 216–17; stability of, 205, 229; as substandard basa, 195, 205; substyles of, 204; madyakrama, 96. *See also* madya
madyangoko, 96. *See also* madya
Malay, 7, 8
Mangkunegara, 54
Mangkurat I, 22
Mangkurat II, 22
Mangkurat III, 23
mbasakaké, 160–61, 182
mechanism of linguistic change, 19, 199, 204
metalinguistic terminology, 4
metapragmatic descriptions: of *bapak*, 136; with basa, 49–50, 87; and contextual presupposition, 13–14; elicitation of, 52–53; of *éyang*, 142; of *gusti*, 64, 136; of honorific directives, 186; of *ibu*, 144; inadequacies of, 51–52; and kin terms, 50, 53, 72, 135–36, 142; of *krama désa*, 201–02; of *kula*, 73; of *ndara*, 80; and normative use, 52, 86; of *mbakyu*, 72; of *nandalem*, 62–66, 71, 73, 76–77; of *panjenengan*, 73; of personal pronouns, 50–51, 53, 62, 65, 105, 121–22, 131, 227; and pragmatic salience, 17–18, 109; of pronominal *dalem*, 62–66, 71–73, 76–77, 121–22, 130–31; of psycho-ostensive particles, 220; of *radèn*, 68–69; and refinedness, 247; of *sampéyan*, 130; and social attributes, 102; from speakers vs. literature, 4, 85–87; and speech style change, 18; and speech style

metapragmatic descriptions (cont.)
structure, 85–86; and speech style use, 48; terminology in, 17; of titles, 53, 68–69, 80, 136. See also kin term use, personal pronoun use, title use

modal demonstrative series, 211

modern use. See conservative vs. modern use

modes of lexical reference: and address style structure, 97; of designations, 248; and evolution of personal pronouns, 116–17, 132; among honorifics, 155; and indexicality, 16, 97, 103, 116, 132, 155, 228, 248; vs. objects of lexical reference, 103; and paradigmatic set structure, 19, 85, 96–97, 132, 228; and psycho-ostensive particles, 223; and speech style structure, 85; and structural change, 131–32

native speaker awareness, 17–20; and normative vs. strategic use, 227–28; and pragmatic salience, 109; and relative nonarbitrariness, 252–53; and speech style change, 108–10, 229; and speech style elements, 232–36. See also metapragmatic descriptions

negative directives. See directives

negative imperatives. See imperatives

ngoko: ambiguity of, 88; vs. basa, 49–50, 87–88; as basic language, 89, 106; as basic to speech style structure, 92; formulaic locutions in, 212–13; imperatives in, 182–84, 186–87, 214–15, 218; and interjections, 222; intralevel variation in, 195; as metalanguage, 153, 191–92; vs. *ngoko alus*, 50. See also ngoko/krama oppositions, ngoko/madya/krama oppositions, honorific/non-honorific oppositions

ngoko alus. See ngoko

ngoko/krama oppositions, 89–95, 197–204; as address style diacritics, 96, 203; analogical sound relations between, 198, 200; delimitation of, 92, 197; demonstrative pronouns in, 207; dialectal significances of, 233–34; extension of, 234; and frequency of use, 92, 163; vs. honorific/non-honorific oppositions, 101; models of change in, 199, 201–04, 230, 234; vs. ngoko/madya/krama oppositions, 89–92, 96, 204; relative nonsalience of, 234; stability of, 195. See also ngoko/madya/krama oppositions

ngoko/madya/krama oppositions, 88–89, 95–98; and address styles, 203; and continuum of refinedness, 96; demonstrative pronouns in, 207; and dialect evolution, 205; and fast-speech processes, 226; frequency of use, 95; in gestural functions, 205; vs. honorific/non-honorific oppositions, 88–89, 100; and invitatives, 218–19; negative directives, 215–16; vs. ngoko/krama oppositions, 89–92, 95–97, 204; nonisomorphic relations between, 205, 216–17; and propositives, 216–17; relative nonsalience of, 229; stability of, 195–96, 204–05, 229, 234. See also demonstrative pronouns, indexing acts, imperatives, address styles

nomarch, 26

normative vs. strategic use: and Brown and Gilman's model, 230, 235; and contextual presupposition, 13–14, 107–08; as Durkheimian social facts, 241; dynamic relations between, 14, 19, 45, 107–09, 240, 246; in face-want analysis, 237–41; and humility, 35, 40–43, 108, 131; and indexicality, 107–08; and interaction, 106; of kin terms, 140, 144; and linguistic etiquette, 40; and *mbasakaké*, 160; and metapragmatic descriptions, 13, 20, 52; and obeisance, 64; of personal pronouns, 51, 120, 122, 126–27, 235–36; and phonological variation, 231–32; and pragmatic devaluation, 115, 239; and pragmatic salience, 109, 115, 232–35; and pragmatic value, 106–07, 228–29, 239; and pronominal change, 133; of speech styles, 4, 10, 228; of titles, 48, 77–84, 103, 108. See also title use, personal pronoun use, kin term use

objects of lexical reference: and honorifics, 139–41; 153, 192–93, 226, 228; vs. modes of lexical reference, 103; and paradigmatic structure, 19; and psycho-ostensive particles, 223;

Index of subjects 287

and speech style structure, 85, 226, 228. *See also* semantic domain
observer's paradox, 52

Pakualam, 54
Pakubuwana I, 23
Pakabuwana II, 22–24
Pakabuwana IX, 56, 63
Pakabuwana X, 46, 57, 63, 81, 141
Pakabuwana XI, 79
palace 24–28, 30–34, 43–44
palace language, 210, 245
parentheticals. *See* vocative use
patron/client relations, 27, 28, 42
performatives, 17, 155, 158–60, 164, 179, 185–92, 245
personal pronouns: in complex expressions, 113, 118–21, 127–29; devaluation of, 125, 129–33, 239; as duplex structures, 96; earlier descriptions of, 104; evolution of, 117–34, 147–48, 228, 239–40; and face wants, 239–40; and fast-speech processes, 119, 124–25, 129–32; vs. figurative expressions, 116–19, 127, 131–33, 150; as honorifics, 102, 155, 160; indexicality of, 15, 103, 105, 113, 132–33, 155, 226–28, 245, 248; in krama, 104; in krama andhap, 155; in madya, 104; in metapragmatic descriptions, 18, 50–51, 53, 105, 109; in ngoko, 50, 104; in other languages, 227; vs. other terms for persons, 111–13; paradigmatic elaboration of, 20, 104–05, 156; in performative imperatives, 185–86; pragmatic salience of, 115, 131, 150; referential and social significances of, 133; referential definiteness of, 111; significative directness of, 112, 132; and speech partner roles, 103, 105, 113, 157, 226–27. *See also* personal pronoun use
personal pronoun use: Brown and Gilman's model of, 230, 235; changes in, 16, 18, 77, 229; in exchange, 93, 155; and genealogical seniority, 71; group styles of, 74–75; in king's family, 61–64; among nobility, 65, 68, 71, 73–75, 117–19, 126–27; to *mbasakaké*, 161–62; normative vs. strategic, 131, 133, 235, 240; priyayi vs. nonpriyayi, 75, 122, 127, 129; in response to summons, 113, 117, 120; and vocatives, 121. See also *dalem, kula, aku, sampéyan, panjenengan, panjenengandalem, nandalem, ijengandika, sampéyan,* personal pronouns
phonological variation, 231
pointing, 16, 36, 196, 211, 223, 245, 249
possessive constructions, 117, 123–24
power, Javanese conception of, 29–34, 31
pragmatic devaluation: of *éyanq,* 141–43, 147; and figurative expressions, 116, 133; of *ibu,* 143–44, 147; of kin terms, 149; of *mas,* 144–47; of *nandalem,* 130; of *ndika,* 131; and normative vs. strategic use, 115–16, 229–30, 239; of *panjenengan,* 125, 128–30; of personal pronouns, 116, 131–33; of pronominal *dalem,* 120–22, 131; of *sampéyan,* 125; of titles, 83–84. See *also* pragmatic salience, normative vs. strategic use
pragmatic range, 158–60, 162, 174
pragmatic salience: of address style elements, 195; and arbitrariness of the linguistic sign, 250–53; and contextual dependence, 150; and devaluation, 115, 131, 229; and dialect variation, 233; honorifics, 243; and indexicality, 237; and interactive instrumentality, 236, 251; of kin terms, 141, 144, 161; of krama, 199, 234; and *mbasakaké,* 161; and metapragmatic descriptions, 17–18, 109; and native speaker awareness, 18, 109, 233–37, 240; of ngoko/krama oppositions, 234; of ngoko/madya/krama oppositions, 229; and normative vs. strategic use, 115, 234–35; of personal pronouns, 115, 133, 150; of phonological variation, 231; of pronominal *dalem,* 124–31; and relative nonarbitrariness, 254; semiotic basis of, 20; and speech partner roles, 133; and structural change, 18–19, 109, 115, 131, 229–37, 250; of terms for persons, 144, 149–51, 234, 235; of titles, 83
pragmatic value, 42, 106–08, 228, 252; and figurative expressions, 116, 119; of kin terms, 137, 141; and normative vs. strategic use, 106–07,

Index of subjects

pragmatic value (*continued*)
115, 228; of *panjenengan*, 127; of personal pronouns, 125, 131; of pronominal *dalem*, 121–23; and structural change, 131, 109; and stylistic opposition, 132. See also pragmatic devaluation

presentation of self: and address styles, 88, 195; and gestures, 196–97; indexical significances of, 249–50; and indexicality, 249–50; and indexing acts, 211–12, 245; linguistic gestures in, 223–24. See also etiquette

priyayi, 2–7, 24–45; and cult of royal glory, 24; as close to the king, 24, 30, 32; change from below among, 201; changing meaning of, 44–45; conceptions of etiquette, 3–4, 10, 24, 34–43, 86–87, 150–51, 224; evaluations of *krama désa*, 200; kin relations between, 54; knowledge of little-known krama inggil, 158, 167; in modern Indonesia, 43–44; as modern urban elite, 6, 9, 77; vs. nonpriyayi, 19, 54–55, 68–69, 82, 199; as standardizers of krama, 195, 197–98; as standardizers of linguistic etiquette, 2, 9, 45; and traditional speech level use, 115. See also conservative vs. modern use

proper names, 11, 111–13, 235, 248
propositive, 196, 216–17, 244–45
psycho-ostensive particles, 196–97, 220, 245, 250

quantitative analysis, 231–34
queen. See wives

refinedness: of address styles, 194, 224; of conduct, 3; and demonstrative pronouns, 205; and flatness of affect, 12, 35, 247; general properties of, 255; and gestural muting, 196, 205, 210, 222–24; 244; and indexicality, 17, 132, 149, 223–24, 244, 246–47, 250; and interjections, 220, 224; of krama vs. madya, 196, 212; linguistic vs. nonlinguistic, 211; and metapragmatic descriptions, 247; modulation of, 197; and negative directives, 213; and propositives, 217; and psycho-ostensive particles, 197, 221, 222; and *rasa*, 247; and referential deixis, 223; and referential indirectness, 150, 192; of sound patterns, 50; of speech, 11, 195; of speech styles, 224; and terms for persons, 112, 150. See also *alus*

response to summons, 113, 117, 121–22. See also vocatives

Roro Kidul, 30
royal cities, 25. See also kingship, kingdom, palace

semantic domain: and avoidance, 170–71; of exchange, 174–78, 183; of honorifics, 89, 98, 103, 139, 152; and honorific set structure, 162; and intimacy, 165–66; of little-known krama inggil, 153, 165; and objects of lexical reference, 85; of person, 103, 111, 227; and pragmatic range, 159; of *pundhut*, 174; and semantic indeterminacy, 153–54, 158, 162–64, 171–85, 226. See also semantic indeterminacy, honorifics, personal pronouns

semantic indeterminacy: of *aturi*, 180–85, 189–90, 243; and exchange, 174–79, 191–92; and face redress, 243; of honorific/non-honorific oppositions, 191; in krama andhap, 157; in krama inggil, 173; of *ngasta*, 173; of *paring*, 177–78; of performatives, 158, 187–90, 192; of *pundhut*, 174–76; and semantic domain, 153–54, 158, 162–64, 171–85, 191–93, 226. See also honorific/non-honorific oppositions

semantico-referential meaning, 12
semiology, 15, 251–54
semiotics: and indexicality, 15–16, 109, 228–29, 246–47; of linguistic and nonlinguistic etiquette, 16, 20, 224, 254–55; and Peirce's logic and phenomenology, 247–50; and pragmatic salience, 20; and refinedness, 246–52; and sign systems, 228

sinking status, 67. See also status
social deixis, 15, 160, 237, 238, 246. See also deixis, indexicality
sociolinguistic models, 230–46. See also R. Brown, A. Gilman, Labov, W., Brown, P., and Levinson, S.

speaker reports. See metapragmatic descriptions

speech levels, 1–4, 10–11, 20. See

Index of subjects 289

also speech styles, linguistic etiquette
speech partner roles: and demonstrative pronouns, 207; and exchange, 105, 155, 159, 192; and honorific use, 101–03; and indexing acts, 208–10; and kin term use, 134, 138, 140; and personal pronouns, 102–03, 105, 113, 150, 155, 157, 226–27; and performatives, 158; and pragmatic range, 158–59; and pragmatic salience, 133; and relative status, 36, 156; and vocative use, 148
speech styles: in address vs. reference, 13–14, 49, 88; vs. address styles, 14, 194, 223–24; change in, 16, 19, 76, 108, 227–29, 251–52; and continuum of refinedness, 96; dialectal significances of, 233; vs. etiquette, 11, 223; exchange of, 93–94, 105; and grammatical categories, 86; indexical significances of, 107; and kin terms, 135; vs. linguistic etiquette, 11–12, 103, 113, 150, 195–96, 228; as linguistic system, 12–13, 17, 86, 92; ngoko vs. basa, 49–50; and personal pronouns, 93, 104–05; and pragmatic salience, 109, 195, 199, 234; and proper names, 113; referential vs. social meanings of: 12–13, 87, 105–06, 108; sociolinguistic models of, 93, 230–46; vs. speech levels, 10–11; vs. speech topics, 244; standard vs. substandard, 3, 19, 233; syntagmatic structure of, 93; structural foci of, 225–27; and *valeur*, 106. *See also* ngoko, madya, krama, krama inggil, krama andhap, speech style use, address styles
speech style use: and affinal seniority, 73; change in, 76–77; as cultural text, 108; in etiquette, 110; genealogical seniority, 70–71; group styles of, 48, 73–76; and humility, 40; and interactive norms, 86–87; and kin term use, 50, 134–35; in king's family, 61–63; metapragmatic descriptions of, 48; among nobility, 65–68, 73–76; normative vs. strategic, 10, 107, 228; and personal pronouns, 50, 105; priyayi vs. nonpriyayi, 77; and relative status, 50; and self-presentation, 88; and social change, 76–77; and status fadeout, 73–76; and titles, 51. *See also* ngoko, madya, krama, krama inggil, krama andhap
Sri Manganti, 33
status: and affinal seniority, 71–73; and birth order, 62; and descent, 53–56, 65–66, 70–71; as distance from king, 31–32, 48, 53, 65; and etiquette, 36, 46; and genealogical seniority, 69, 71–72; in governmental hierarchies, 46; and group styles, 48, 74, 76; among kin relations, 65; in king's family, 56–64; among nobility, 65–69; and titles, 47–48; priyayi vs. nonpriyayi, 55. *See also* king's family, descent, speech style use, titles
strategic use. *See* normative vs. strategic use, pragmatic salience
structural change: and fast-speech processes, 131; among kin terms, 136–48; in krama, 197–204; among personal pronouns, 115–34, 148–49; and pragmatic salience, 18–19, 131; and pragmatic value, 18, 115, 131, 229; and strategic use, 149
Sultan Agung, 22, 54
Surakarta, 2, 4–8, 22, 43, 54, 121
symbol, 247. *See also* semiotics, semiology

taboo vocabularies, 165, 170, 191
teknonymous usage, 145. *See also* kin terms
titles: change in, 18, 77–83; as collective designations, 47, 55–56, 67, 77, 83, 113; in complex expressions, 145; of crown prince, 59; and descent, 54–55, 66–67; devaluation of, 80; as interactional mediators, 47–48, 77, 83; vs. kin terms, 111, 135–36, 147, 228; of king, 58; of king's children, 59–61; and linguistic etiquette, 11; and noble status, 55; of office, 46–47; in other languages, 227; referential indefiniteness of, 111, 113–14; and sinking status, 67; and status fadeout, 48, 66, 74; as status markers, 47–48; and status of mother, 59–61, 65–66. *See also* title use, status
title use: of *(be)ndara*, 67–68, 79–82; and Brown and Gilman model, 235;

title use (continued)
of (gus)ti, 63–64, 79–80; and humility, 64, 83; among king's children, 59, 63, 64; and linguistic inflation, 83; among lower nobility, 67, 68, 81; of mas, 143, 145–47; in metapragmatic descriptions, 53, 64, 80–81, 135; among nonpriyayi, 68, 69; normative vs. strategic, 83, 84, 108; official vs. unofficial, 48, 54–56, 63–64, 67–69, 77–83; of (ra)dèn, 68, 81–82; in reference vs. address, 51, 114; and speech style use, 51; in vocatives, 51, 64, 67, 114. See also gusti, bendara, radèn, mas, titles

vagueness, 170
variable rule analysis, 232
valeur, 106. See also pragmatic value

vocative use: of bapak, 137–38, 148; of bendara, 67, 81; full vs. short forms in, 138; of gusti, 64; indexicality of, 134, 150, 228; of kakang, 144–46; of kin terms, 51, 114, 134, 136–39, 148, 228, of mas, 146–48; of mbakyu, 138–39, 148; vs. referential use, 51, 111, 114, 138, 145; vs. response to summons, 113, 121; stylistic variation, 137

wives: as jural vs. biological mothers, 61; in king's family, 57–58, 64; in lower noble families, 74; in noble families, 65–66; queen vs. others, 57. See also pramaiswari, priyantun dalem, priyantun nèm, priyantun sepuh, garwa.

Yogyakarta, 2, 4, 5, 54, 121

University of Pennsylvania Press

Conduct and Communications Series

Erving Goffman and Dell Hymes, Founding Editors
Dell Hymes, Gillian Sankoff, and Henry Glassie, General Editors

Erving Goffman. *Strategic Interaction.* 1970
William Labov. *Language in the Inner City: Studies in the Black English Vernacular.* 1973
William Labov. *Sociolinguistic Patterns.* 1973
Dell Hymes. *Foundations in Sociolinguistics: An Ethnographic Approach.* 1974
Barbara Kirshenblatt-Gimblett, ed. *Speech Play: Research and Resources for the Study of Linguistic Creativity.* 1976
Gillian Sankoff. *The Social Life of Language.* 1980
Erving Goffman. *Forms of Talk.* 1981
Dell Hymes. *"In Vain I Tried to Tell You."* 1981
Dennis Tedlock. *The Spoken Word and the Work of Interpretation.* 1983
Ellen B. Basso. *A Musical View of the Universe: Kalapalo Myth and Ritual Performances.* 1985
Michael Moerman. *Talking Culture: Ethnography and Conversation Analysis.* 1987
Dan Rose. *Black American Street Life: South Philadelphia, 1969–1971.* 1987
Charles L. Briggs. *Competence and Performance: The Creativity of Tradition in Mexicano Verbal Art.* 1988
J. Joseph Errington. *Structure and Style in Javanese: A Semiotic View of Linguistic Etiquette.* 1988